And So We Moved to Petaca

And So We Moved to Petaca

Portrait of a New Mexico Community

PHOTOGRAPHS BY LYNN ADLER

EDITED AND WITH AN INTRODUCTION BY BILL SHAPIRO

University of New Mexico Press | Albuquerque

To the Hispano community of Petaca, who, in the early 1970s,
embraced my activist friends with warmth and enthusiasm;
and to my activist friends, who ventured far from the familiar
to settle in this rural, remote community.

INTRODUCTION

And So We Moved to Petaca

Bill Shapiro

Lynn Adler made these photographs between 1970 and 1974 while visiting friends who had left their lives in San Francisco and New York City to move to a tiny village in Northern New Mexico that few people had ever heard of. The village was called Petaca. In some ways, it was a strange choice for these politically active twenty-somethings: Petaca was home to about fifty very traditional Hispano Catholic families with roots in the area going back well over a hundred years. At the time, Petaca had no schools, no hospital, no stoplights; it had one church, one bar, one dry-goods store, and a single gas pump. Spanish was nearly everyone's first language, and the only real employment for locals had been a mineral mine, but that had shut down in the '50s. Recently, the nearby sawmill had laid off many of its workers. In Petaca, most families got by as subsistence farmers, with a few animals and small gardens in which they grew corn, chiles, tomatoes, and beans. Summers were scorching and winters bit hard, but if you were set on living off the grid, Petaca seemed as good a place as any.

In the early '70s there weren't many women photographers, and fewer still used their camera to make ethnographic studies. Truth be told, Adler, a self-taught photographer using an old 35 mm that had been her mother's, didn't set out to do that. She just wanted to take pictures of her friends making their way in this remote, unfamiliar world. But

Adler's instinct for seeing the collision of cultures, along with her savant's eye for constructing beautiful frames, captured a moment both rare and spectacular. Her photographs show her friends deep in the hard work of homesteading and raising families; they show the locals tending their crops and looking after their animals; they show the times when members of both groups came together.

You could say that Adler's big-hearted, intimate pictures tell a fish-out-of-water story, and that would be true. But they also tell the story of a moment when soaring idealism met an earthy protectionism, when activism rubbed up against a quiet fear of land loss and gentrification. Adler's friends had big dreams—they planned to build their own homes, grow their own food, start a newspaper, maybe even construct a school—but despite their best efforts, they were still considered outsiders at a time when outsiders seemed to pose a threat.

For a few years, everyone got along. The well-intentioned but somewhat bumbling gringos respected the local culture and accepted advice (and hands-on help) from the town elders, played with the local children, did what they could to fit in. But in the end, Adler's friends were forced to leave Petaca. There was no time for good-byes or final photos. A chapter closed as quickly and unexpectedly as it had begun.

It's been half a century since Adler last looked through her viewfinder at Petaca and pressed the shutter. Today, the town is even smaller than it was in the early '70s, its population hovering in the mid double digits. The hand-painted signs visible in her photos have been painted over. The cars junked. The children who ran through her pictures are now deep into middle age if they haven't already passed. The old people gone. If Adler hadn't brought her camera to Petaca, if she hadn't carried it around town and made pictures when the spirit moved her, this fleeting moment would have been lost to time, and this story of community and conflict would never have been remembered, let alone told. The truth is, in a community

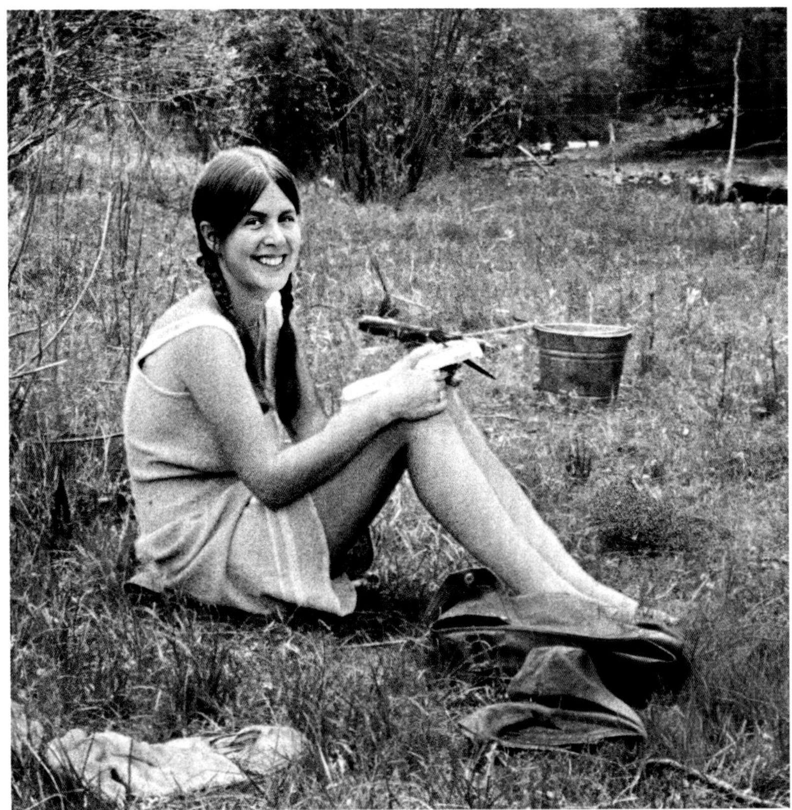

as poor as Petaca, it's unlikely that anyone else had a professional-quality camera, and it's even more unlikely that anyone would have felt comfortable enough to approach the long-haired Anglos to take their picture.

And so Adler's revealing photographs are all that remain to tell the cultural history of this brief era in the life of a small community in Northern New Mexico, a time when a few idealistic young Anglos tried to restart their lives in a traditional town. For the locals, however, the photographs tell a more personal story—the story of a previous generation of whom precious few photos exist. A few years ago, when word got out that Adler had posted pictures of the town and its residents from the early '70s, she received a handful of heartfelt notes. "I know the people in the pictures," one woman wrote. "Very touching to see all the ones who are no longer with us," said another. And one message read, "I'm the great-granddaughter of Jesusita Martinez. These are the only pictures of her I will have. I'm so glad you photographed her."

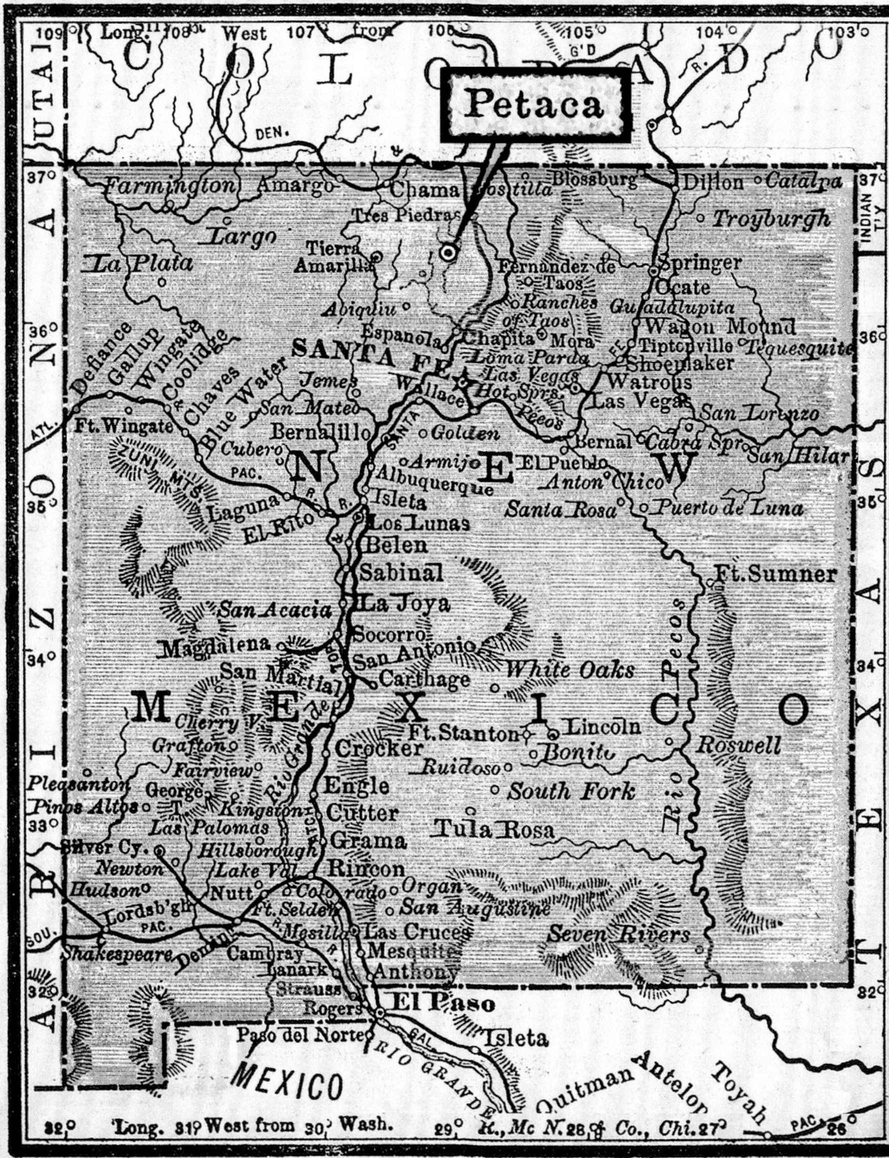

Petaca

Long. 108° West 107° from 106° 105° 104° 103°

COLORADO

UTAH

ARIZONA

NEW MEXICO

TEXAS

INDIAN T'Y

MEXICO

DEN. & R. G'D

Farmington
Amargo
Chama
Costilla
Blossburg
Dillon
Catalpa
Tres Piedras
Troyburgh
Largo
Tierra Amarilla
La Plata
Fernandez de Taos
Springer
Ocate
Ranches of Taos
Guadalupita
Abiquiu
Espanola
Chapita
Mora
Wagon Mound
Tiptonville
Tequesquite
Loma Parda
Shoemaker
SANTA FE
Las Vegas Hot Sprs.
Watrous
Las Vegas
Wallace
Pecos
Defiance
Gallup
Wingate
Coolidge
Chaves
Blue Water
Jemes
San Mateo
San Lorenzo
Ft. Wingate
Bernalillo
Golden
Bernal
Cabra Spr.
San Hilar
Cubero
Armijo
El Pueblo
Anton Chico
ZUNI MTS.
Albuquerque
Isleta
Laguna
El Rito
Santa Rosa
Puerto de Luna
Los Lunas
Belen
Sabinal
Ft. Sumner
San Acacia
La Joya
Socorro
Magdalena
San Antonio
San Martial
Carthage
White Oaks
Cherry V.
Ft. Stanton
Lincoln
Grafton
Crocker
Bonito
Roswell
Fairview
Ruidoso
Pleasanton
George T.
Engle
South Fork
Pinos Altos
Kingston
Cutter
Las Palomas
Tula Rosa
Silver Cy.
Hillsborough
Grama
Newton
Lake Val.
Rincon
Hudson
Nutt
Colorado
Organ
Lordsb'gh
Ft. Selden
San Augustine
Mesilla
Las Cruces
Seven Rivers
Shakespeare
Deming
Cambray
Mesquite
Lanark
Anthony
Strauss
Rogers
El Paso
Paso del Norte
Isleta
Rio Grande
Rio Pecos
Quitman
Antelop
Toyah

ATL. & PAC. R. R.
SOU. PAC.
ATCH. TOP. & SANTA FE R. R.
GAL.

Long. 31° West from 30° Wash. 29° R., Mc N. & Co., Chi. 27° 26°
32° 28°

PHOTOGRAPHS

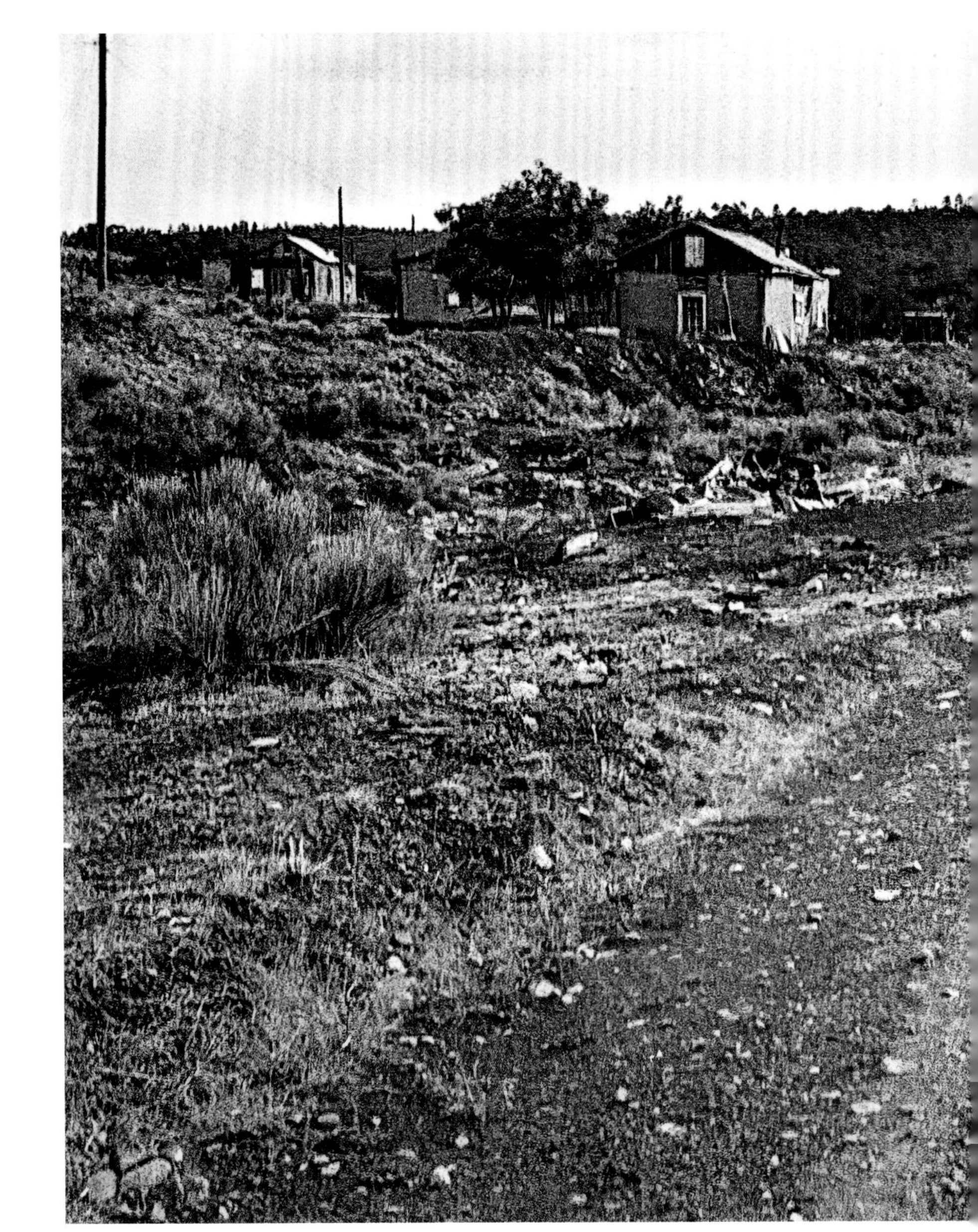

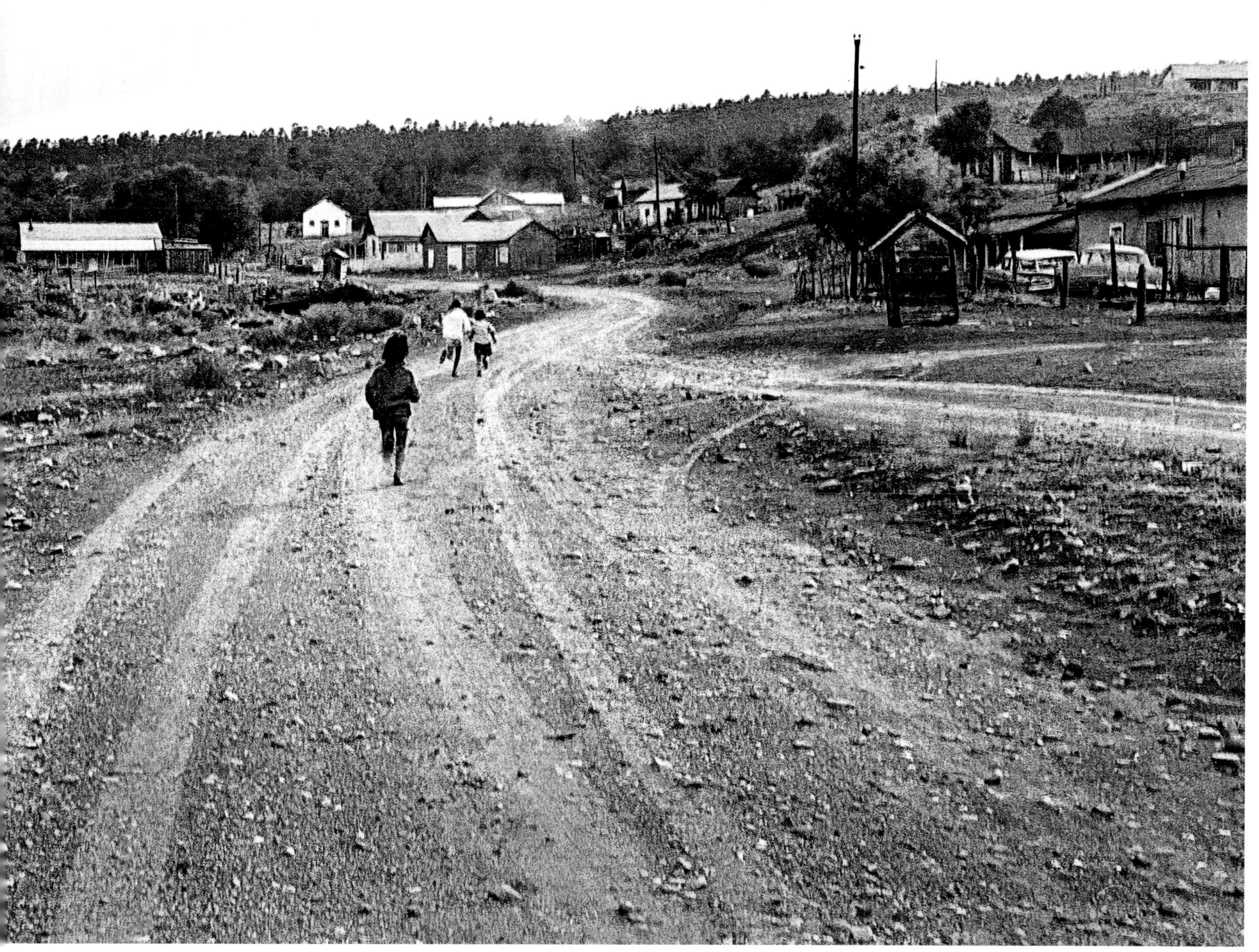

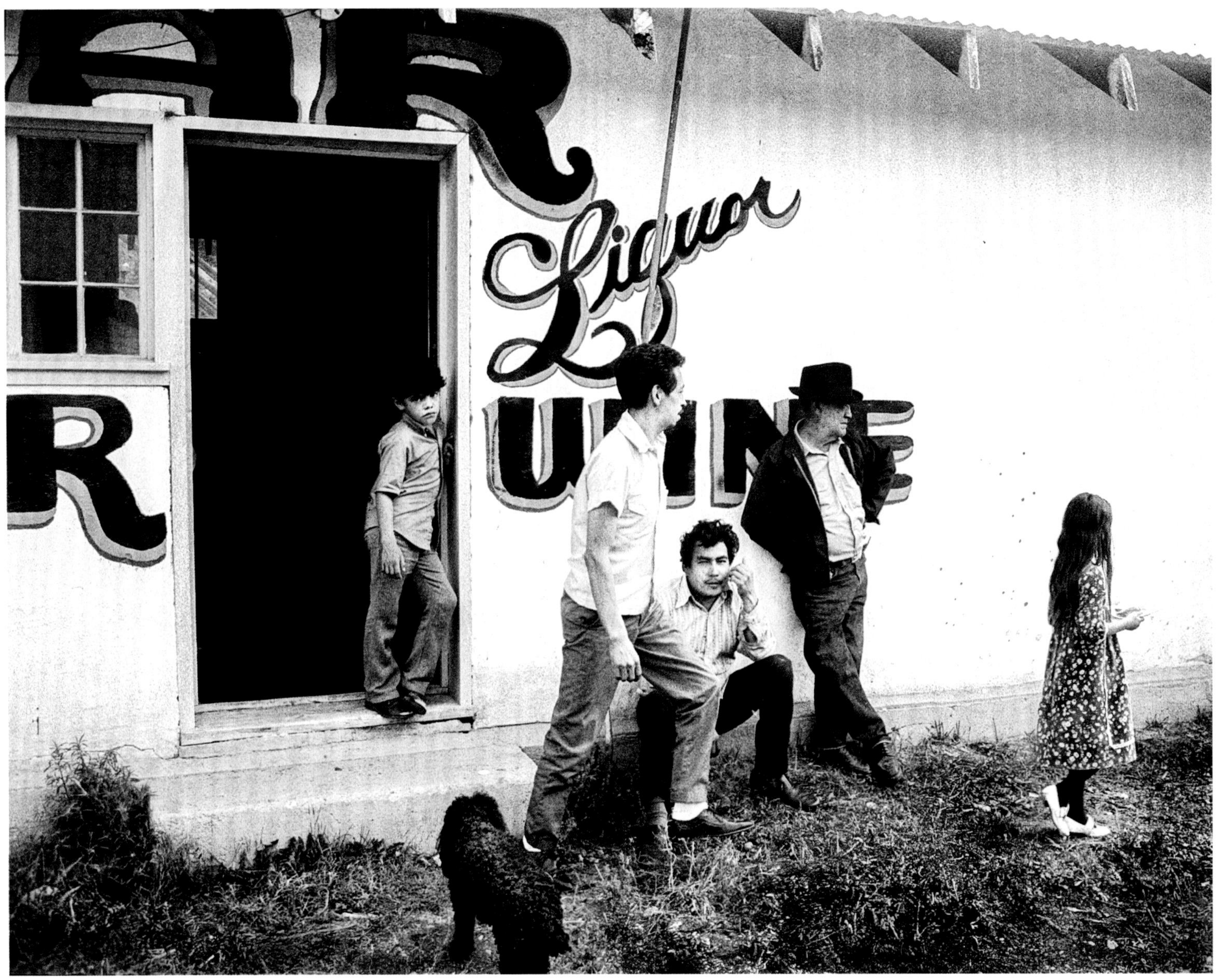
Liquor

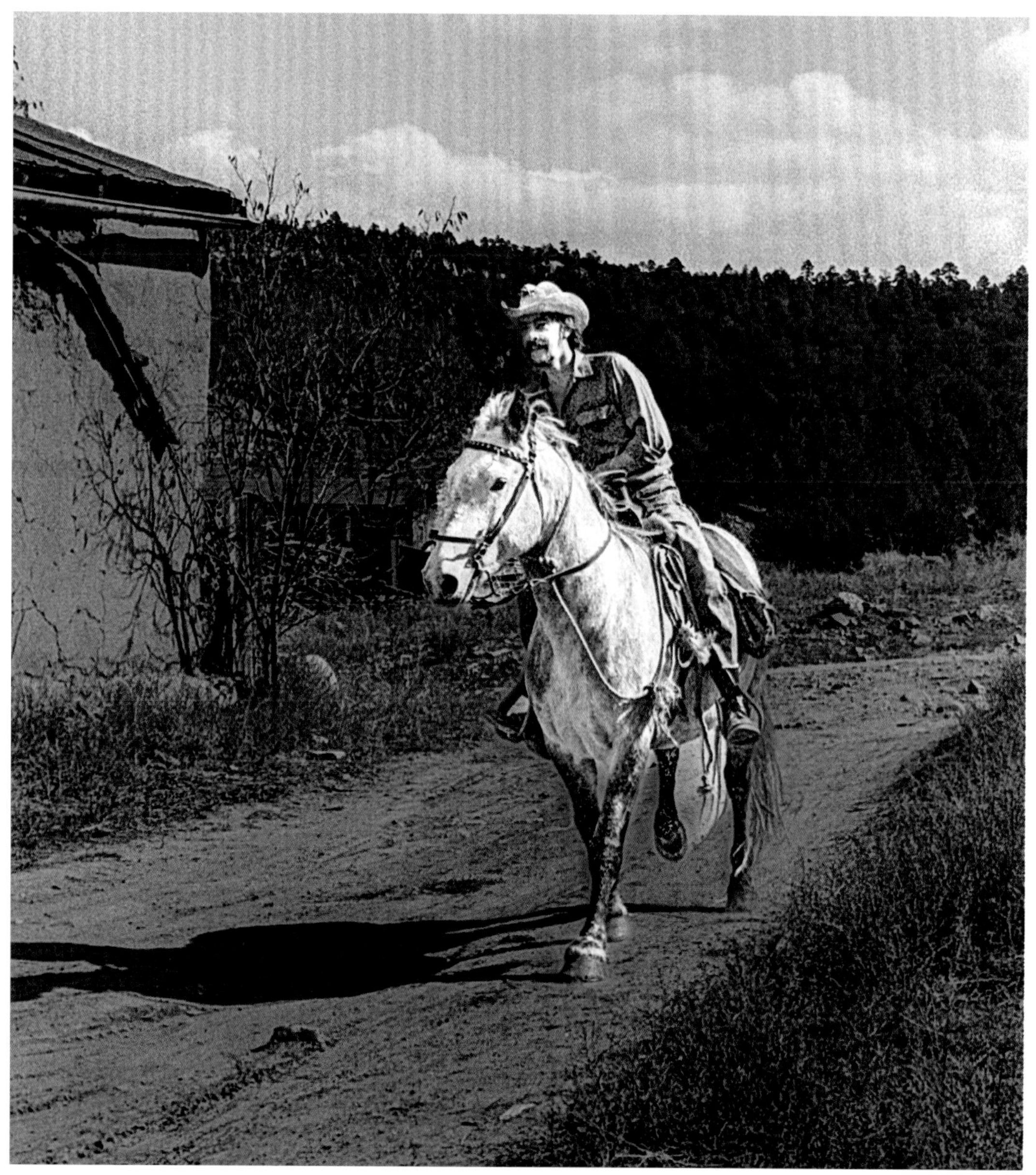

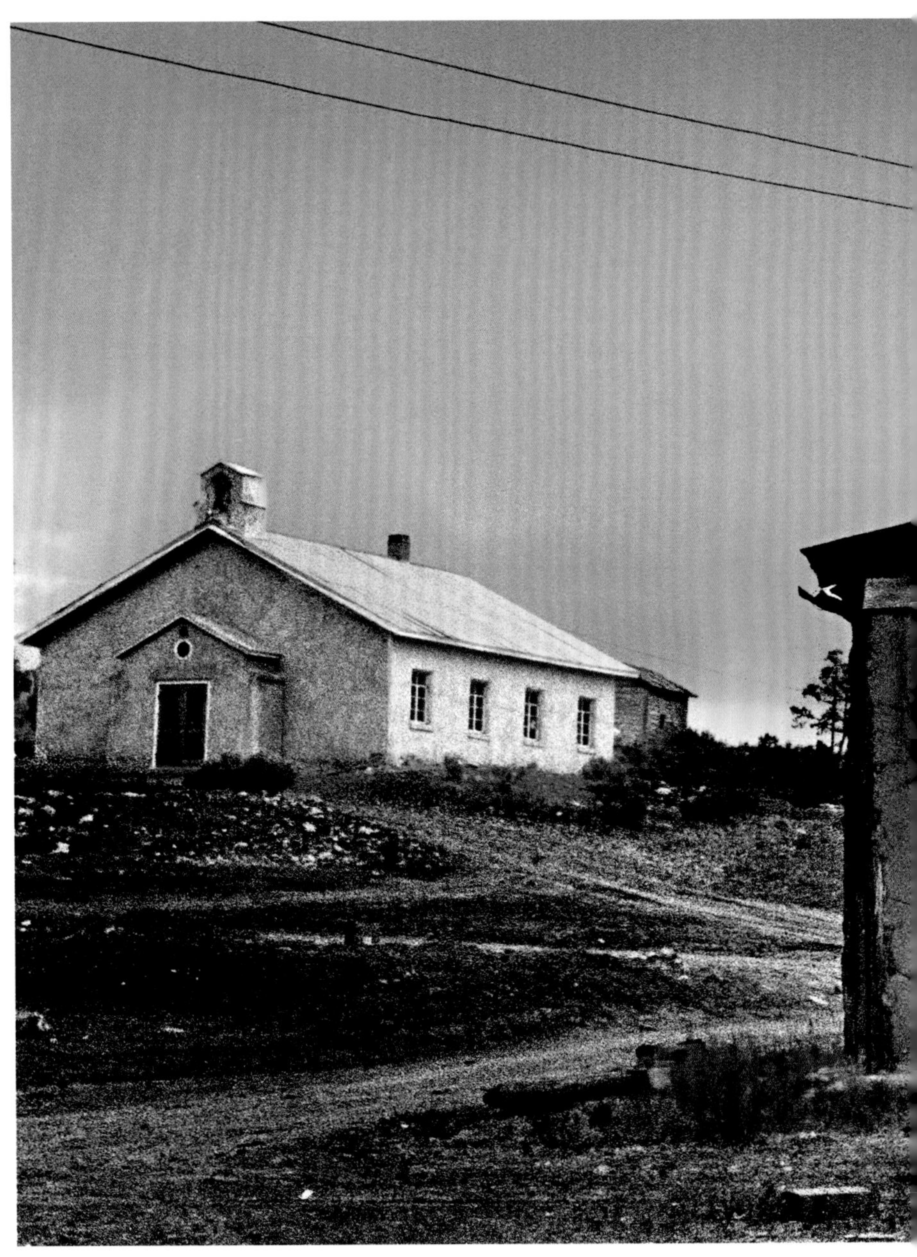

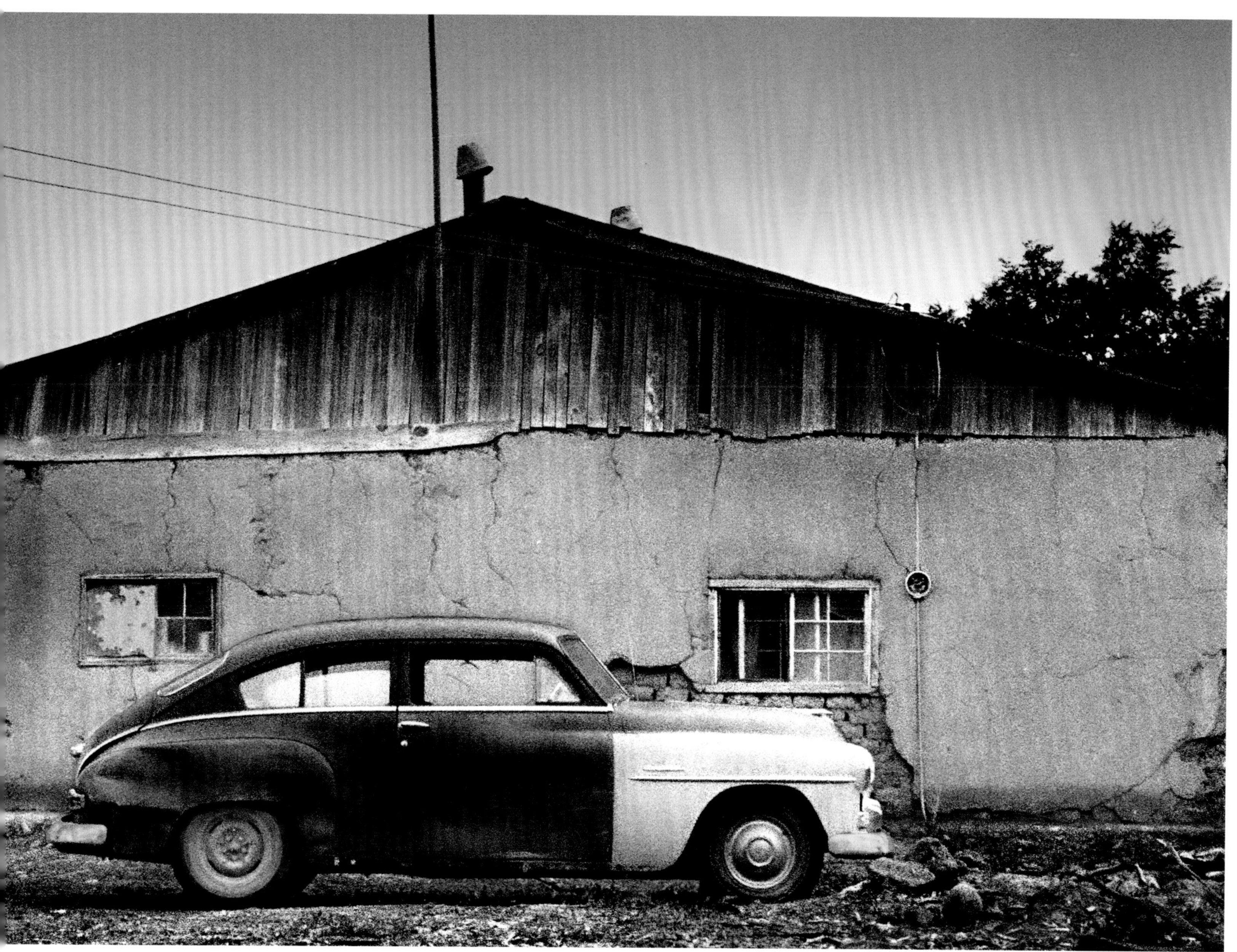

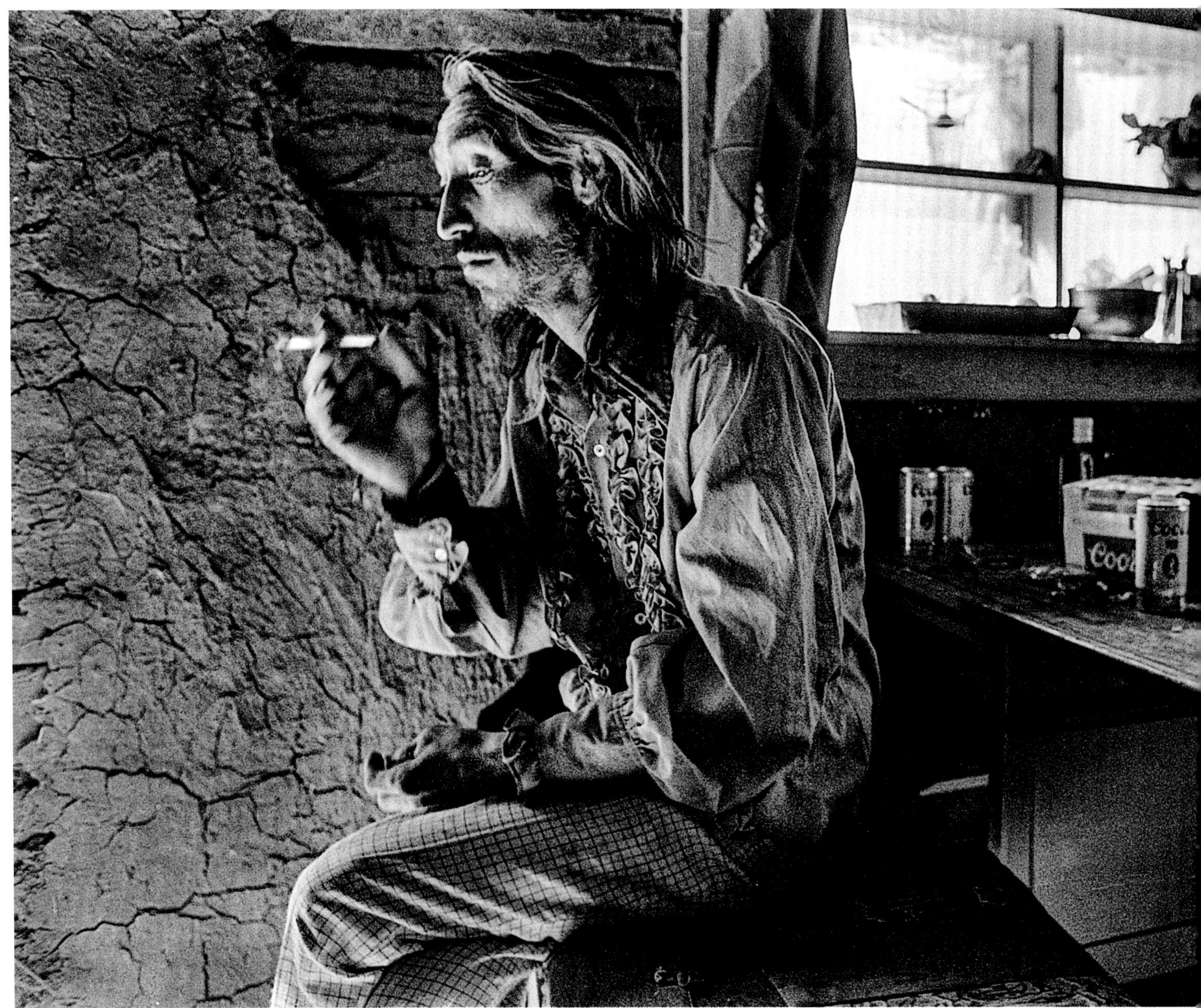

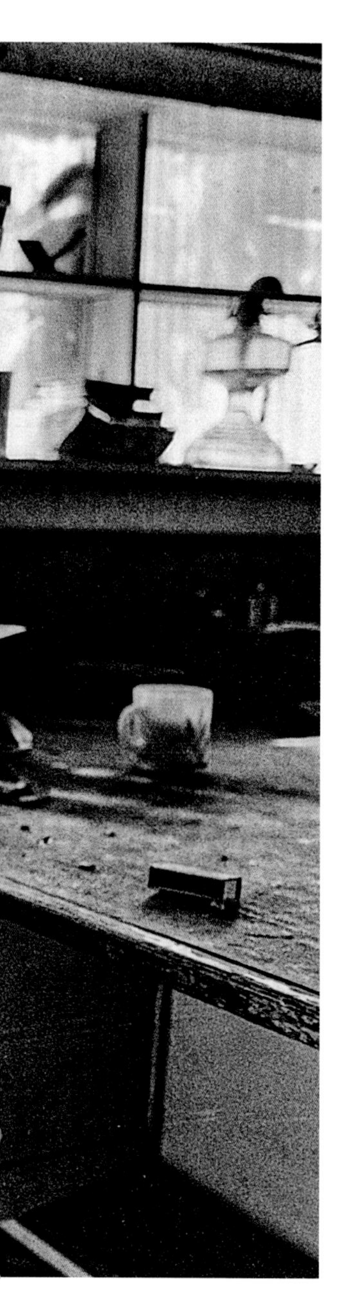

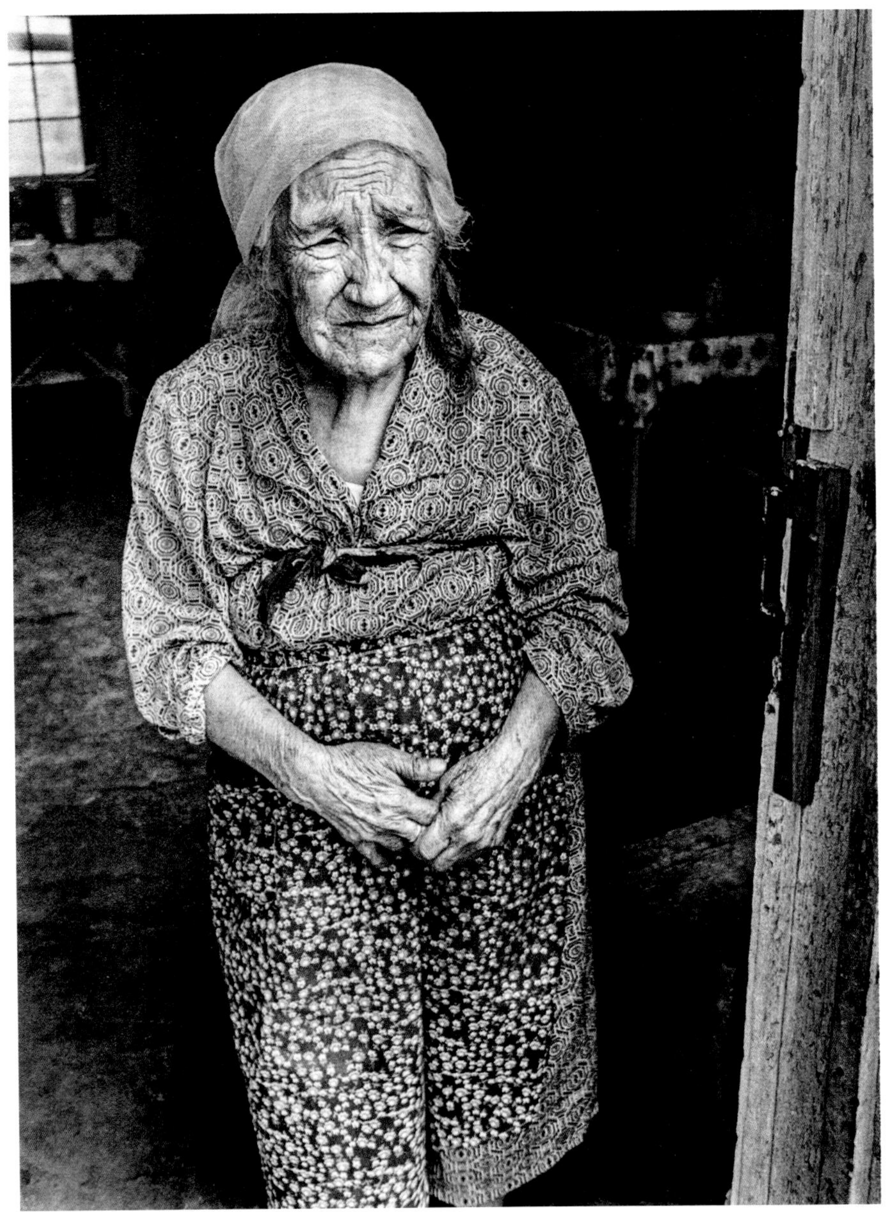

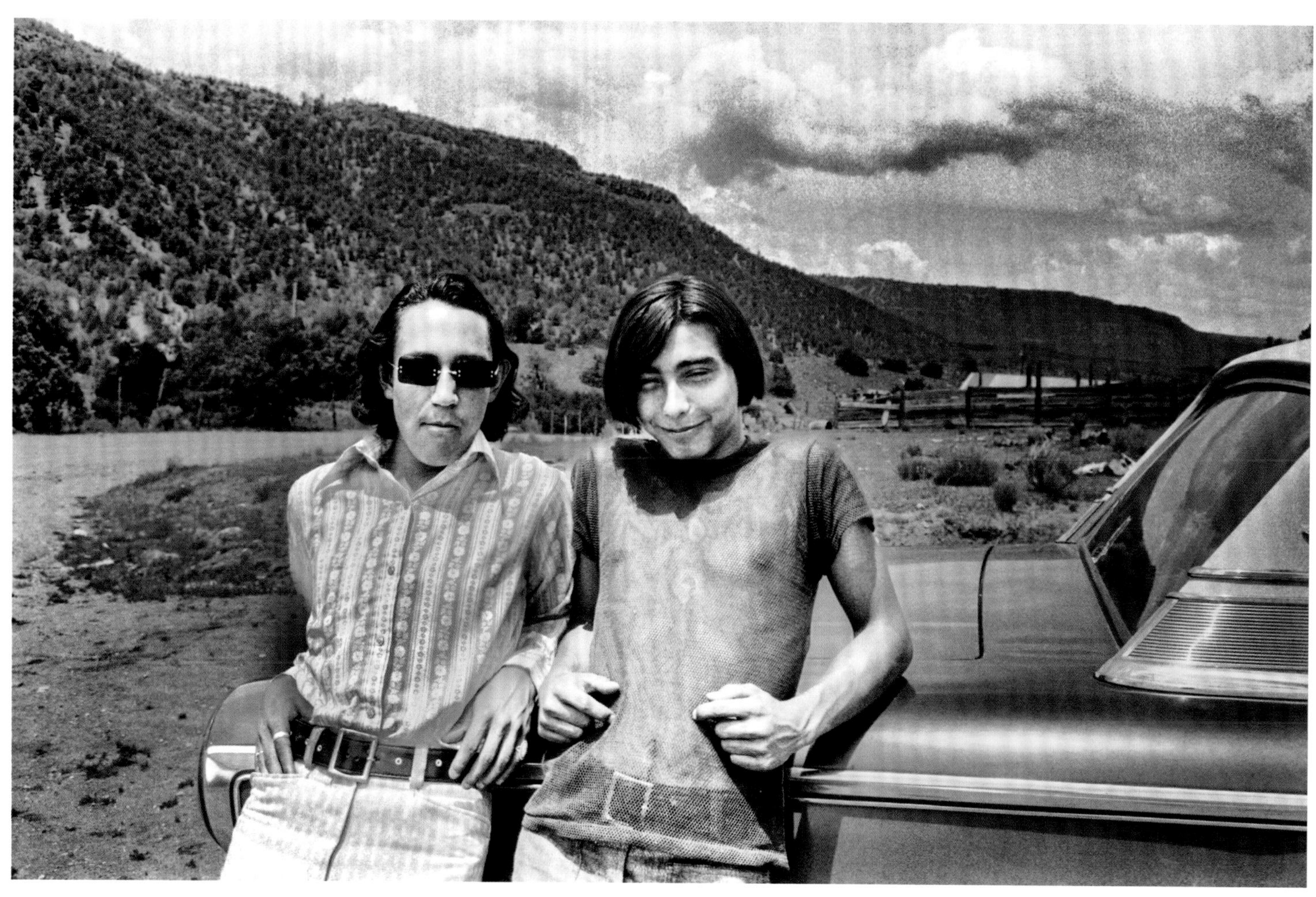

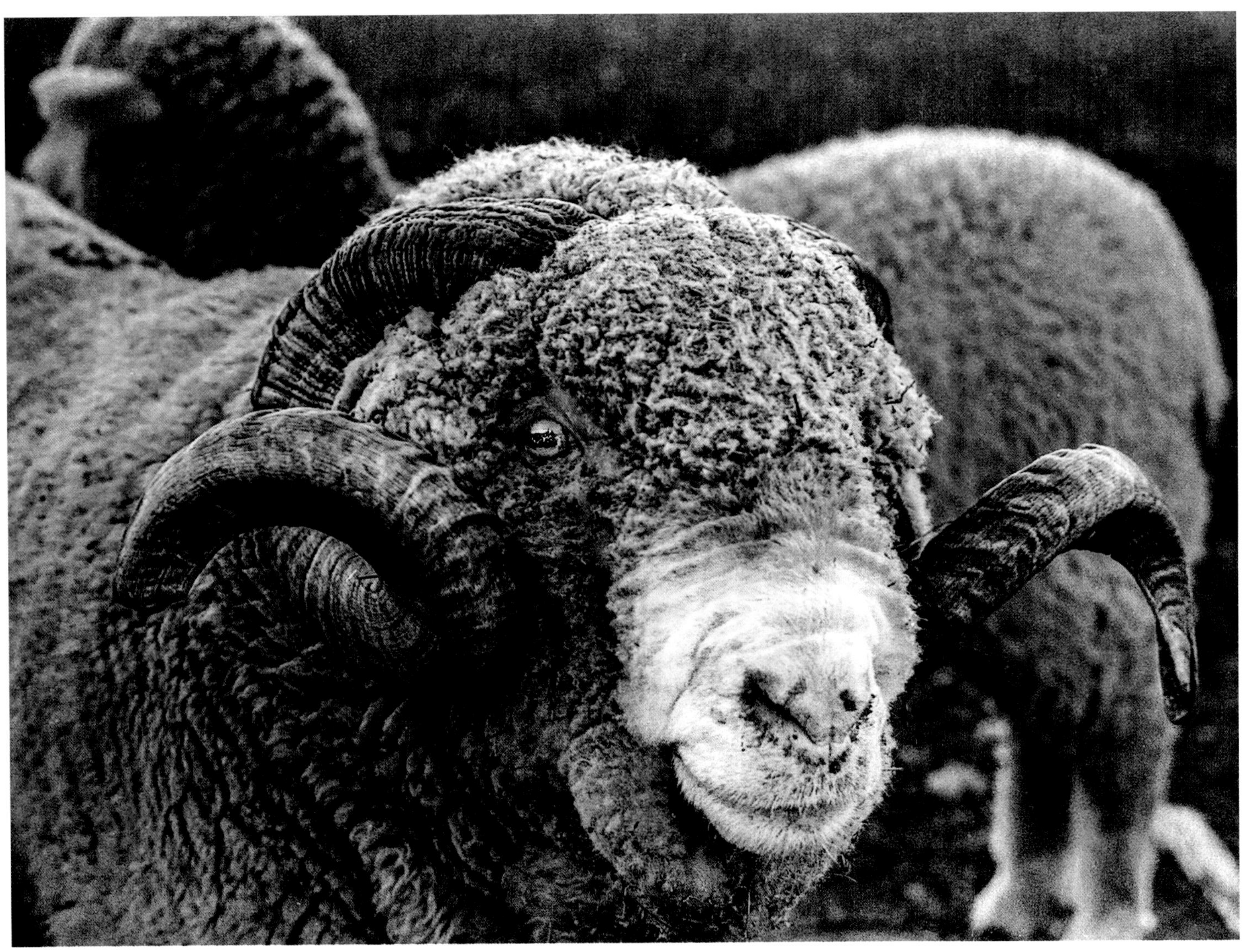

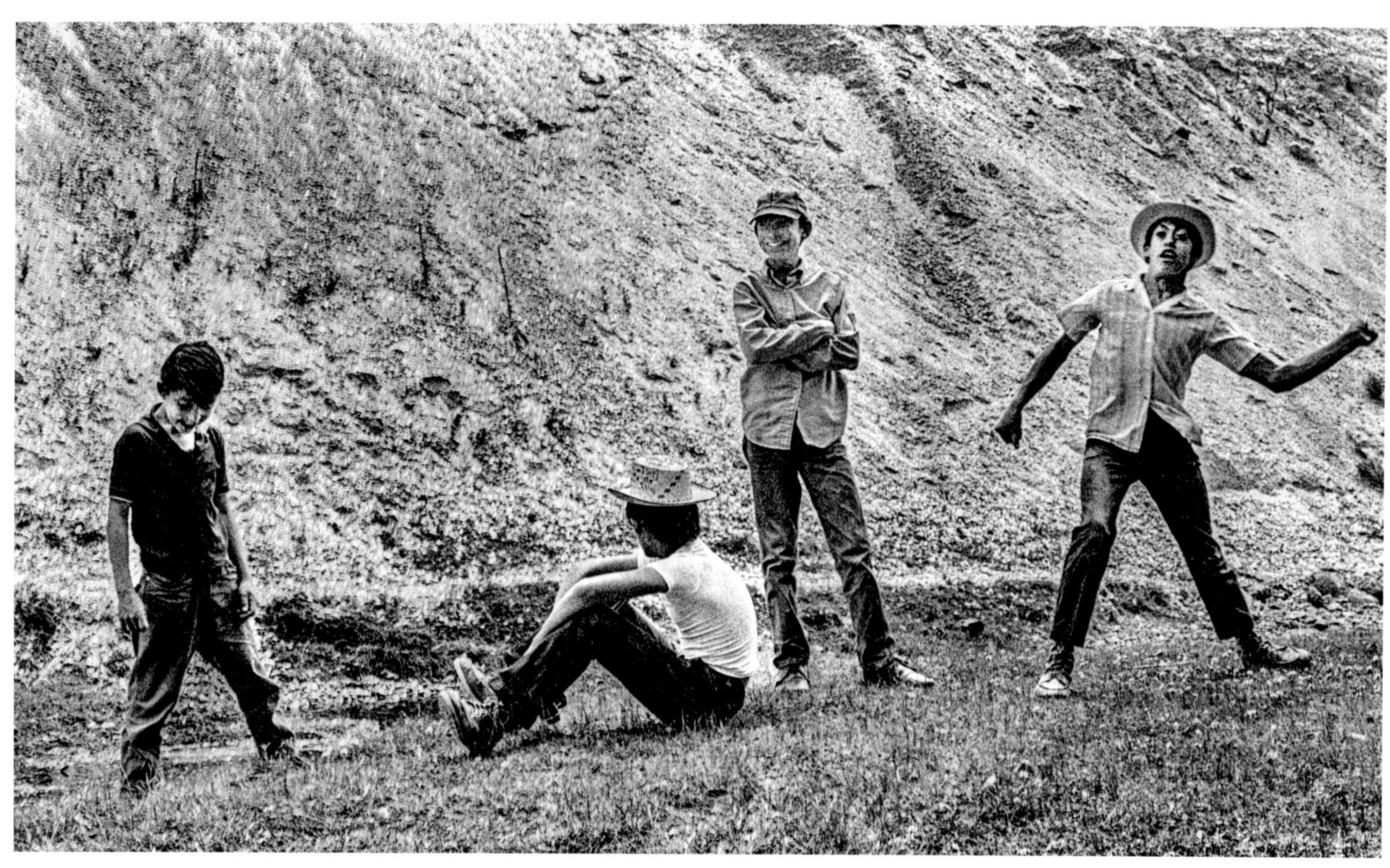

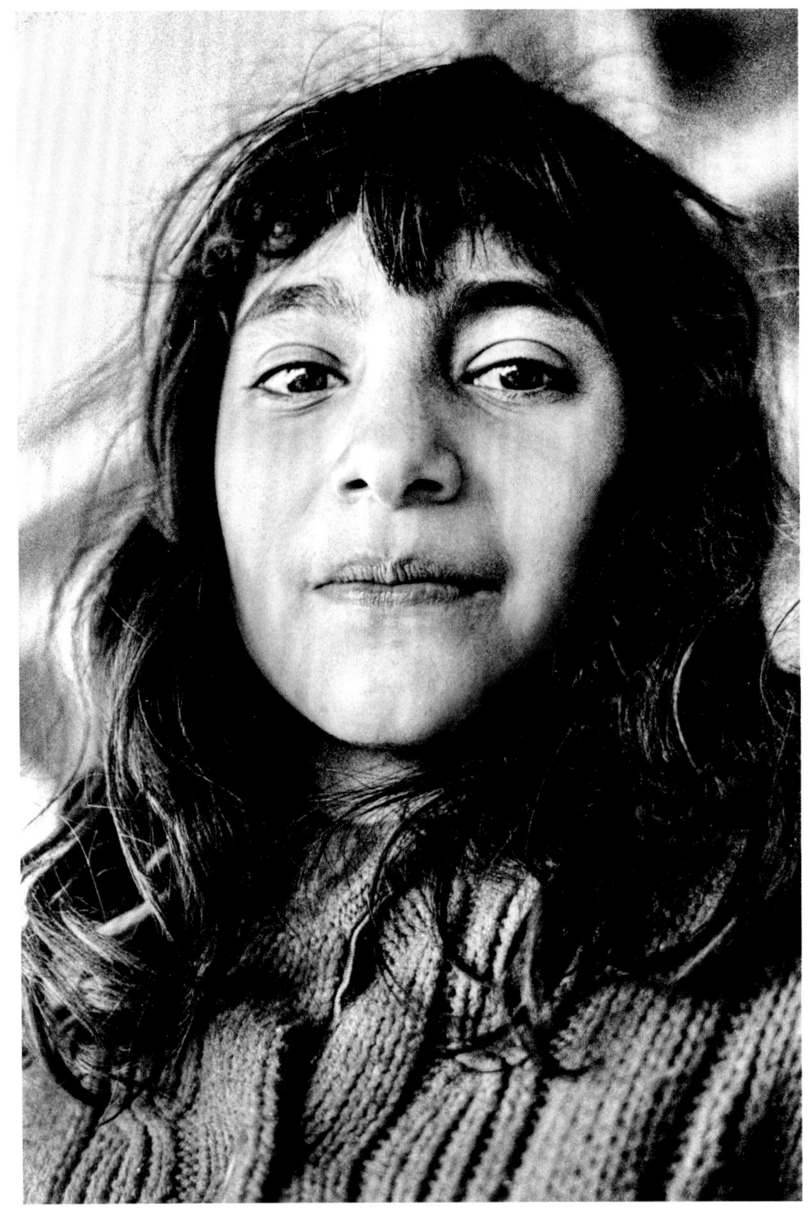

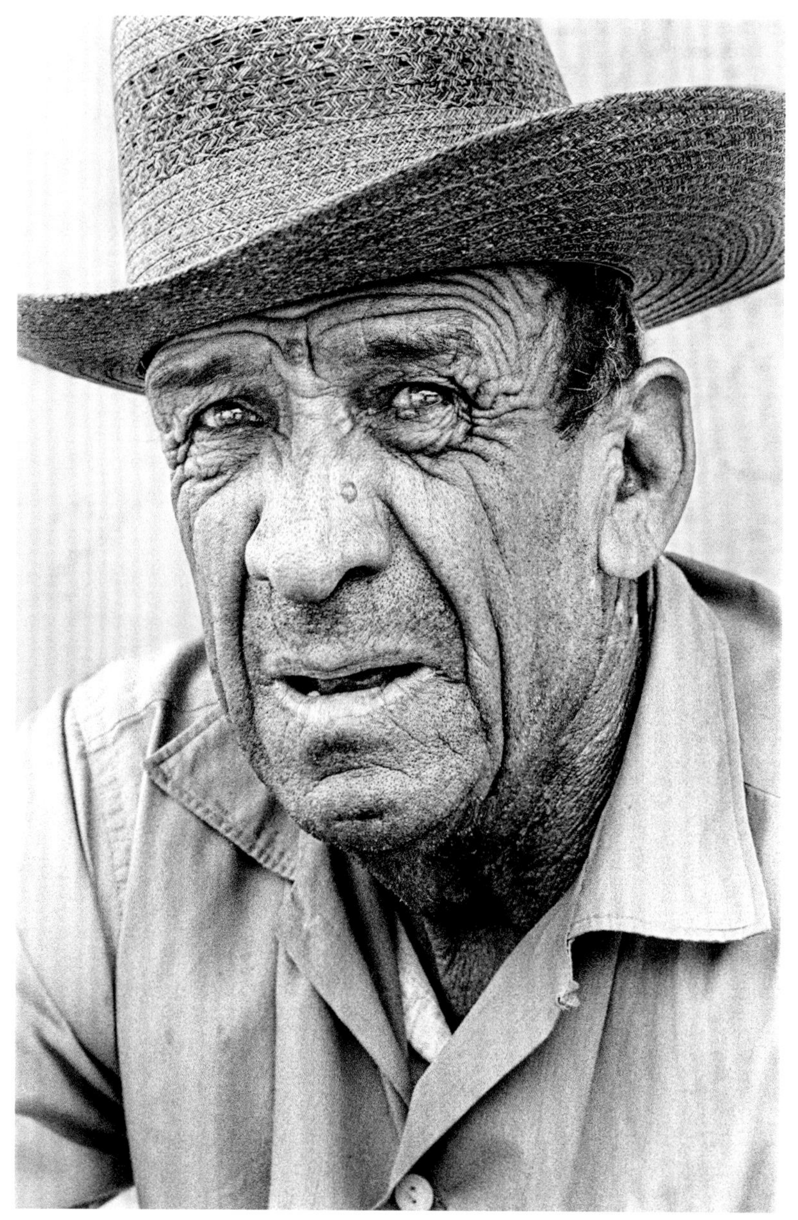

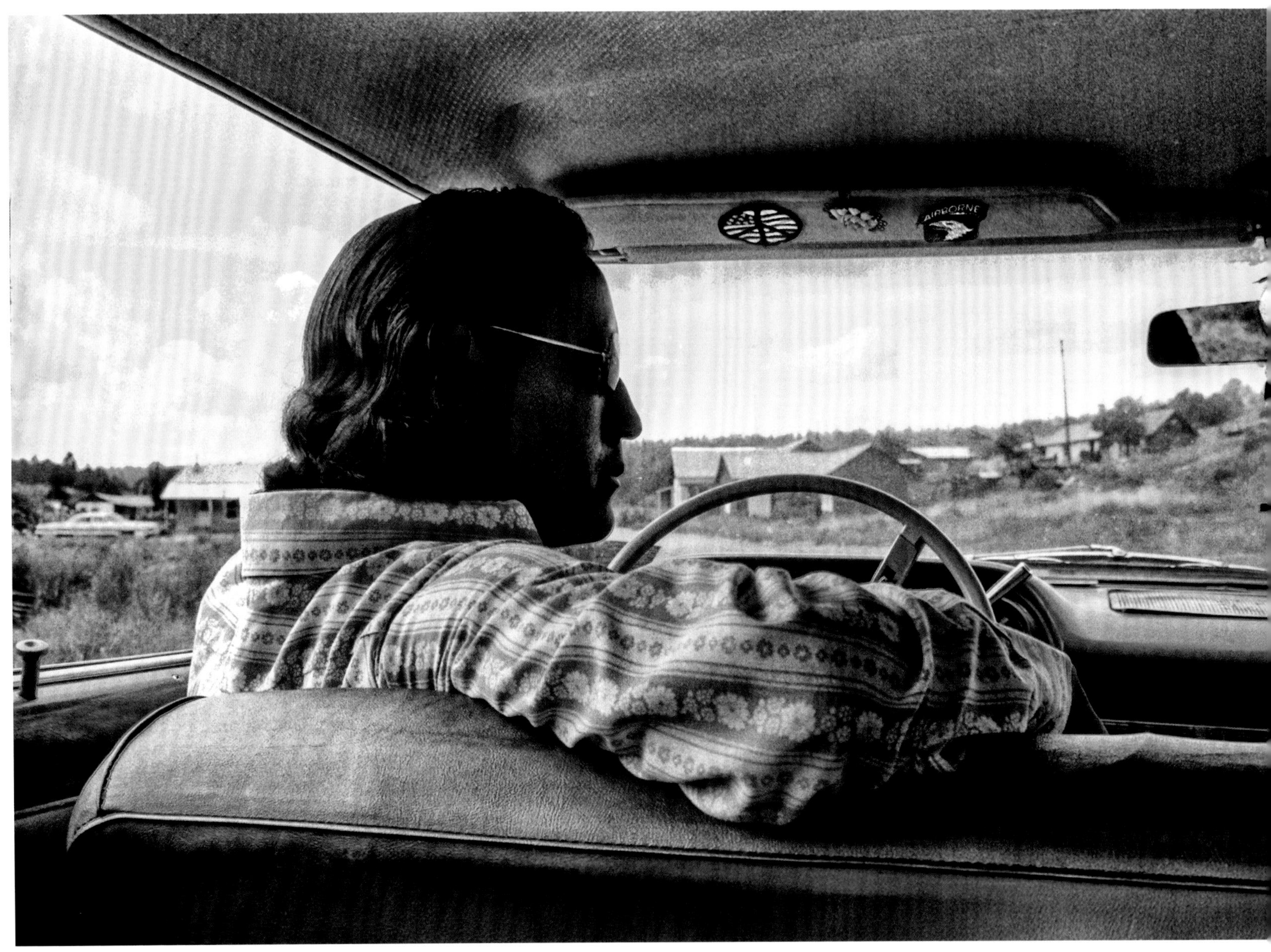
AIRBORNE

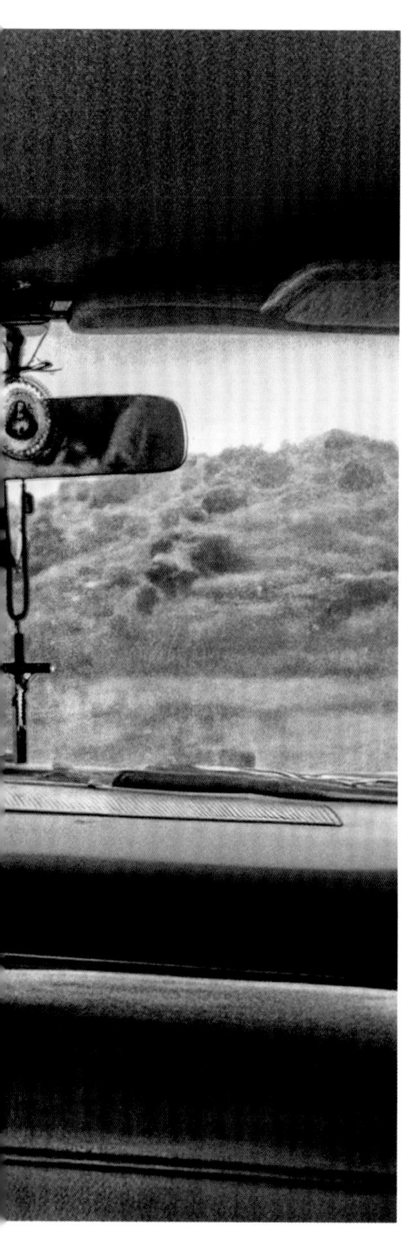

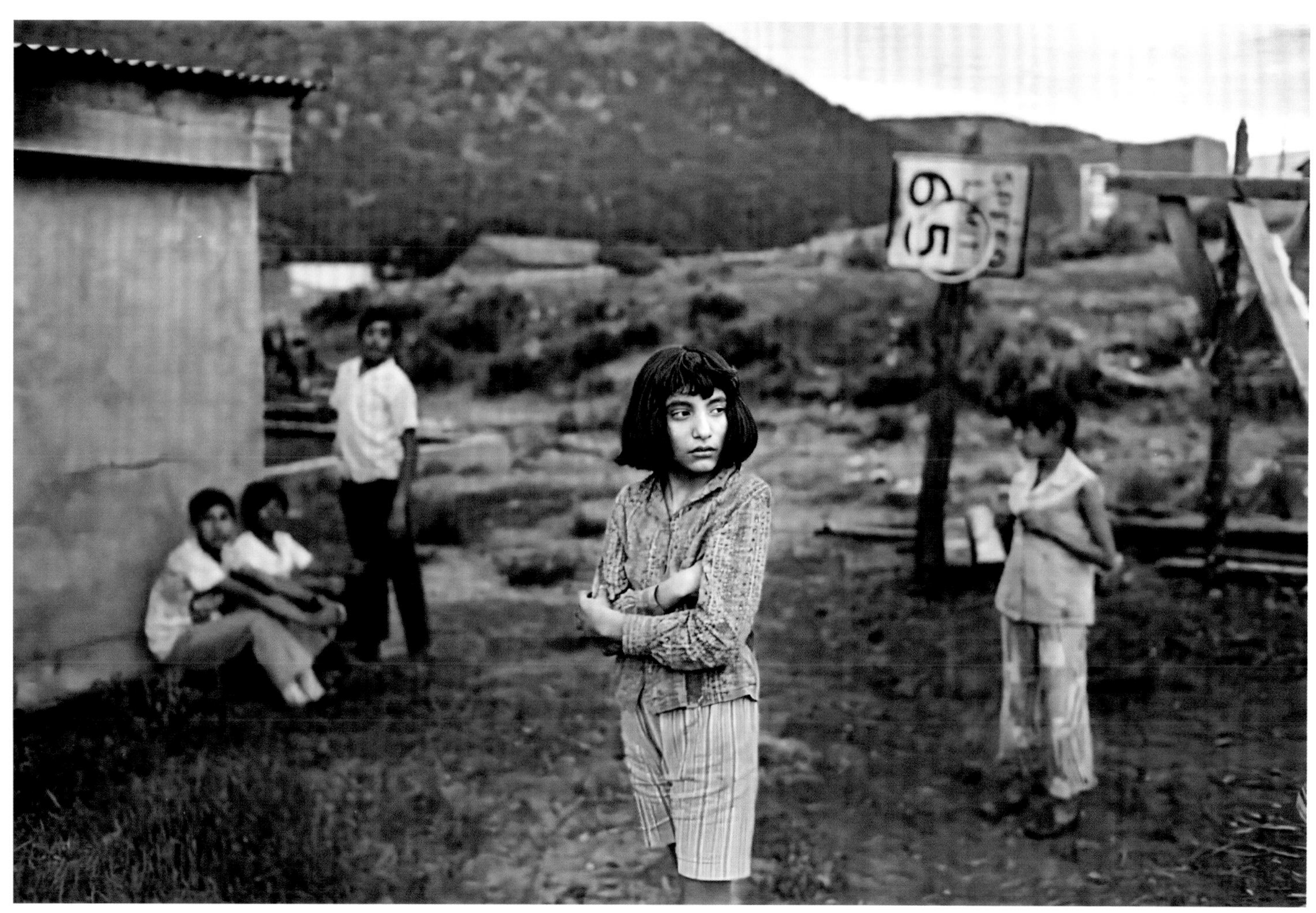

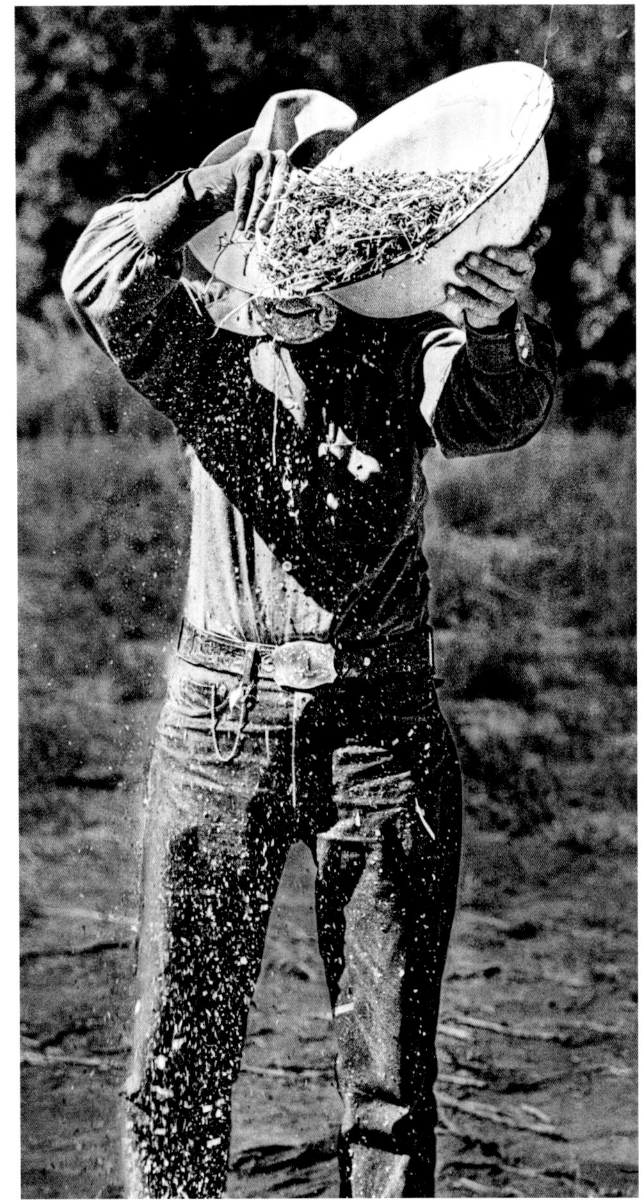

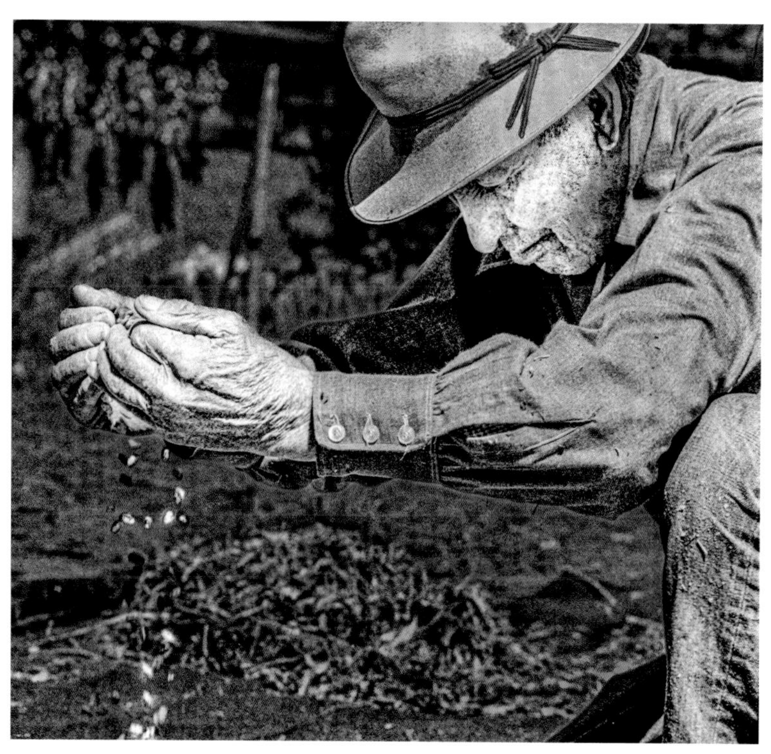

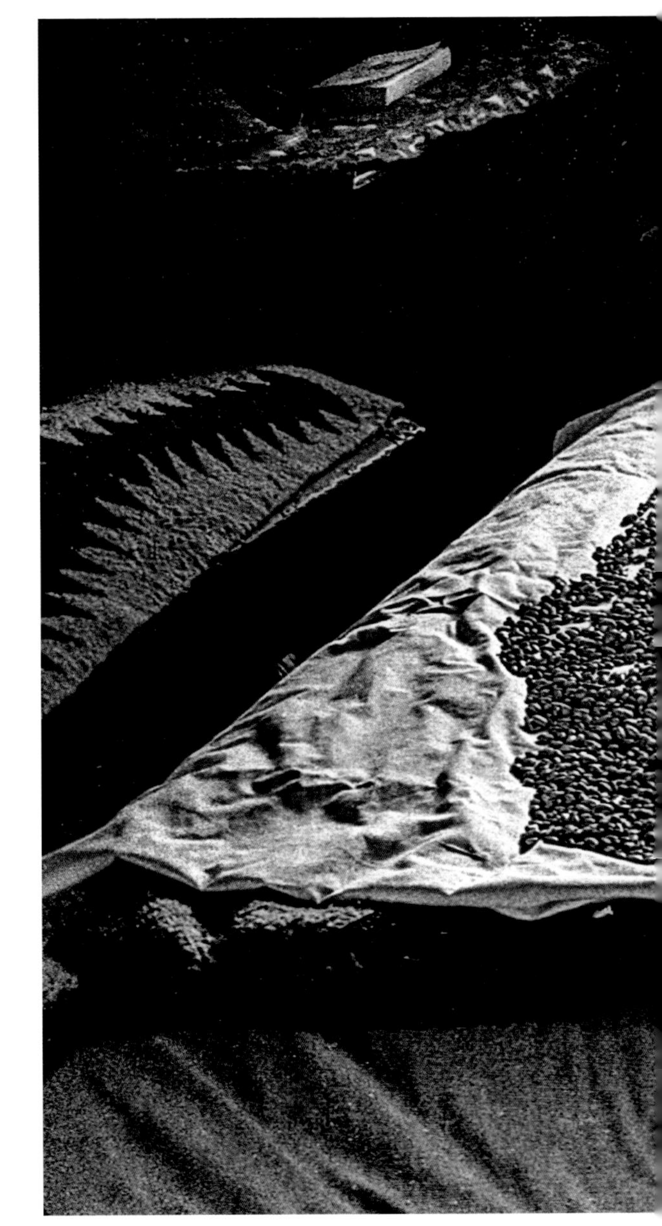

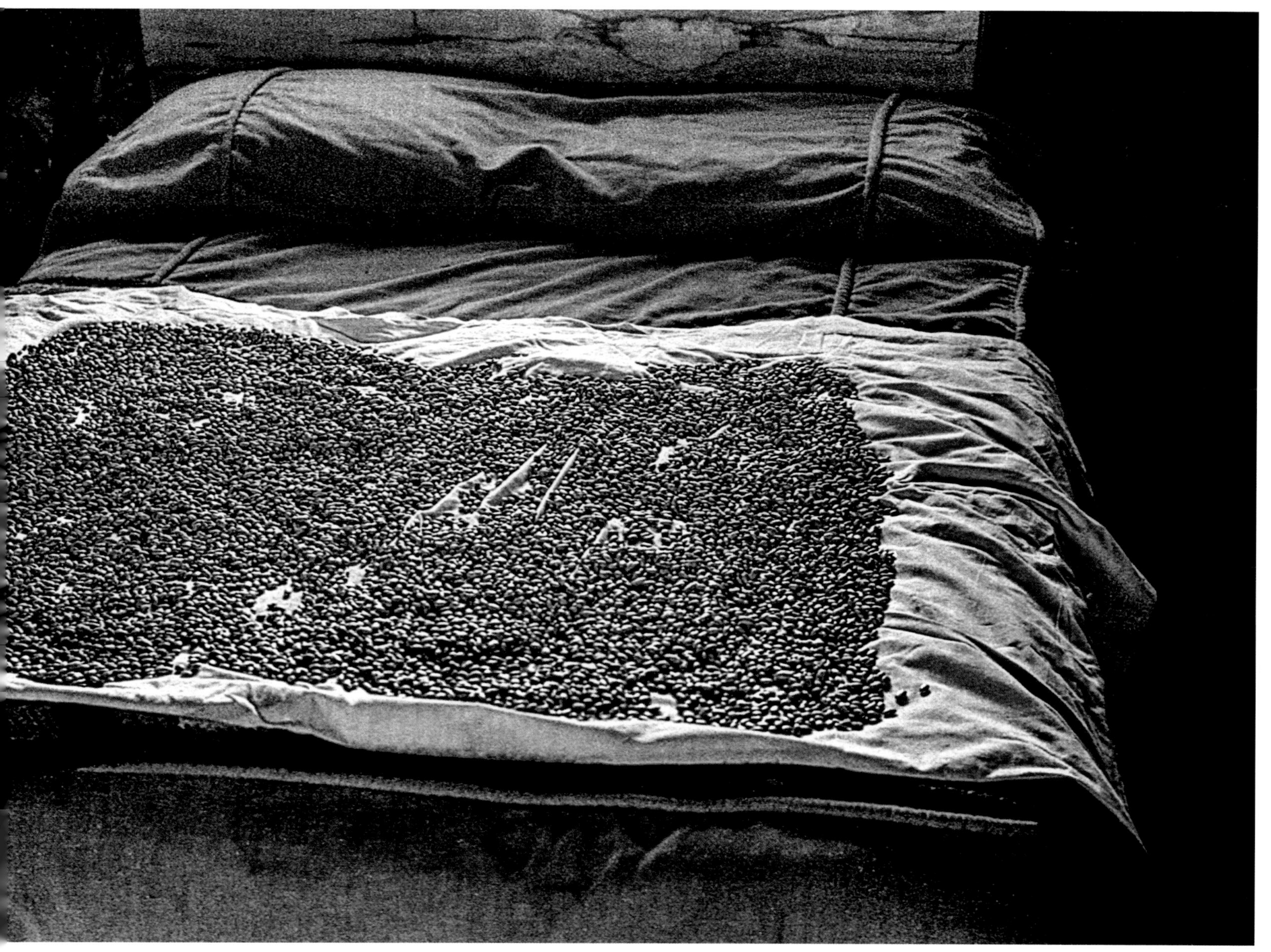

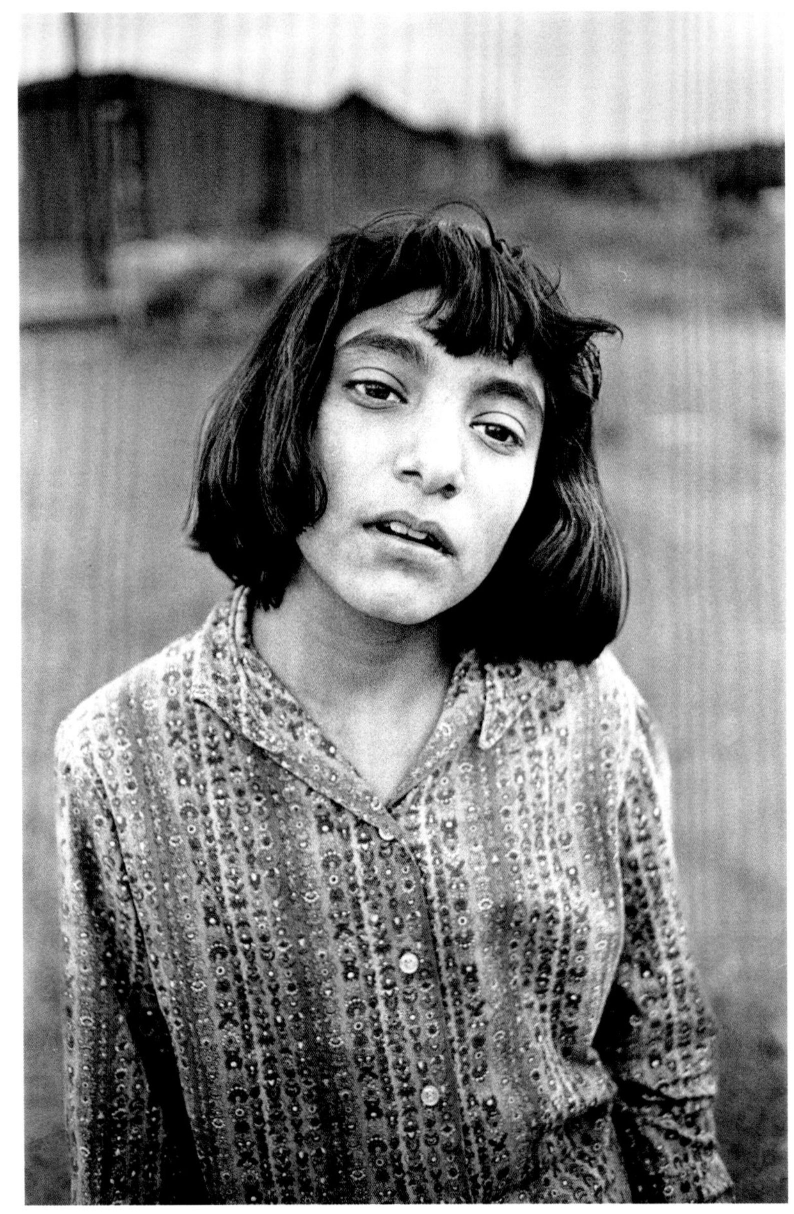

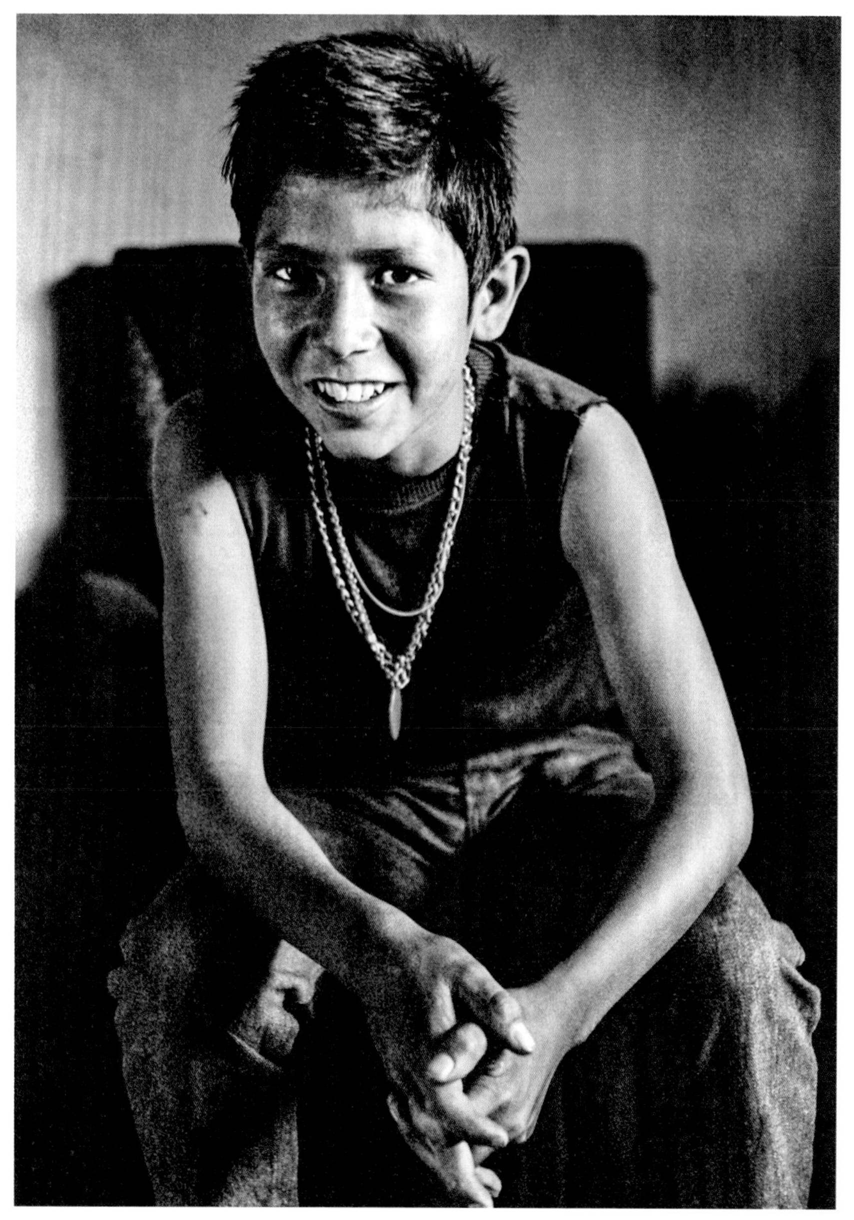

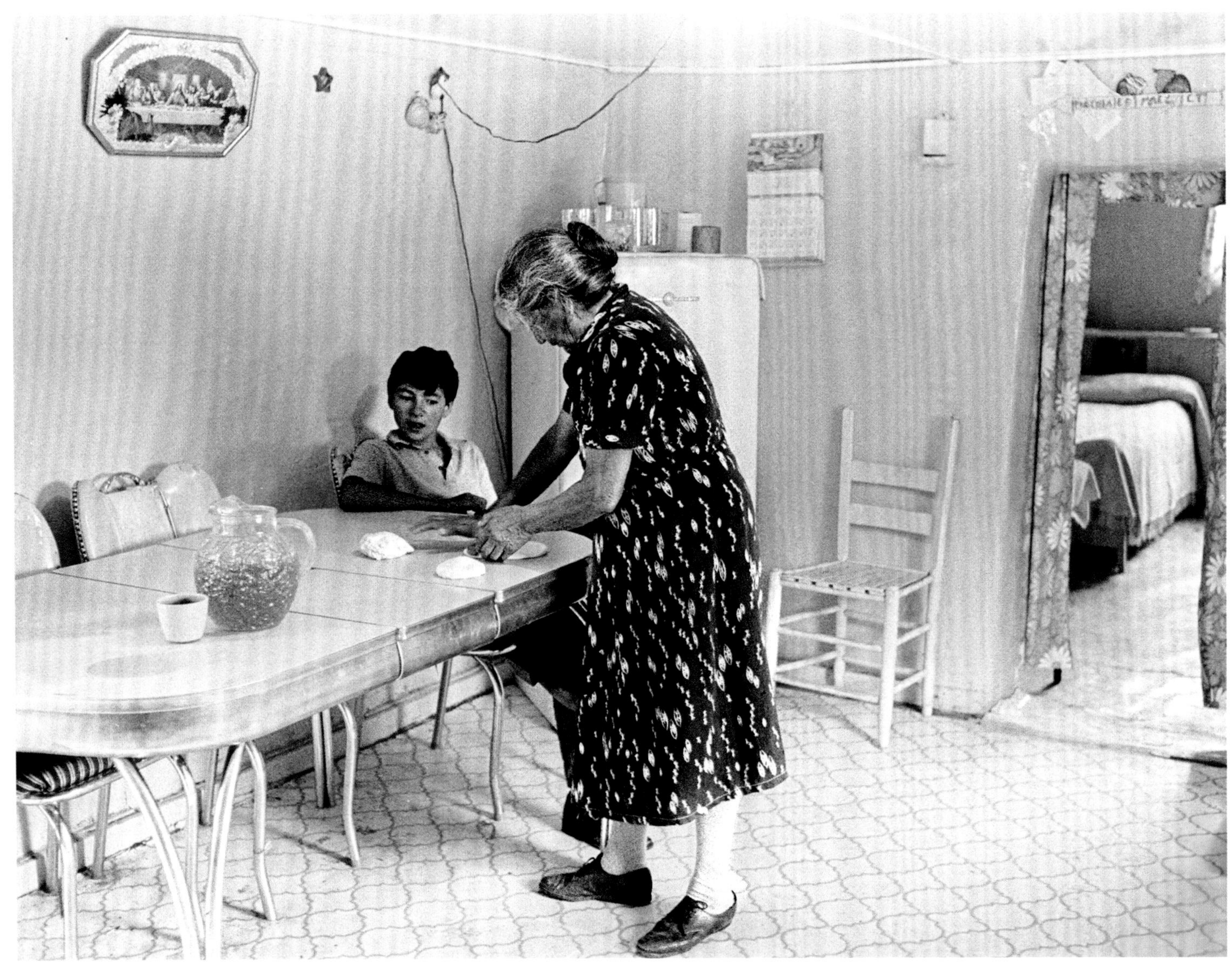

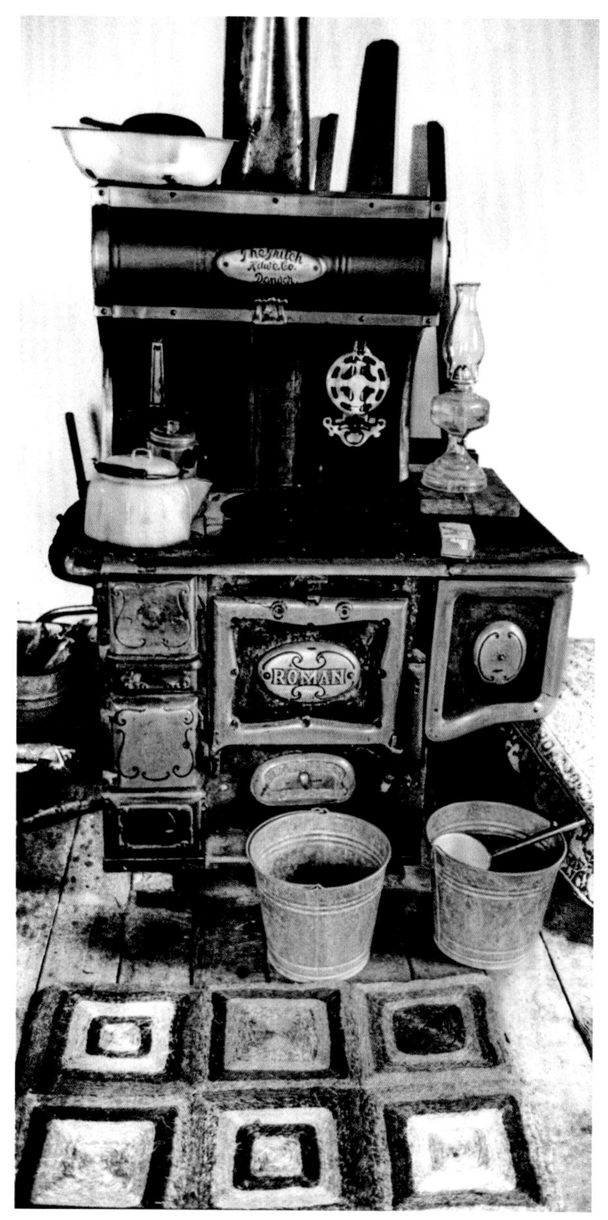
ROMAN

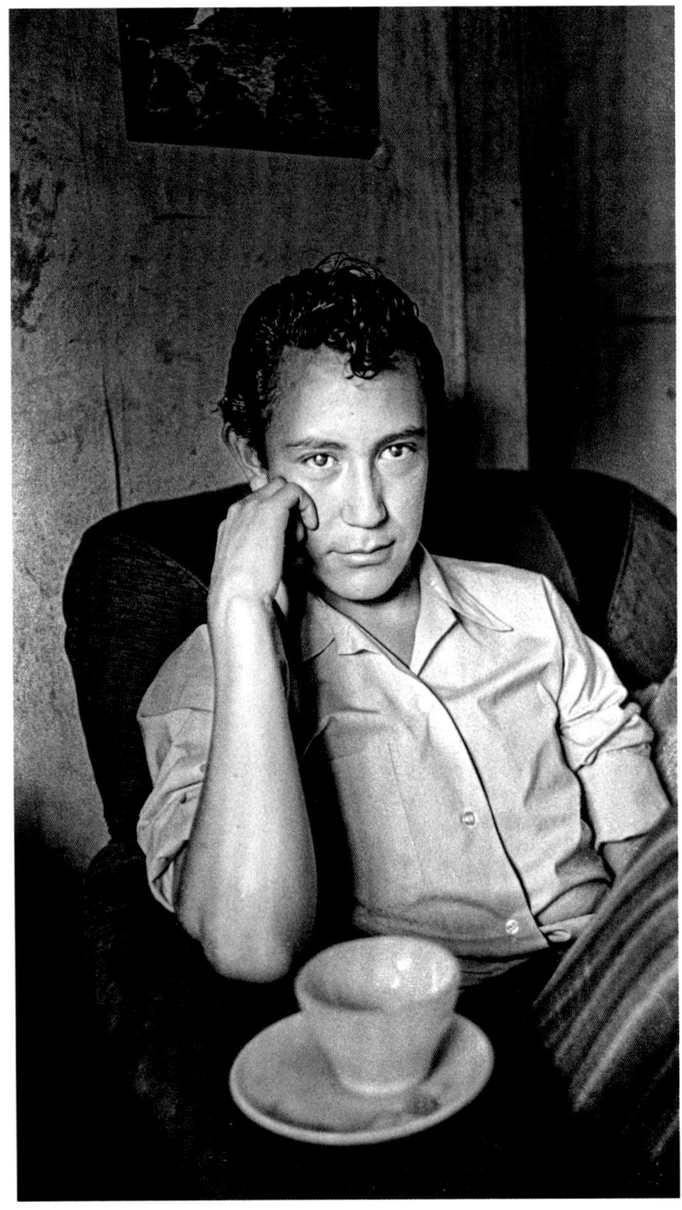

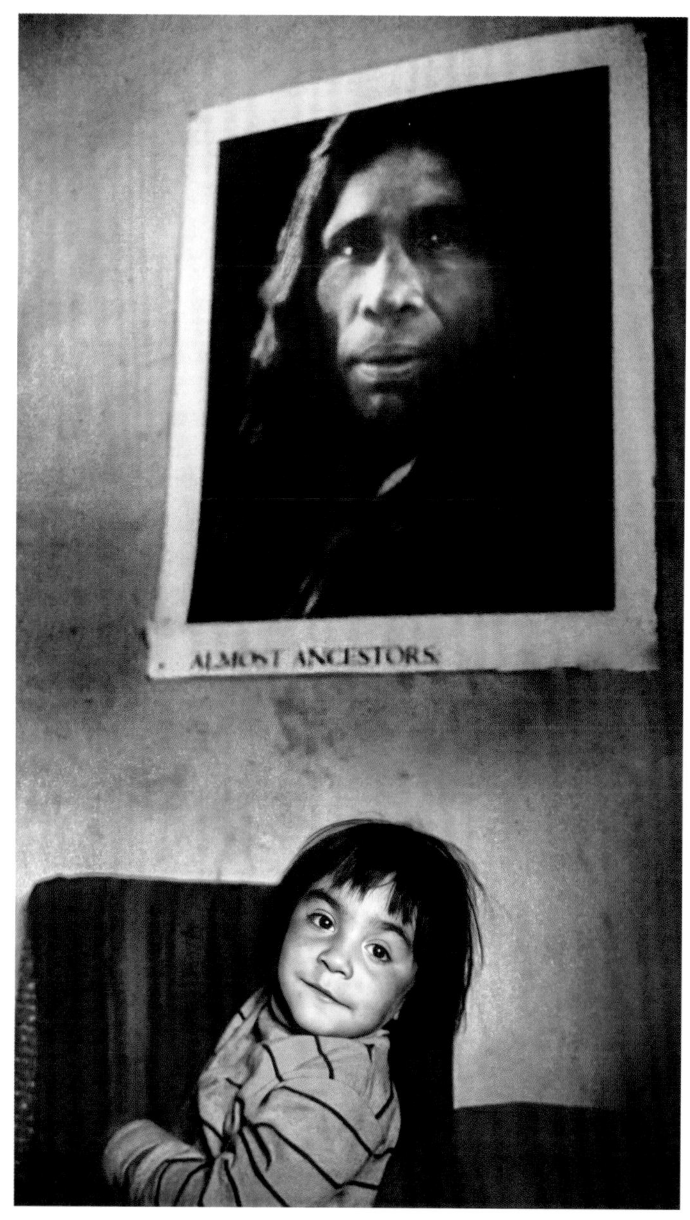
ALMOST ANCESTORS

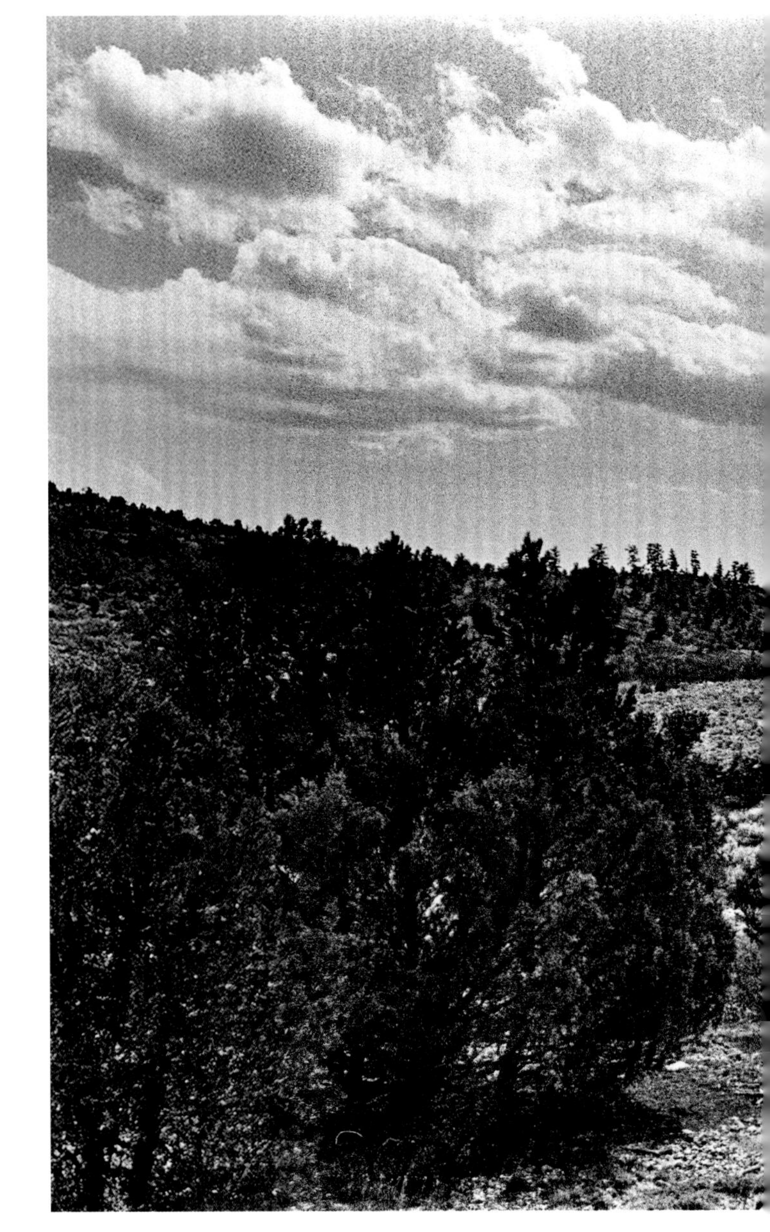

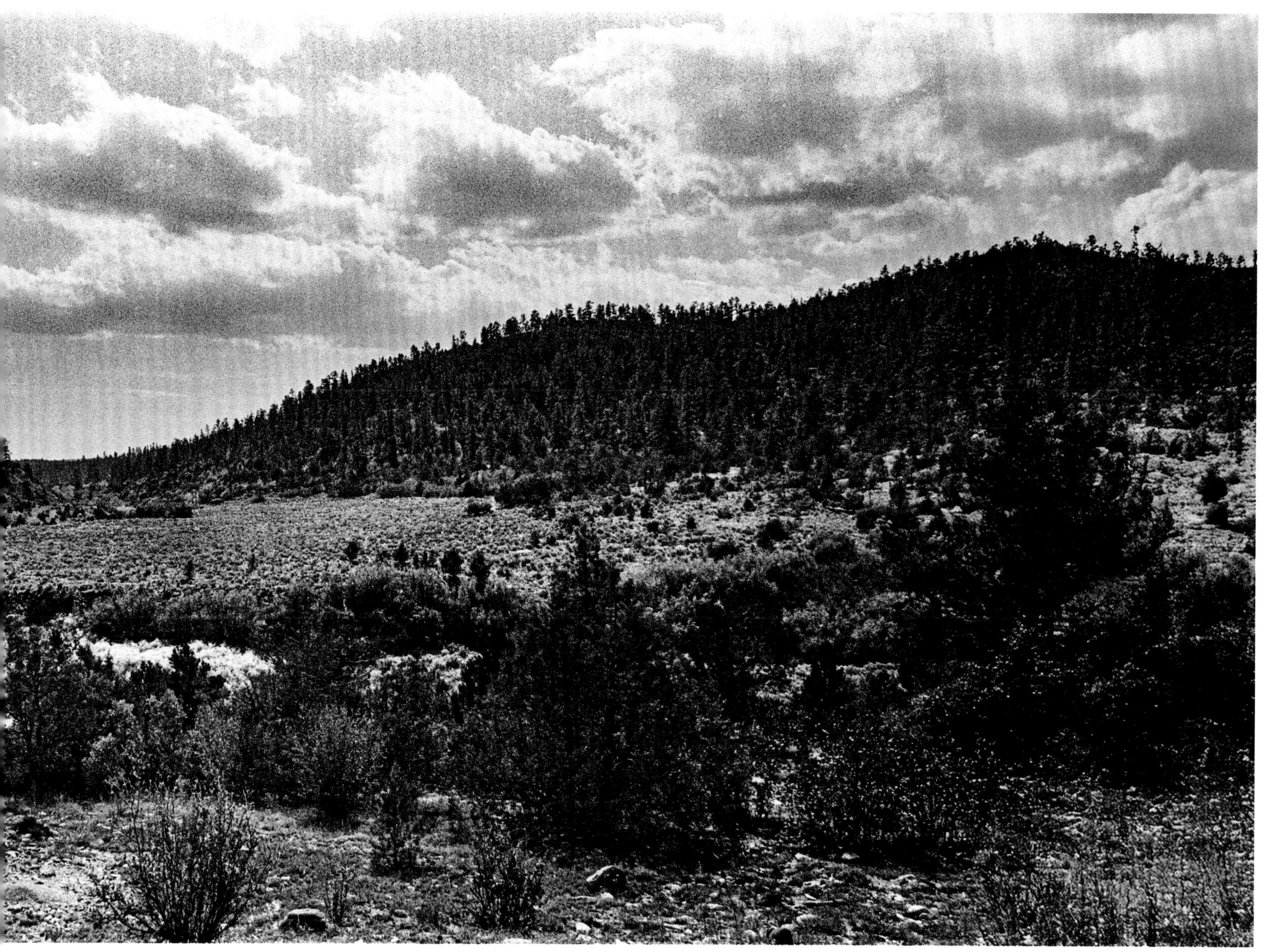

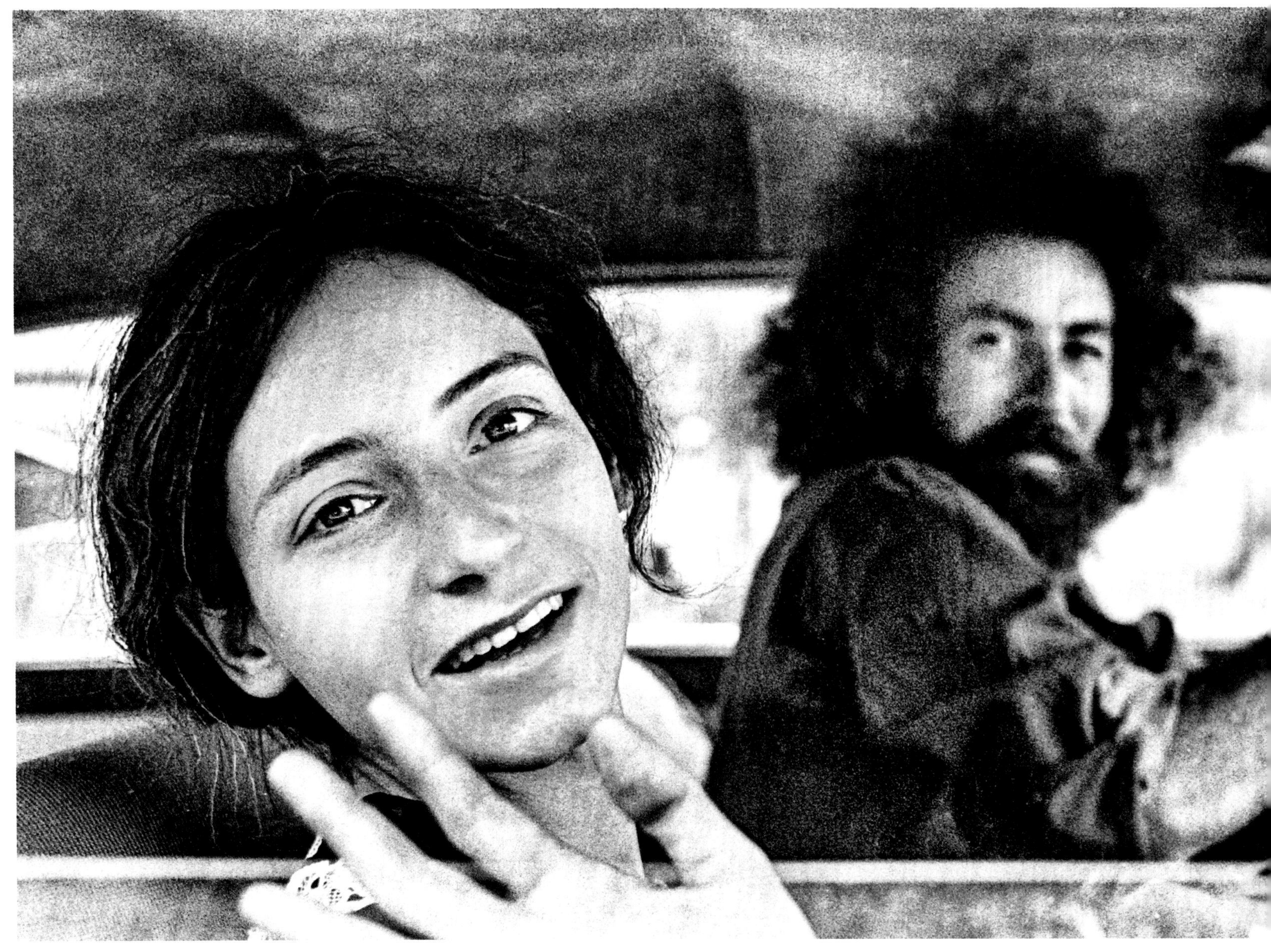

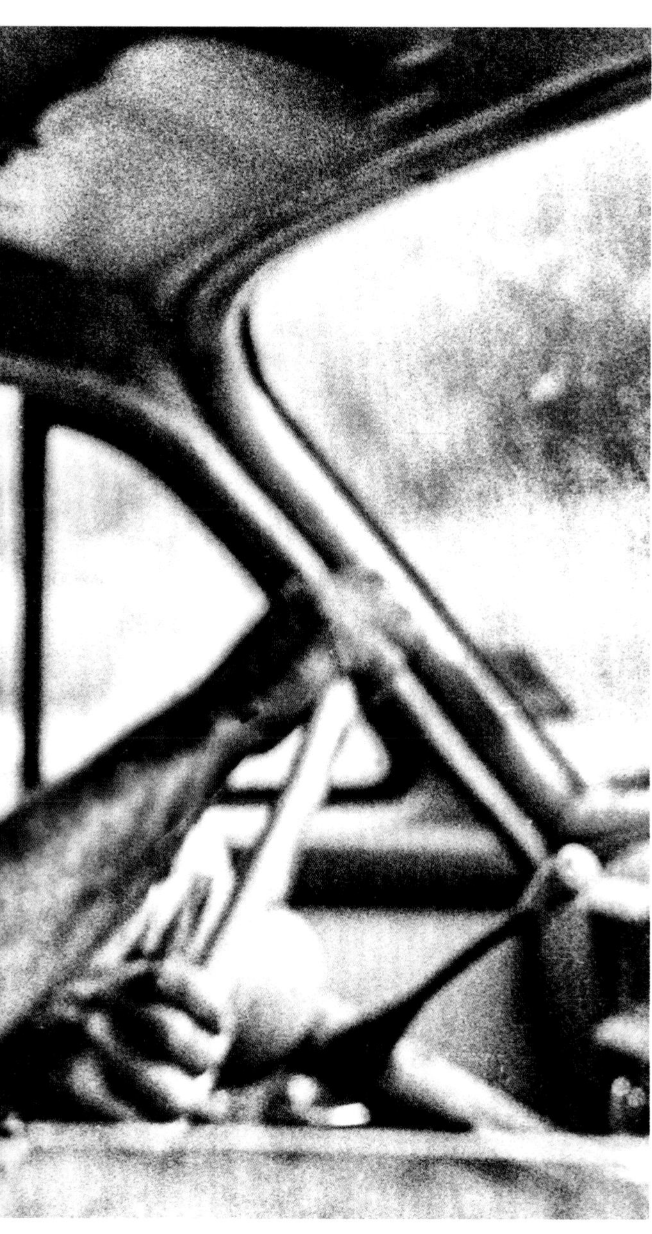

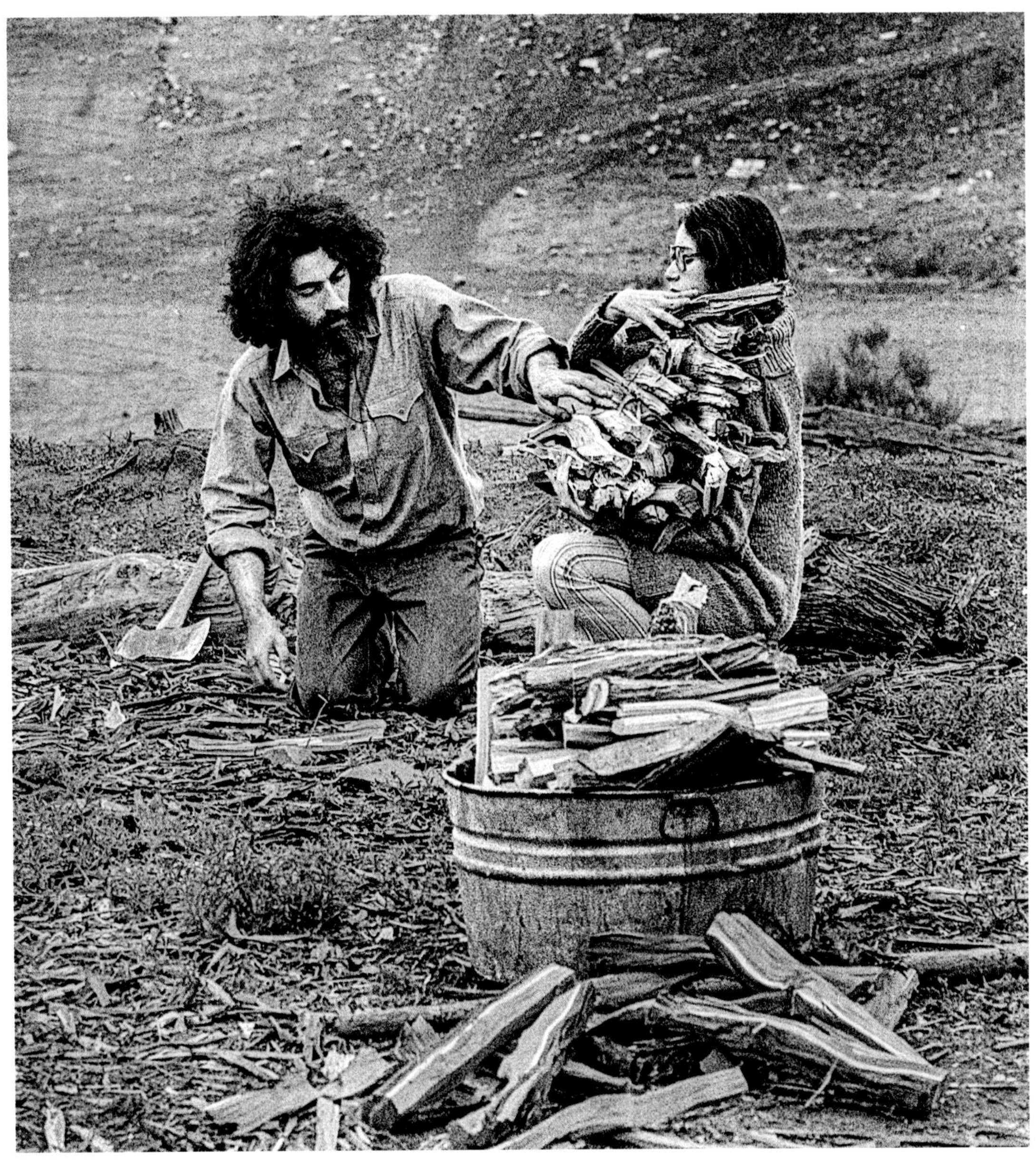

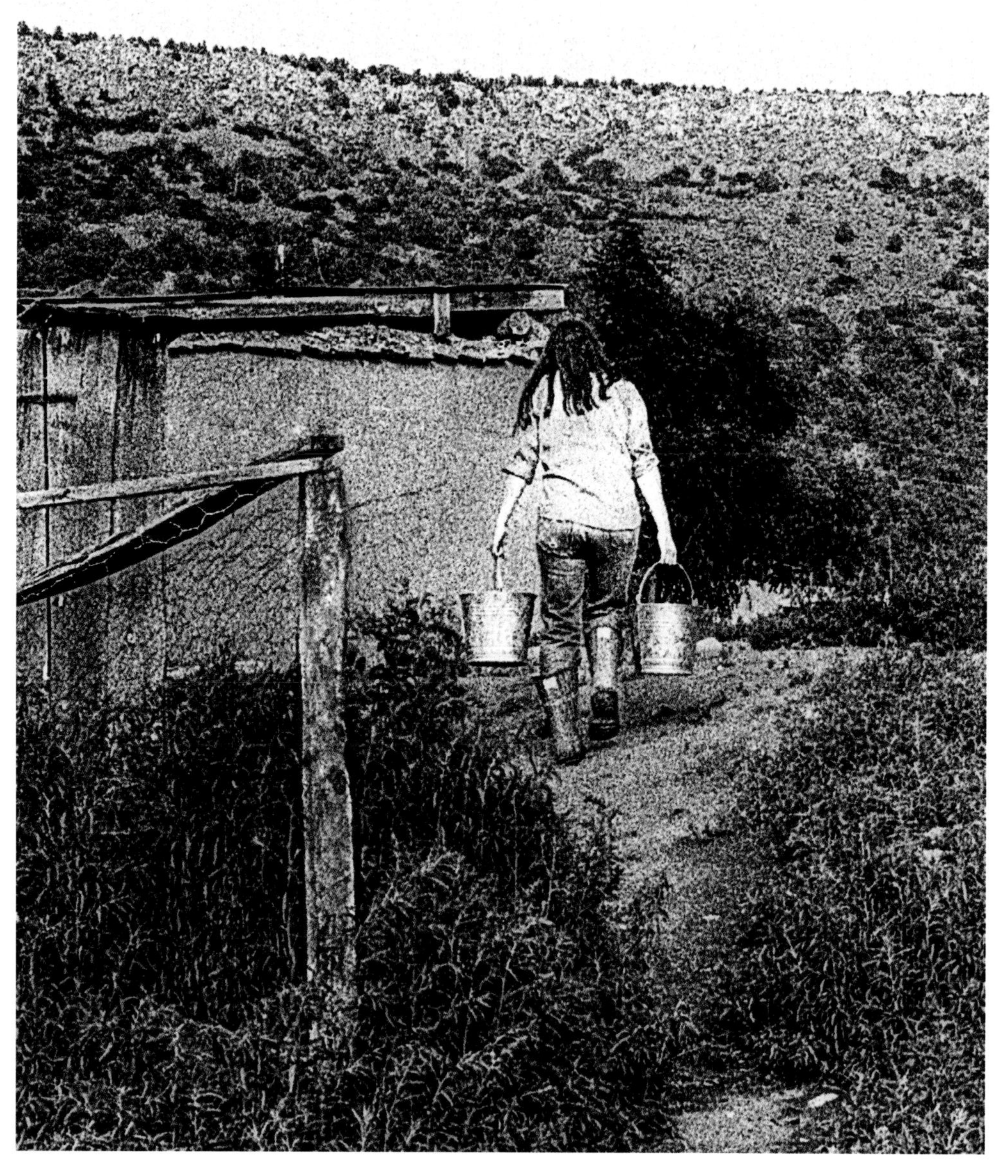

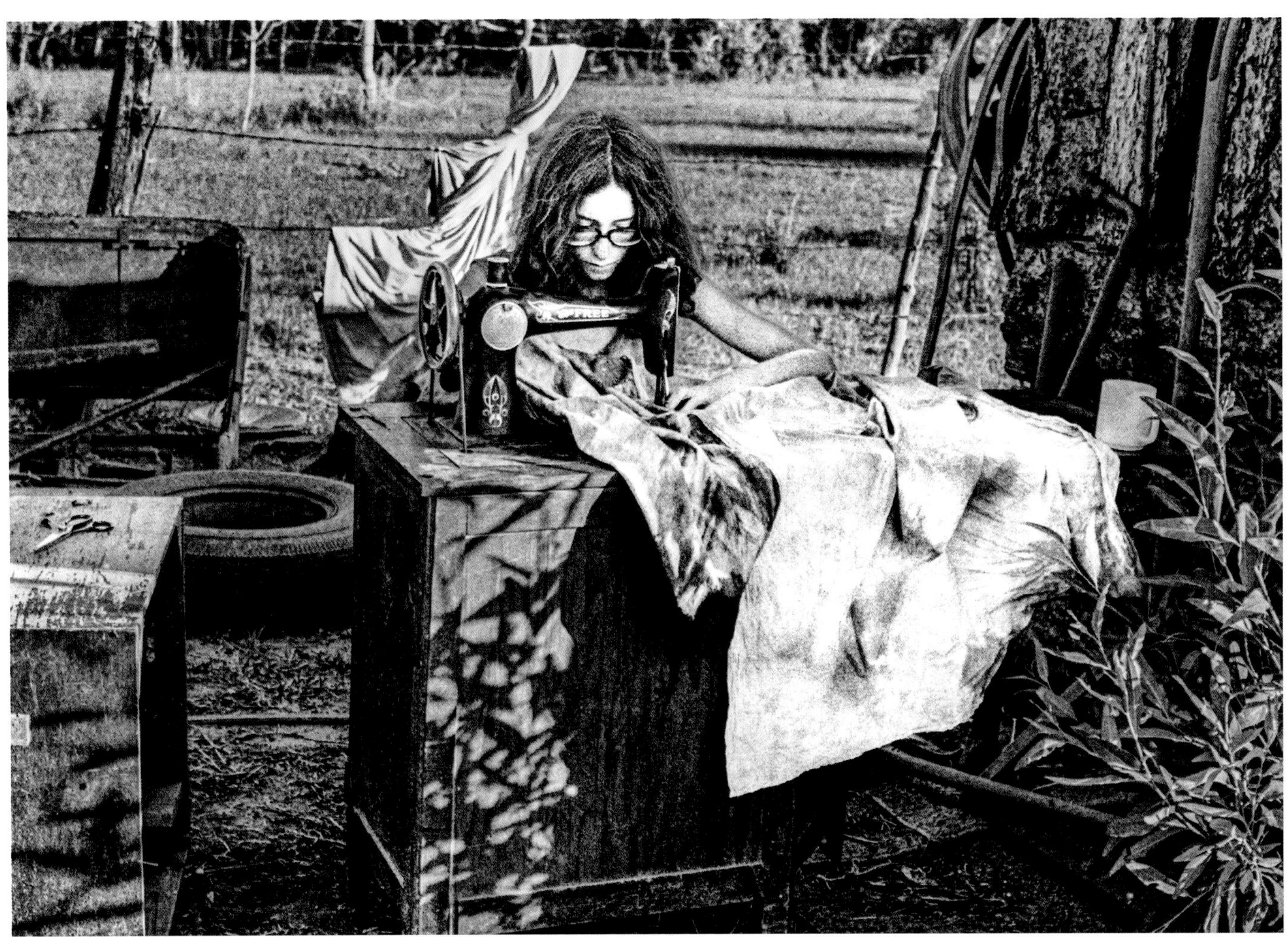

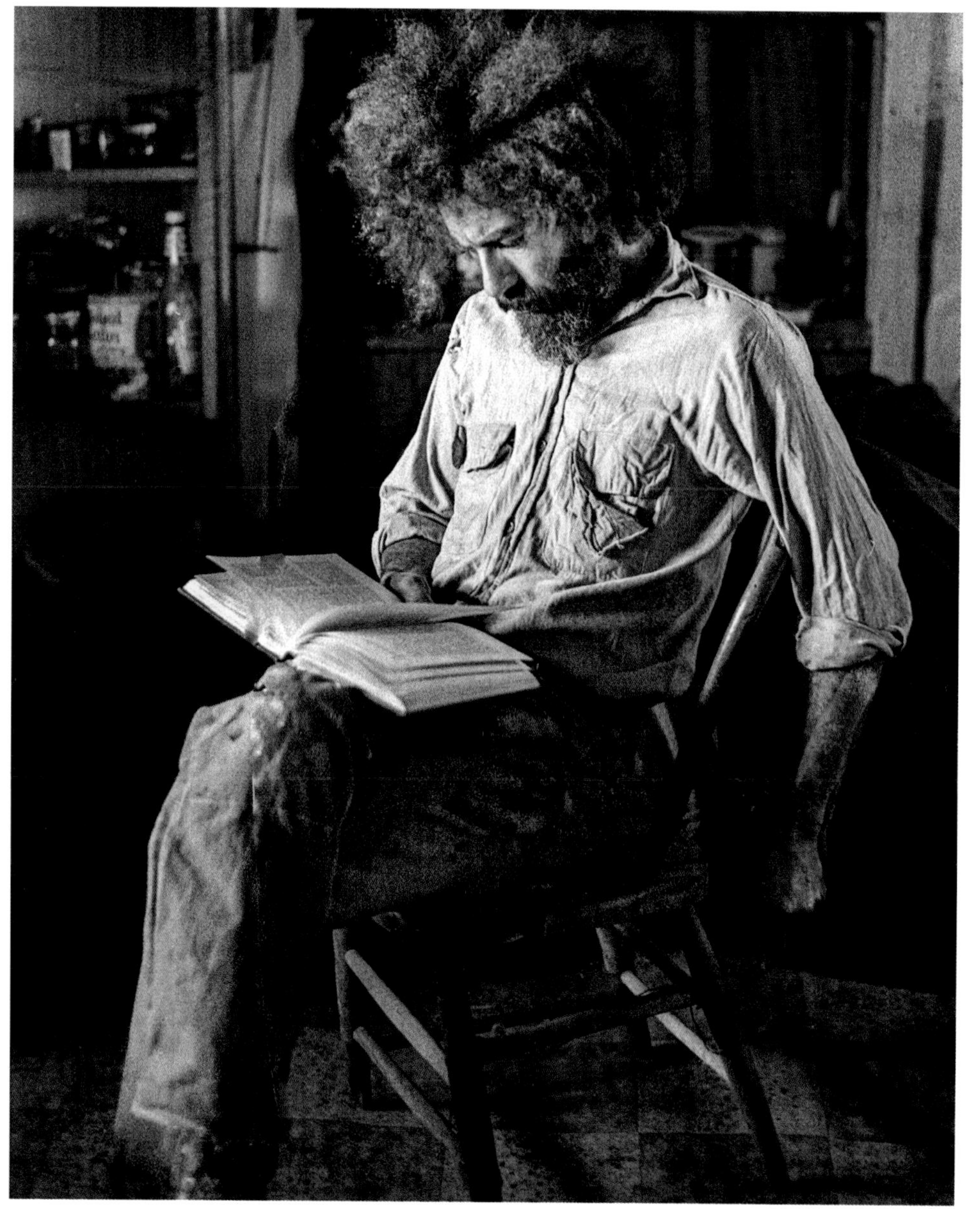

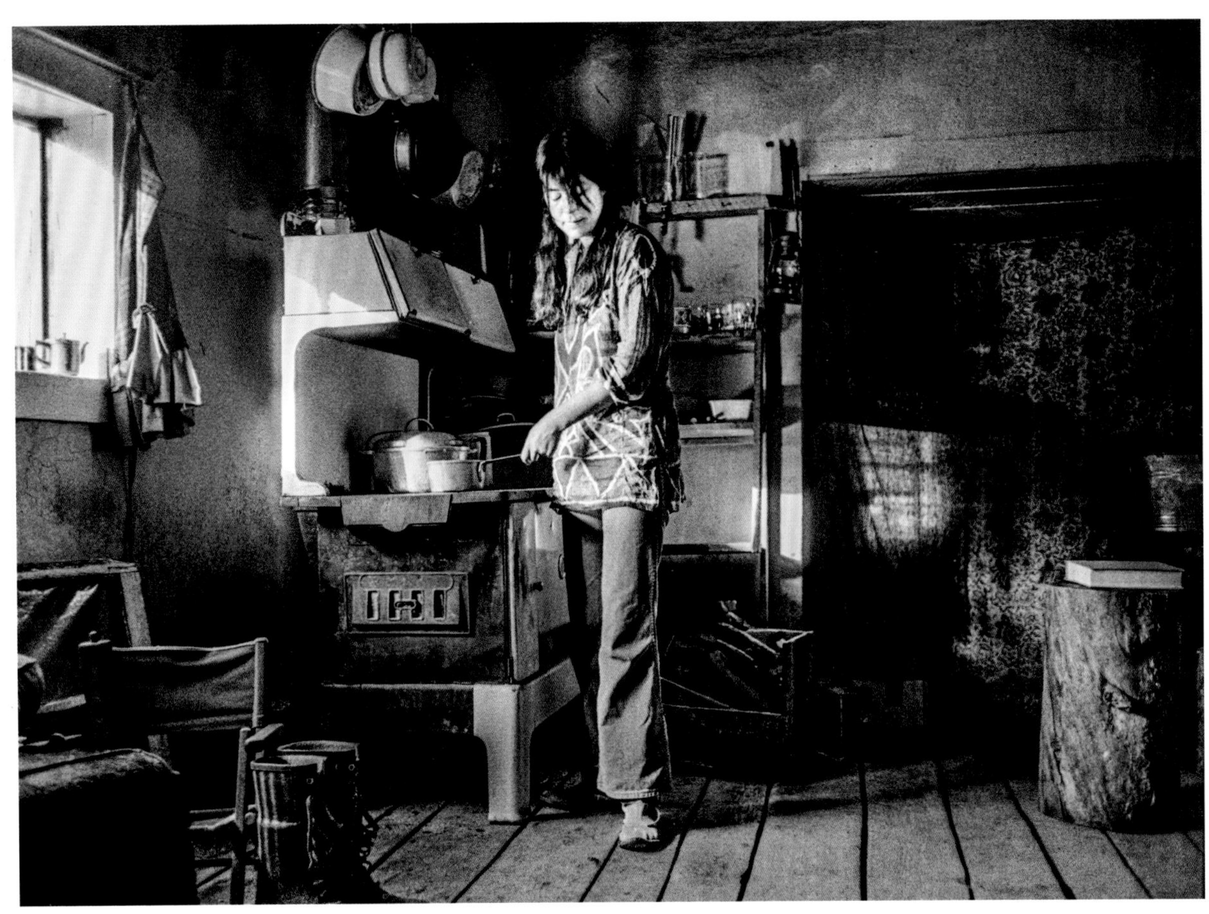

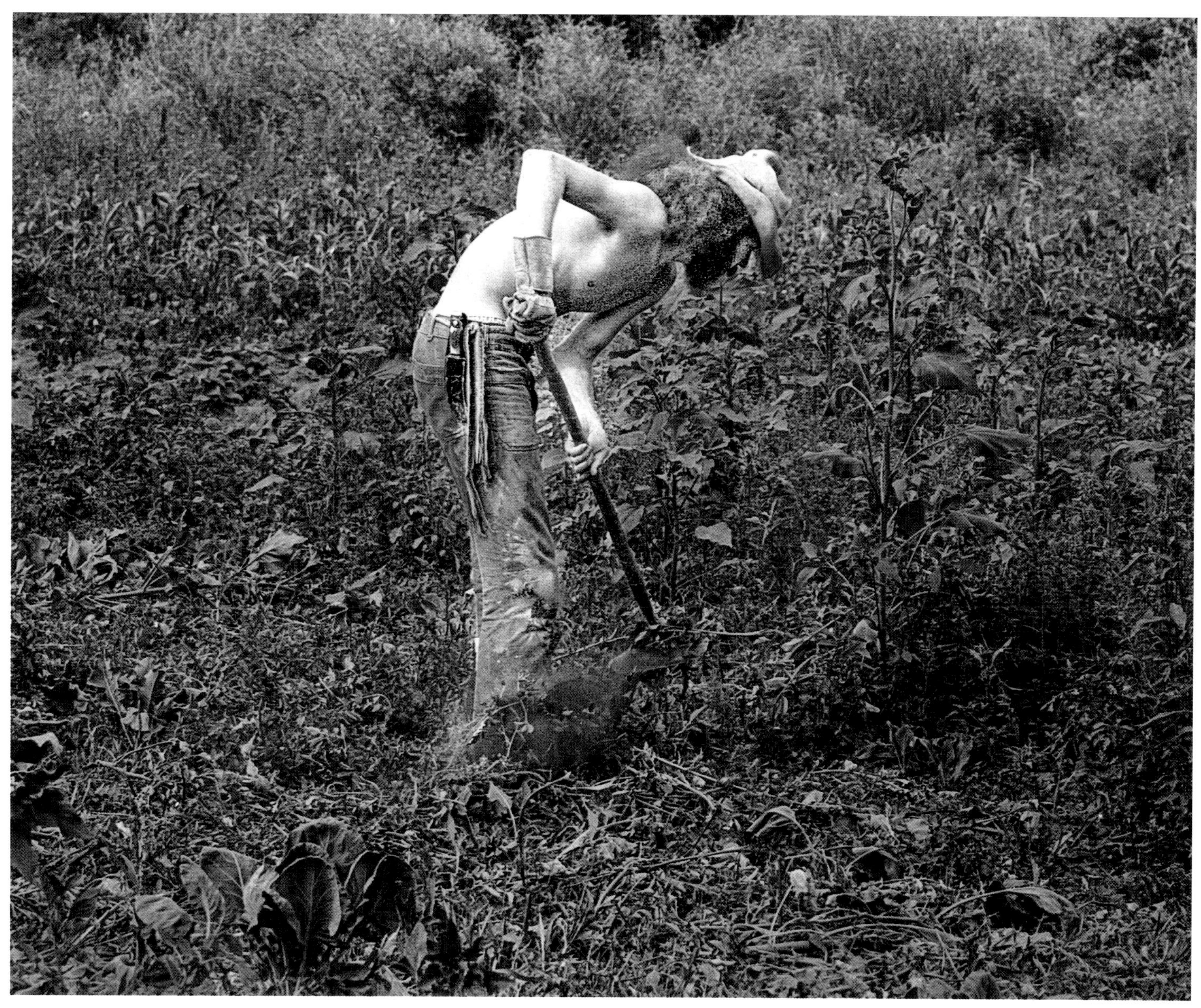

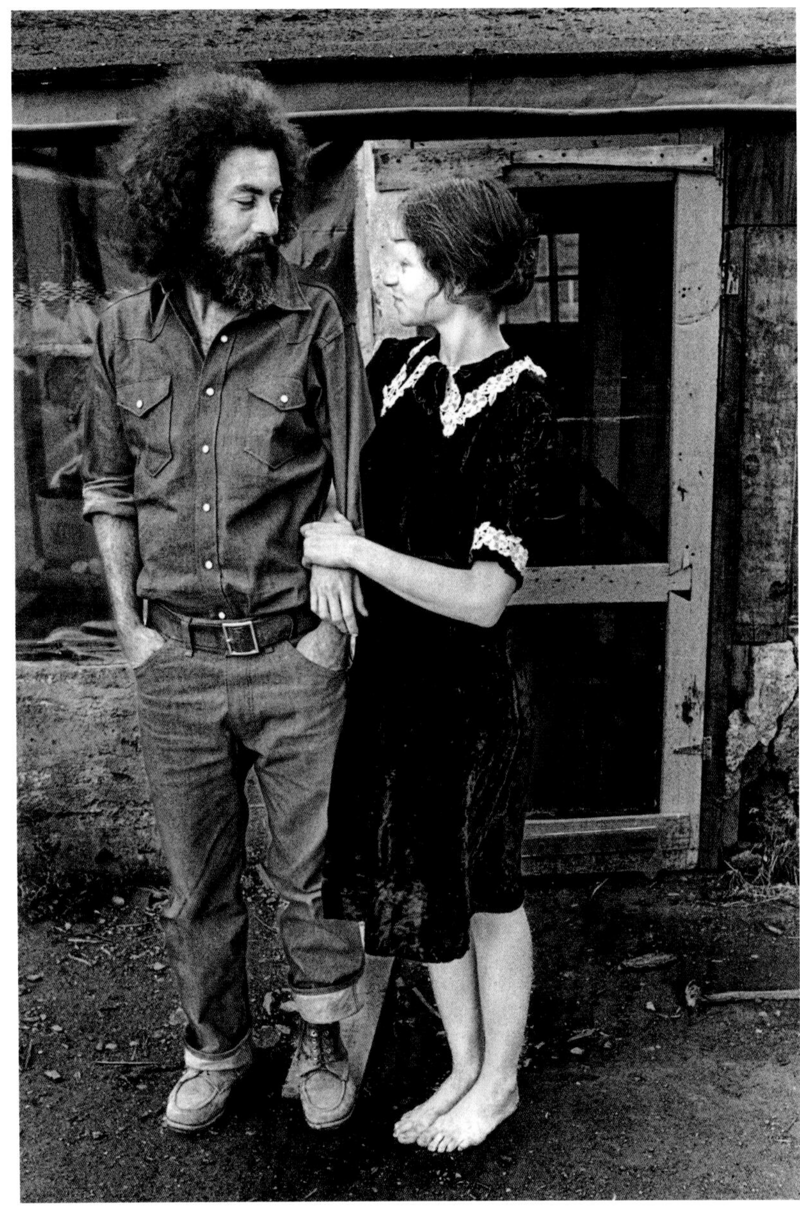

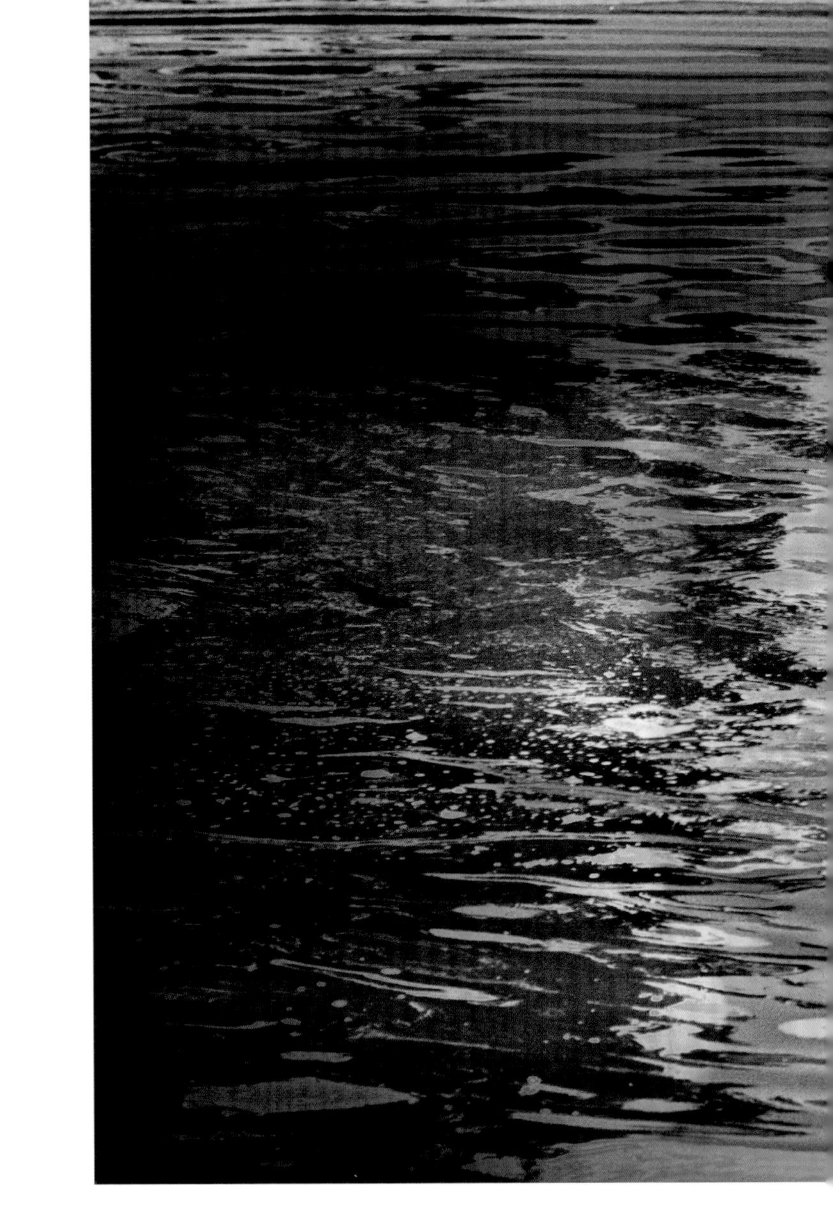

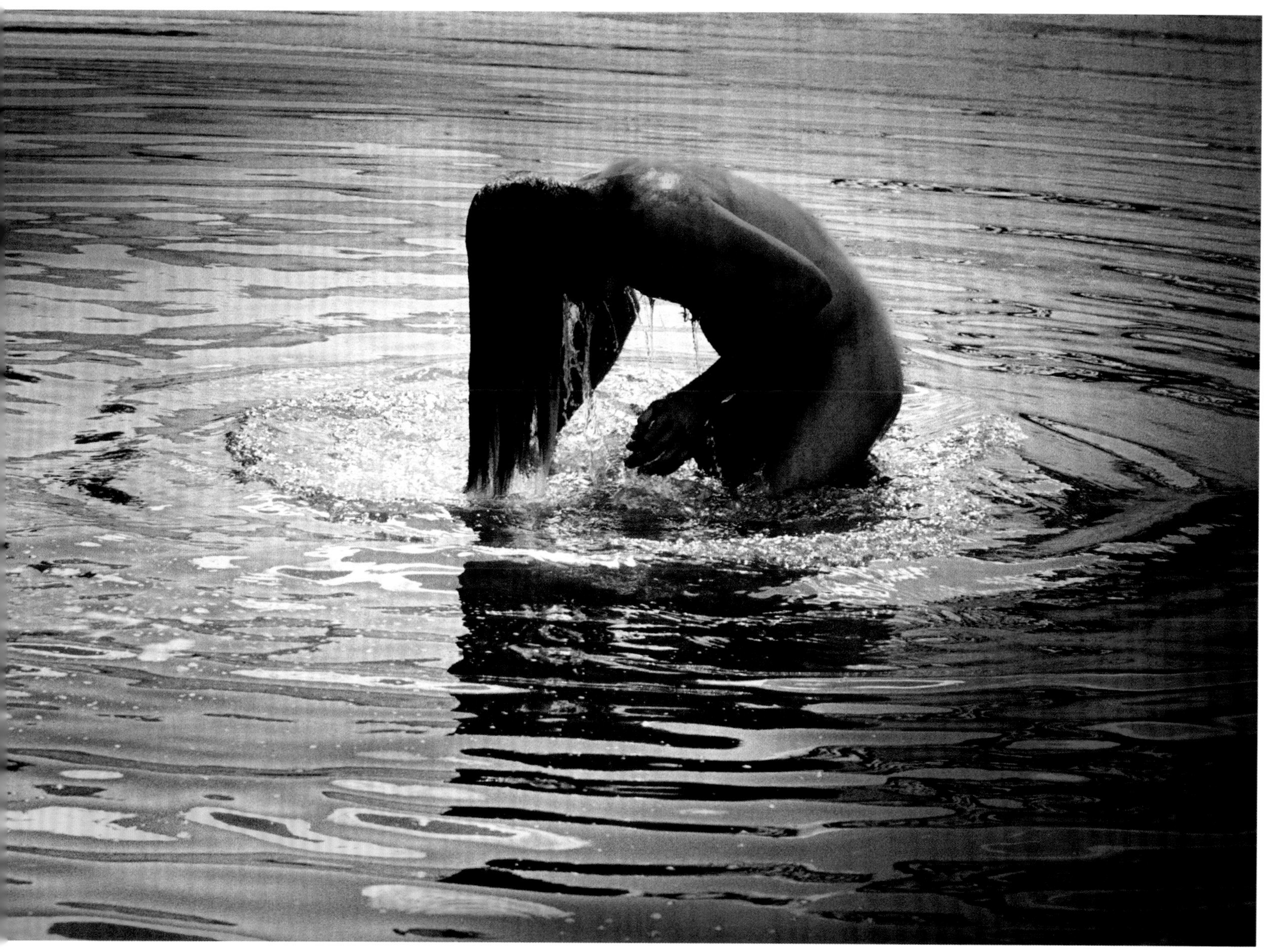

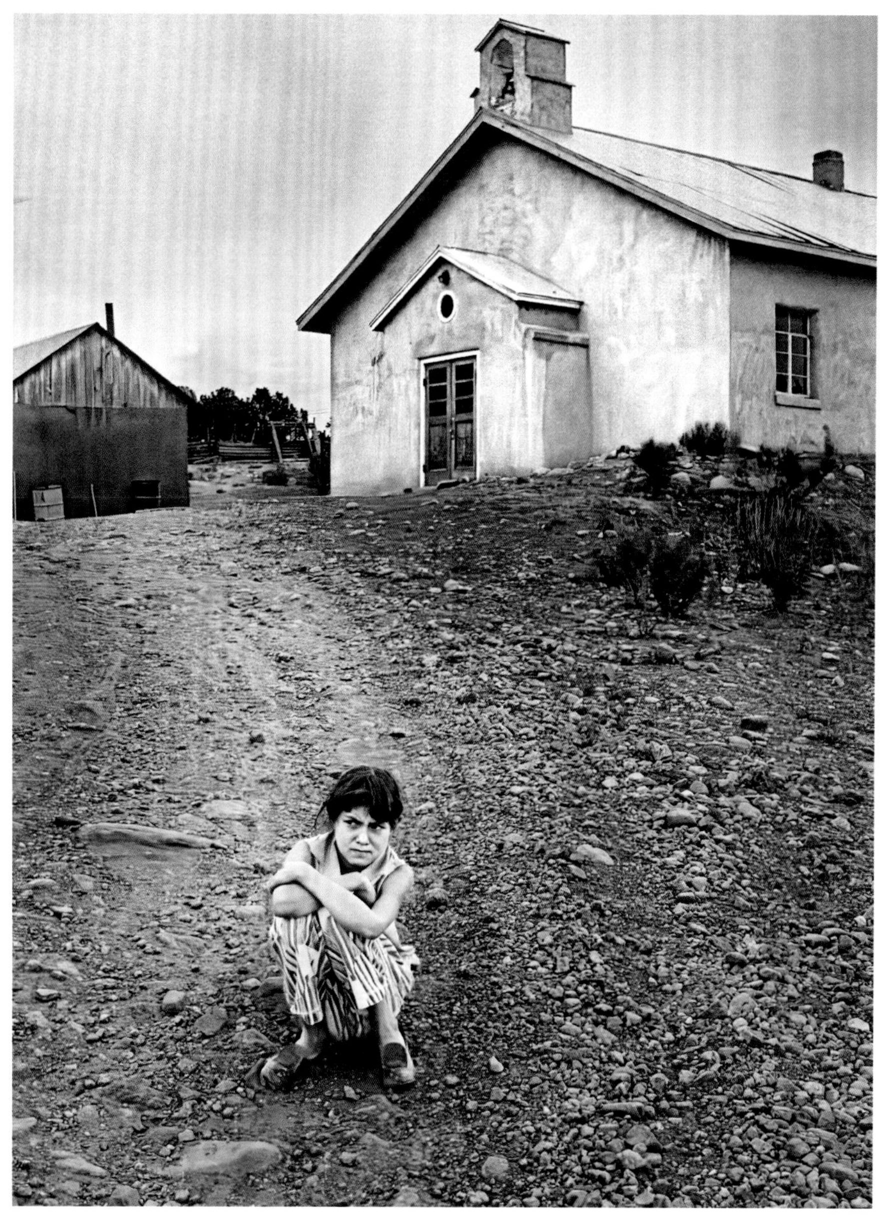

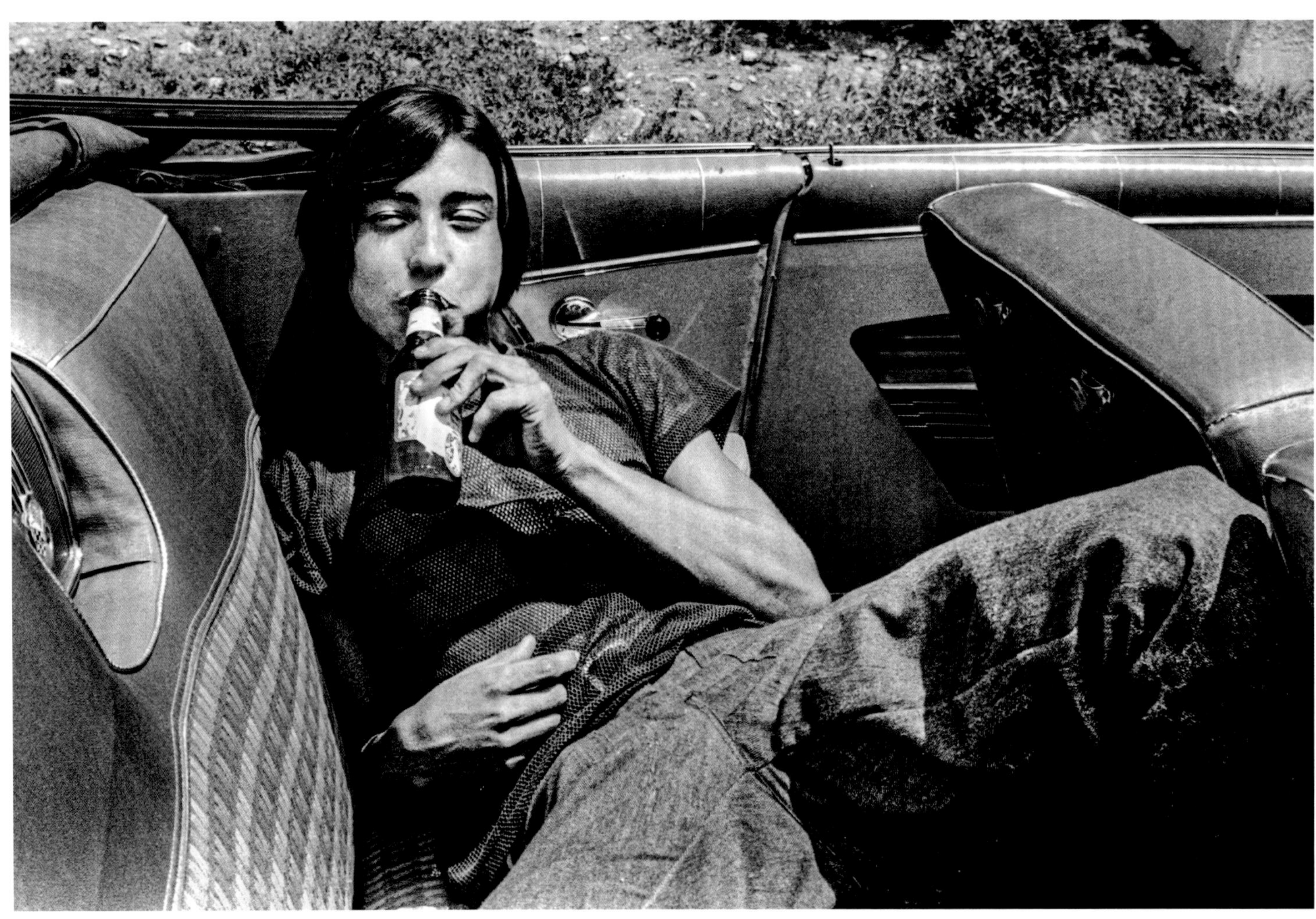

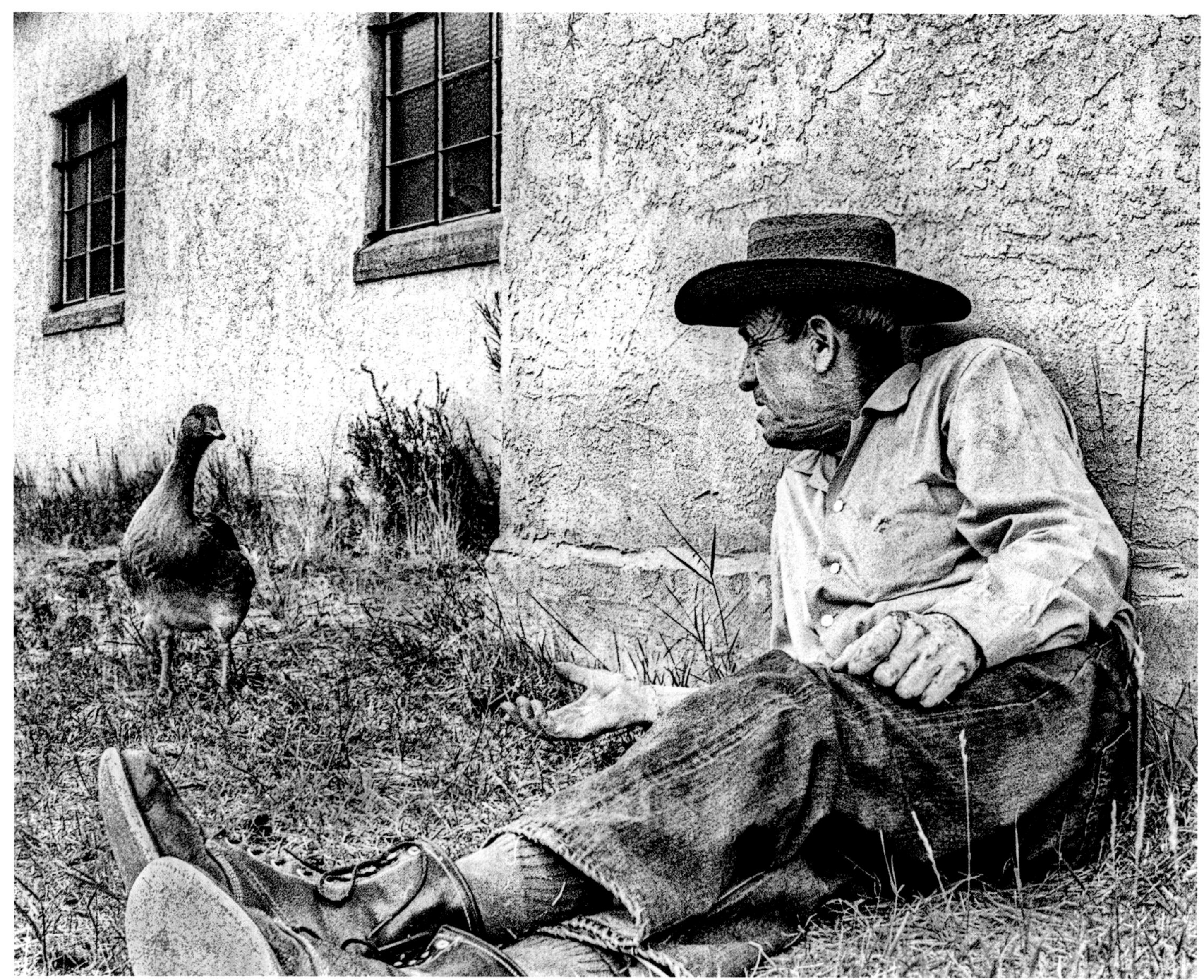

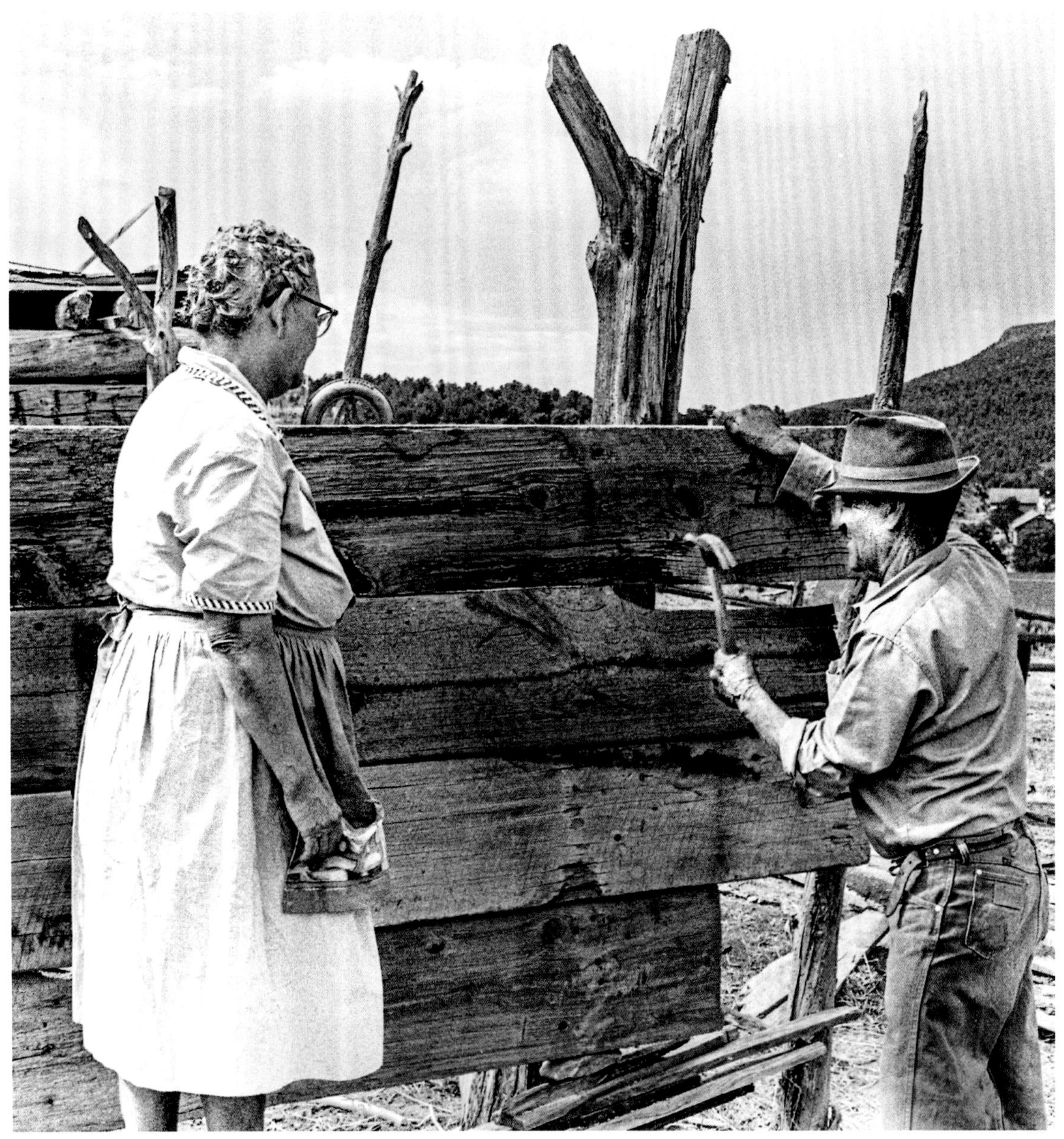

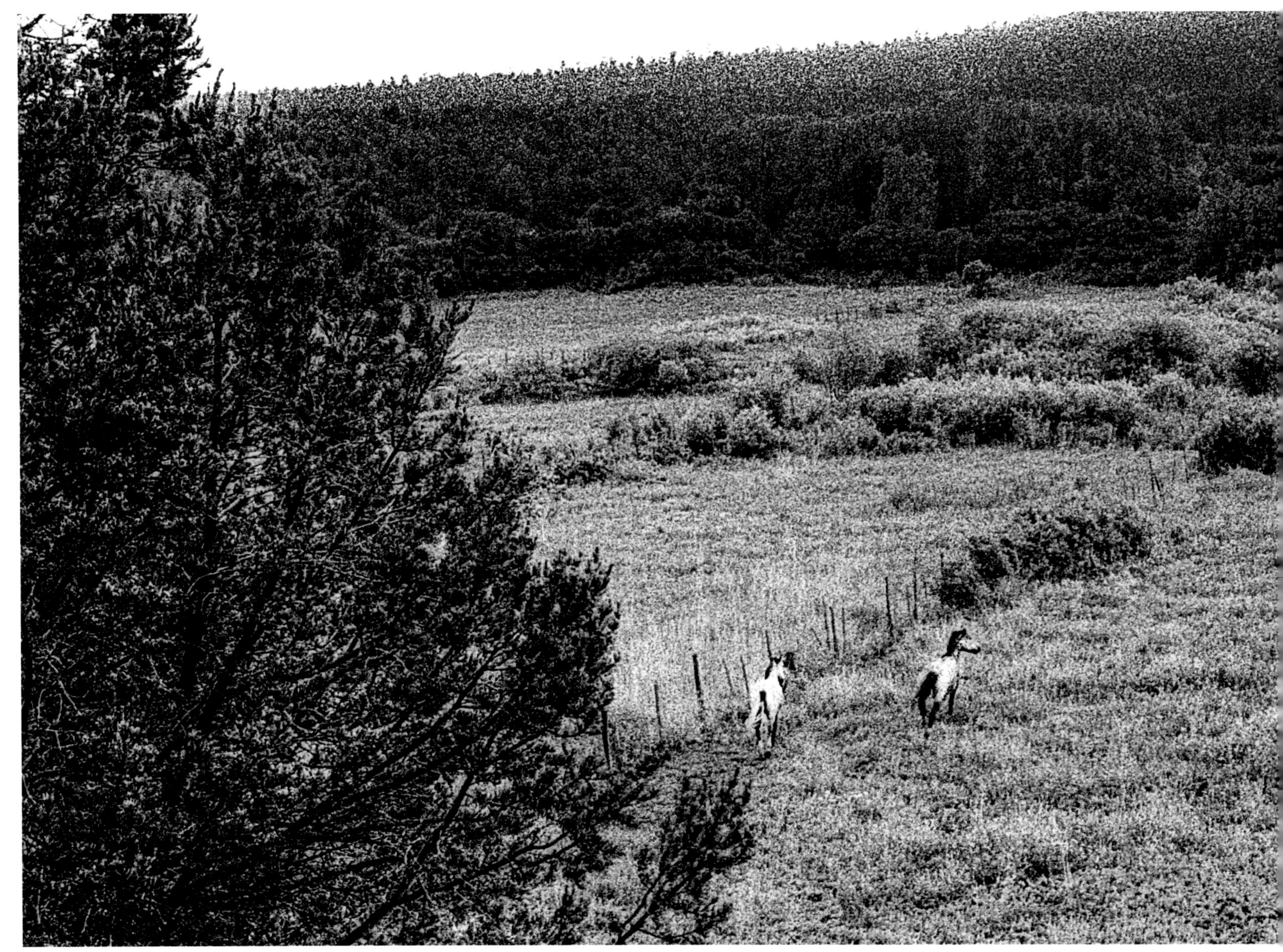

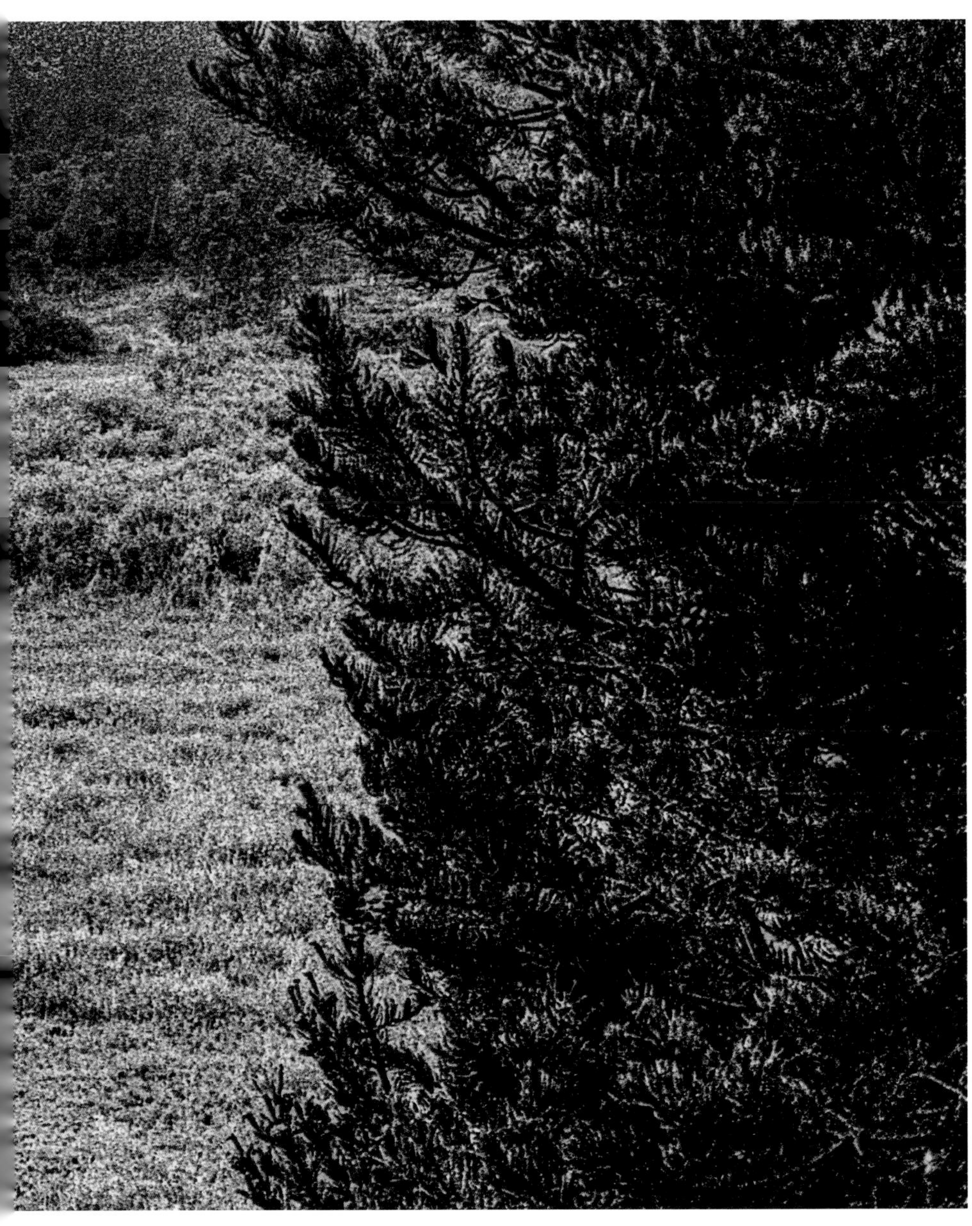

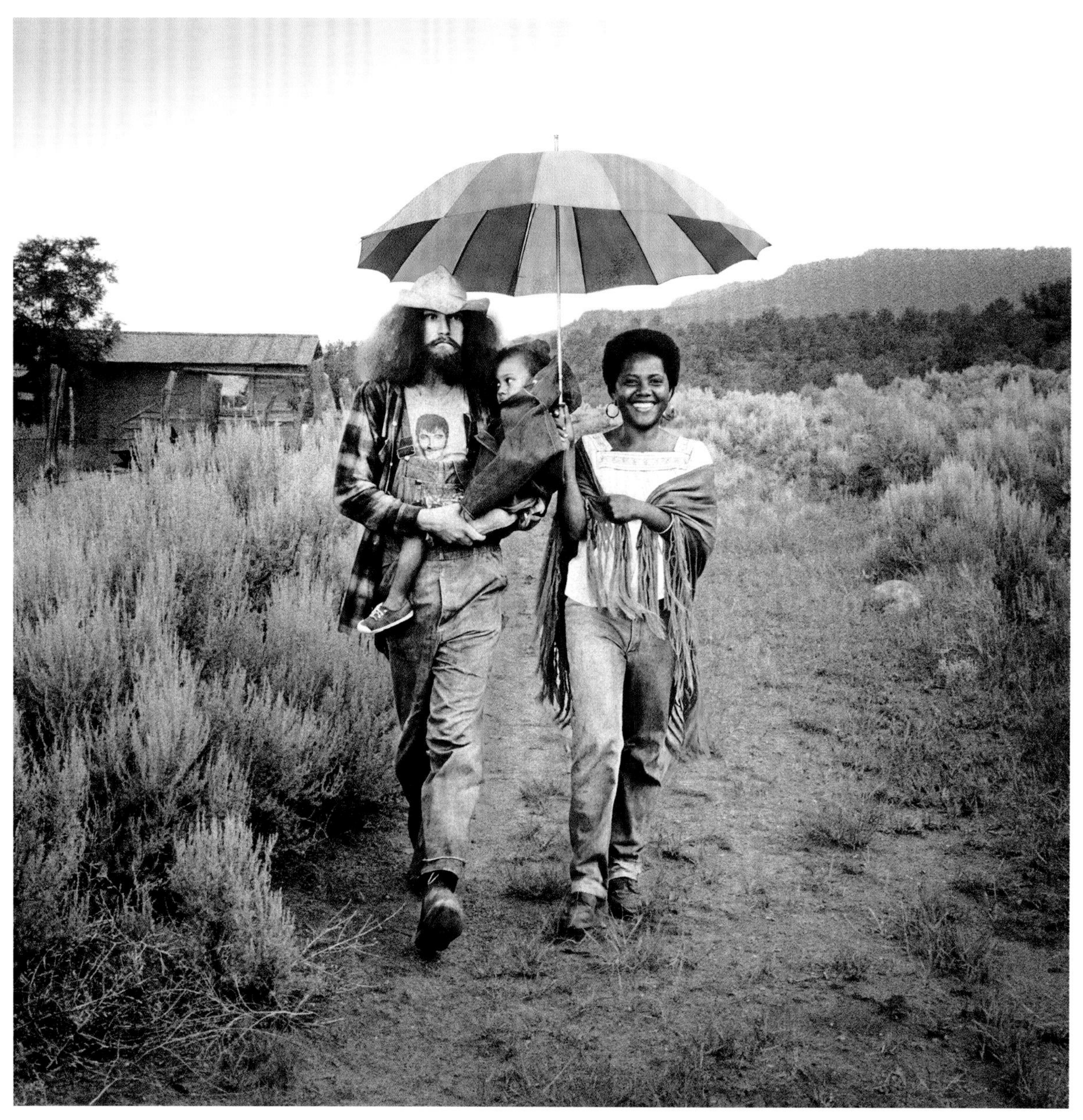

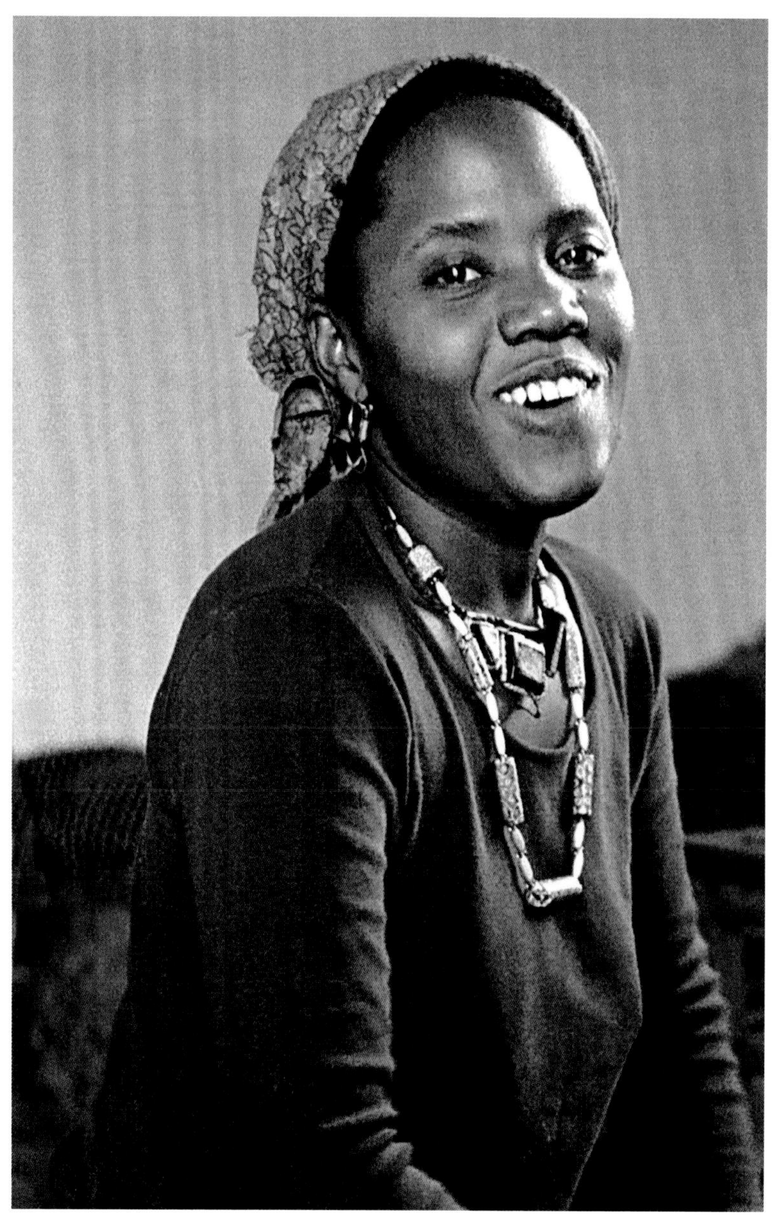

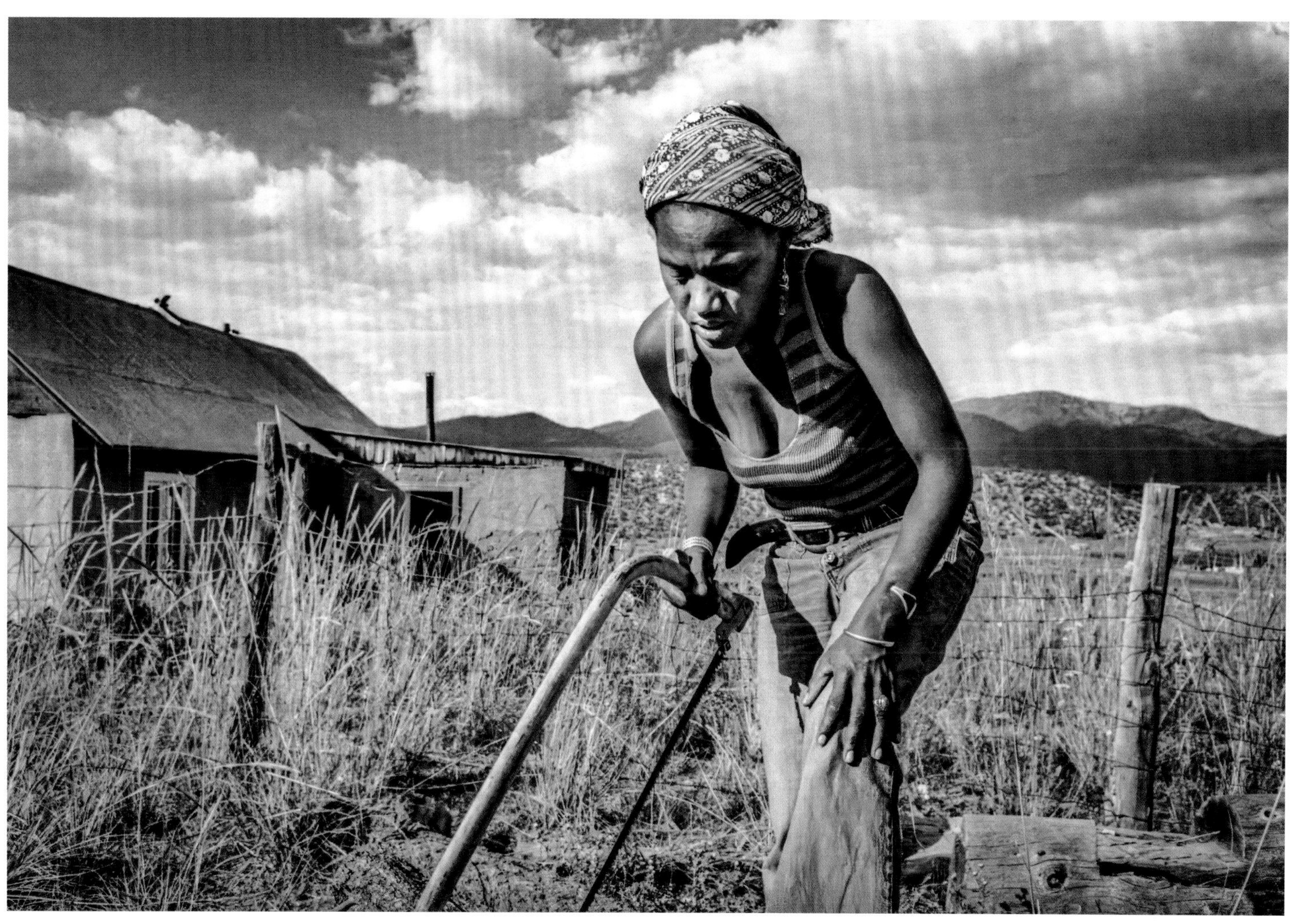

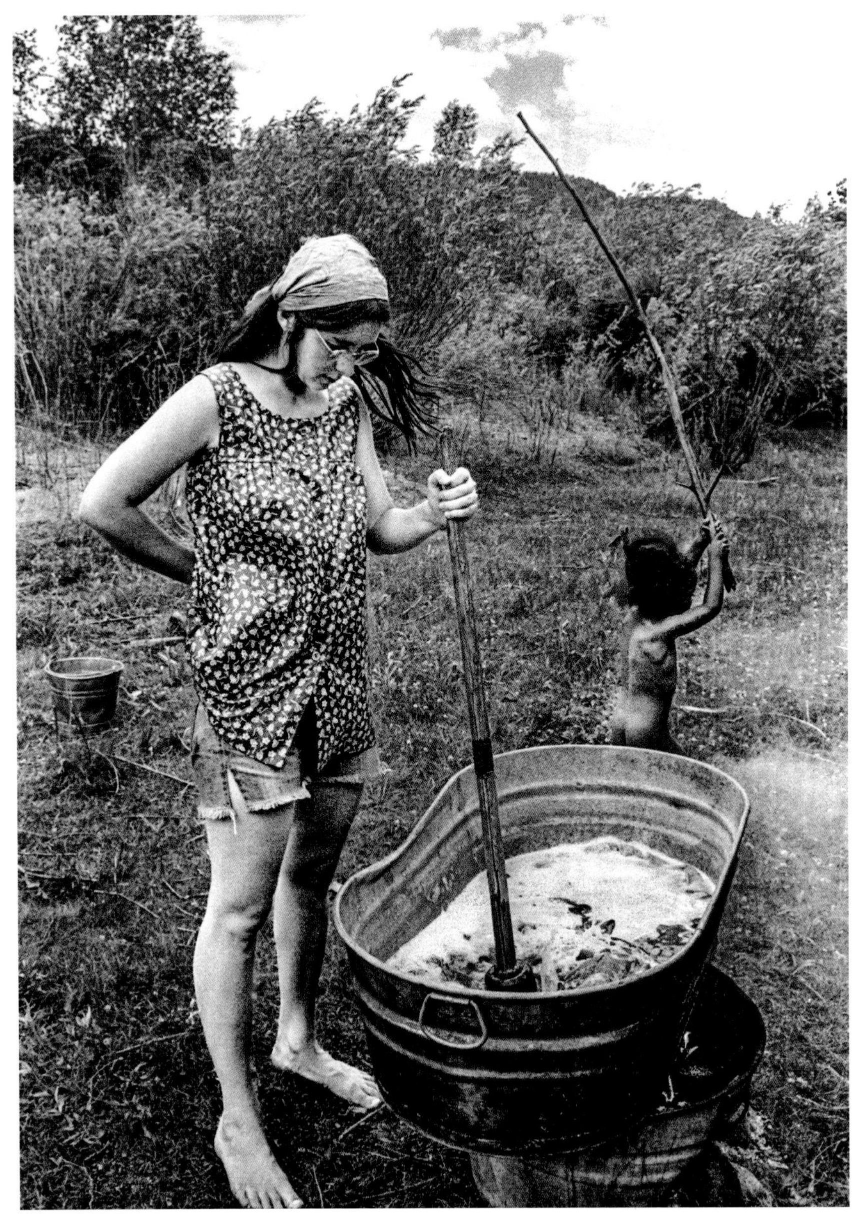

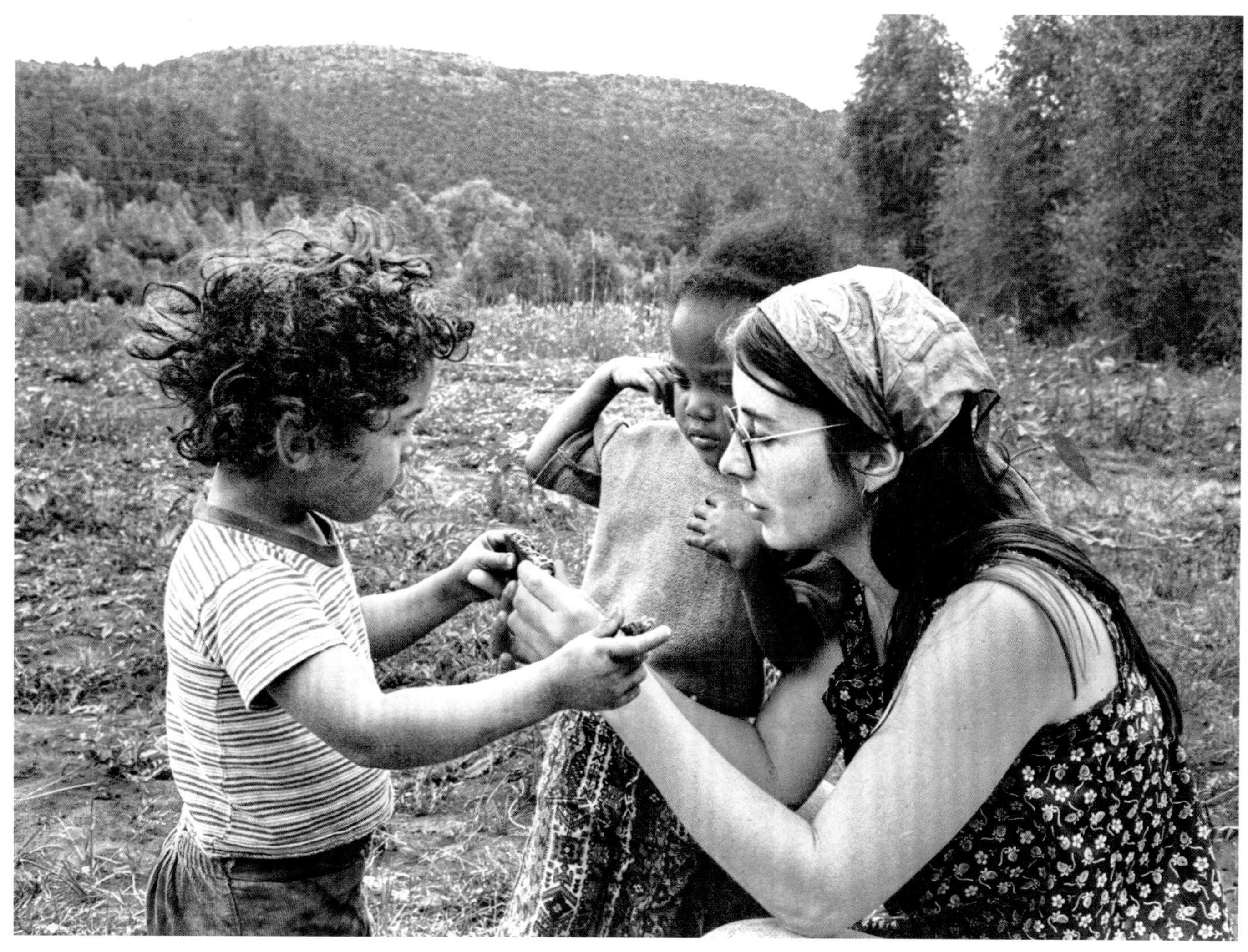

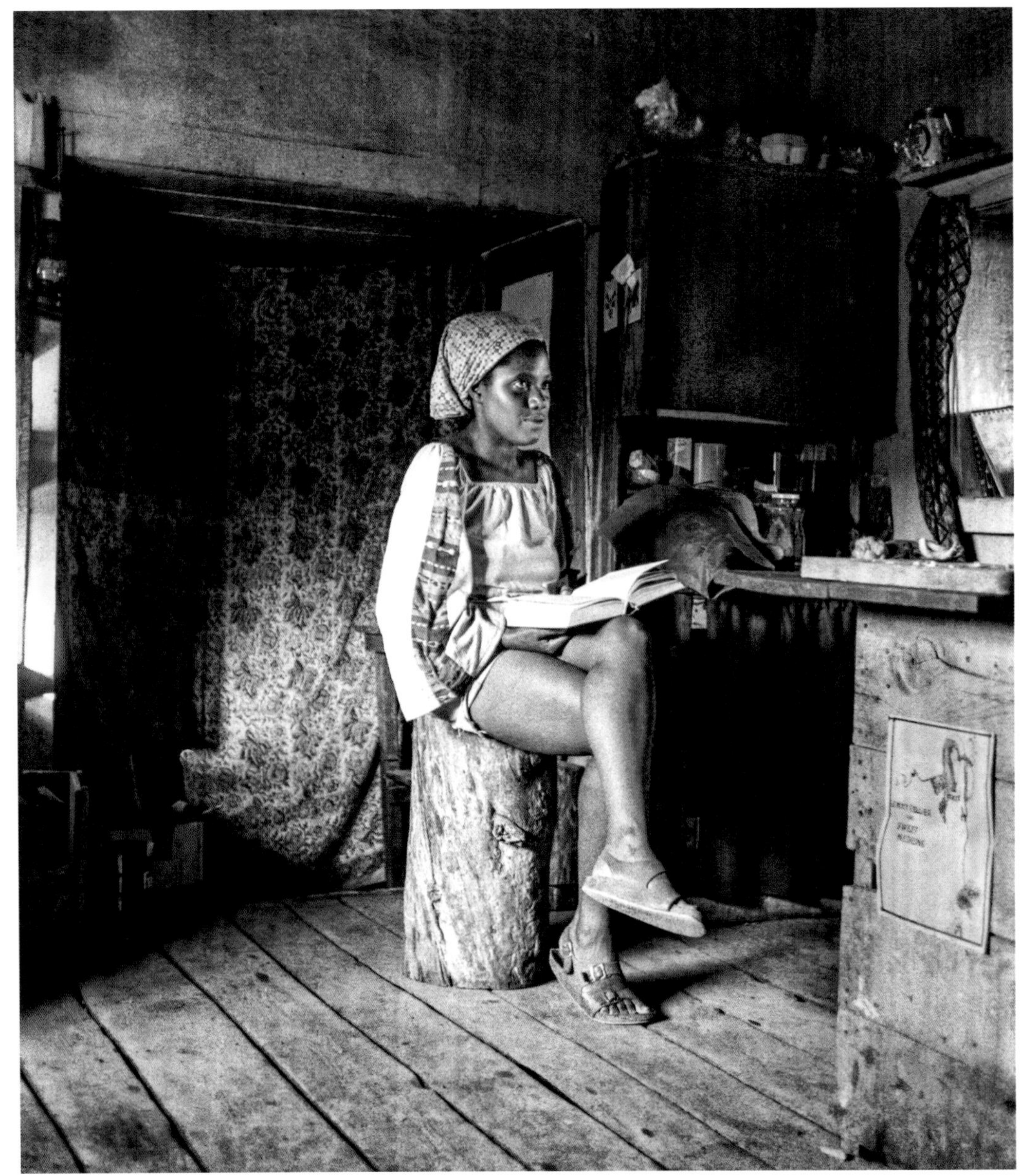

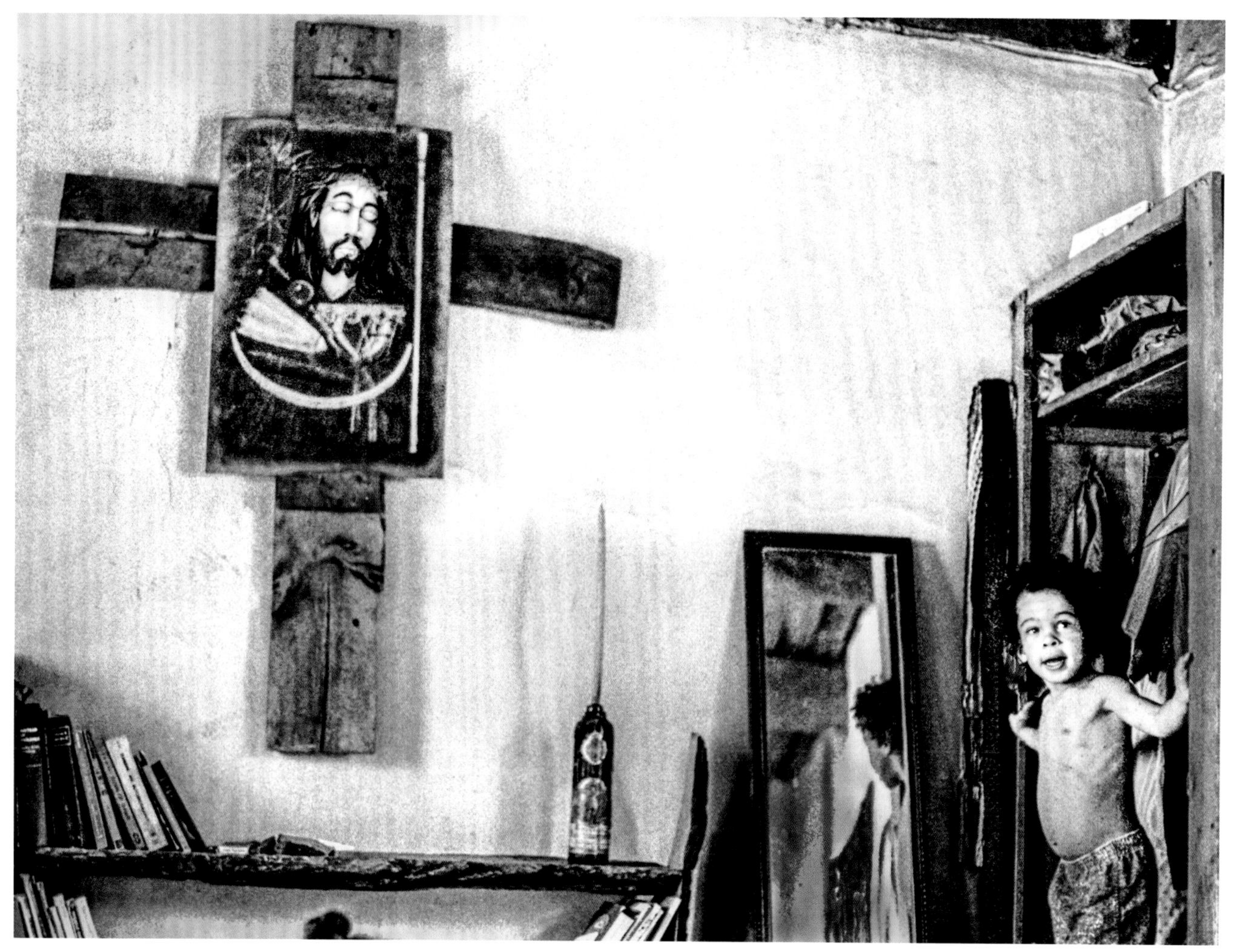

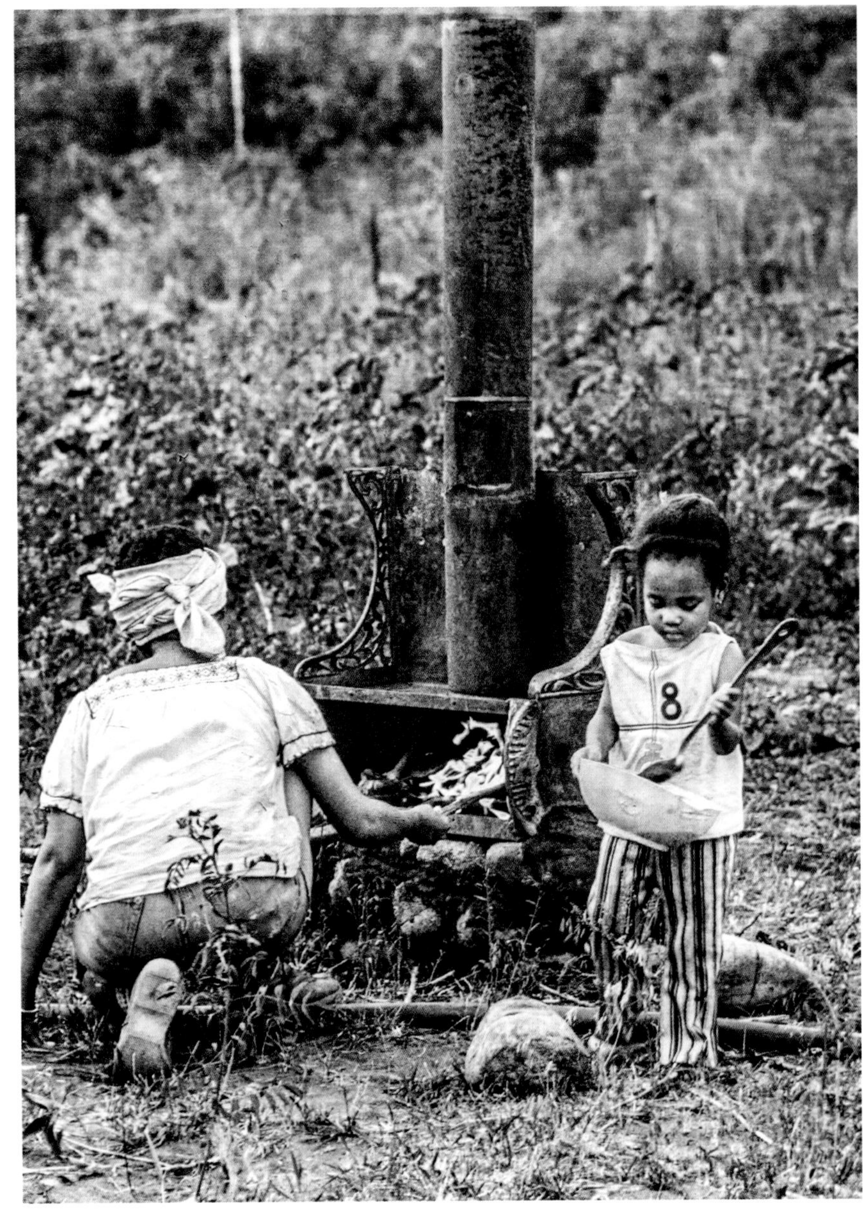
8

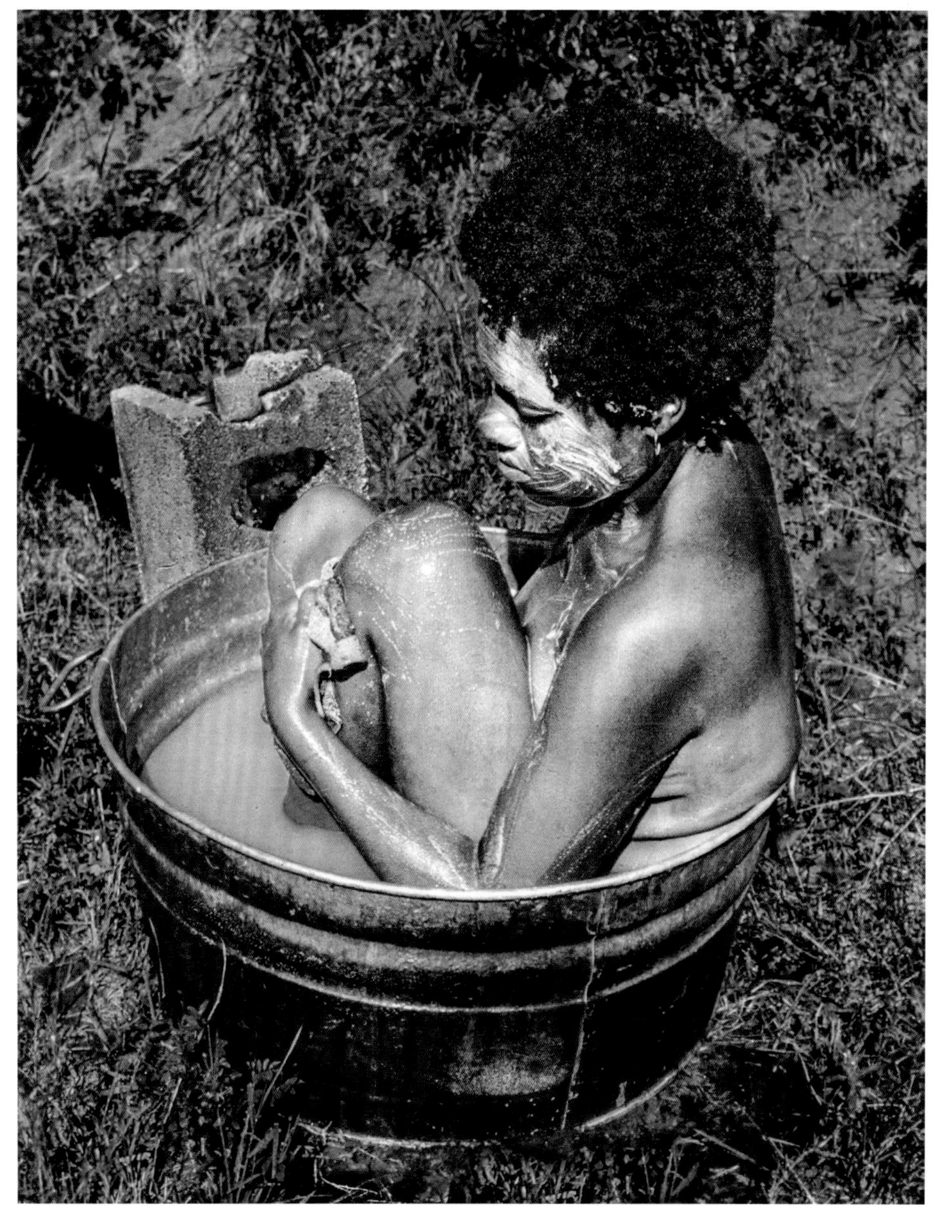

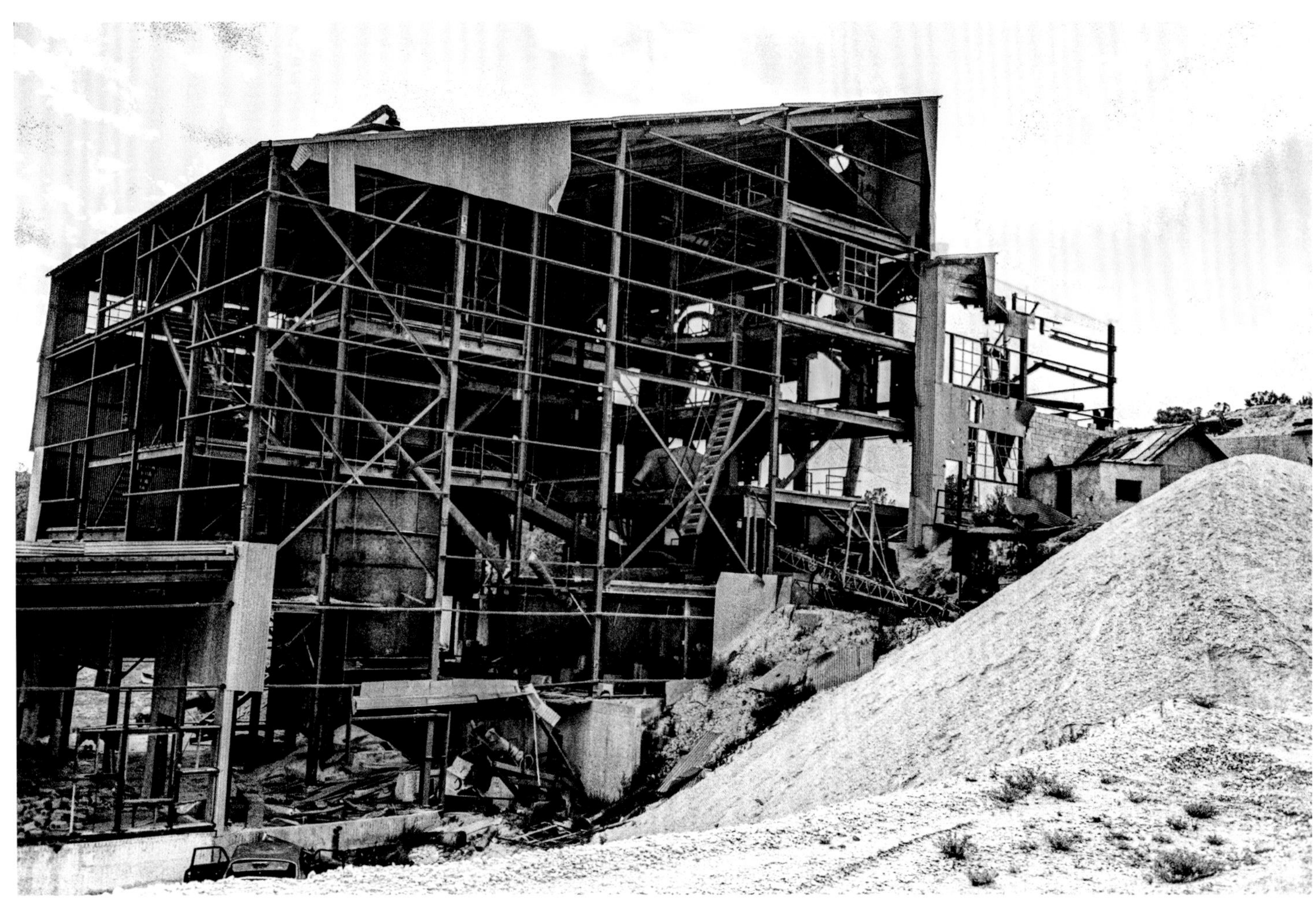

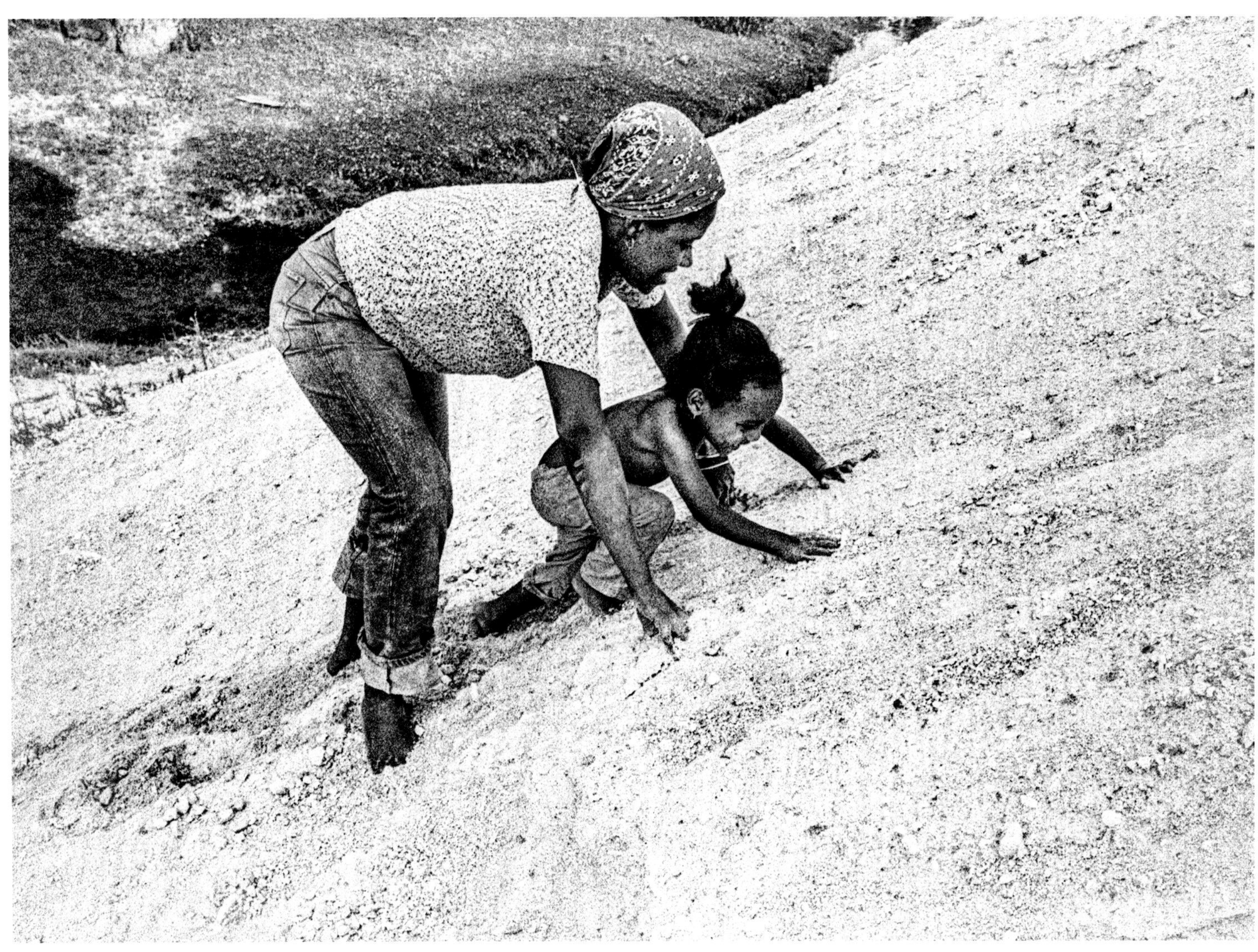

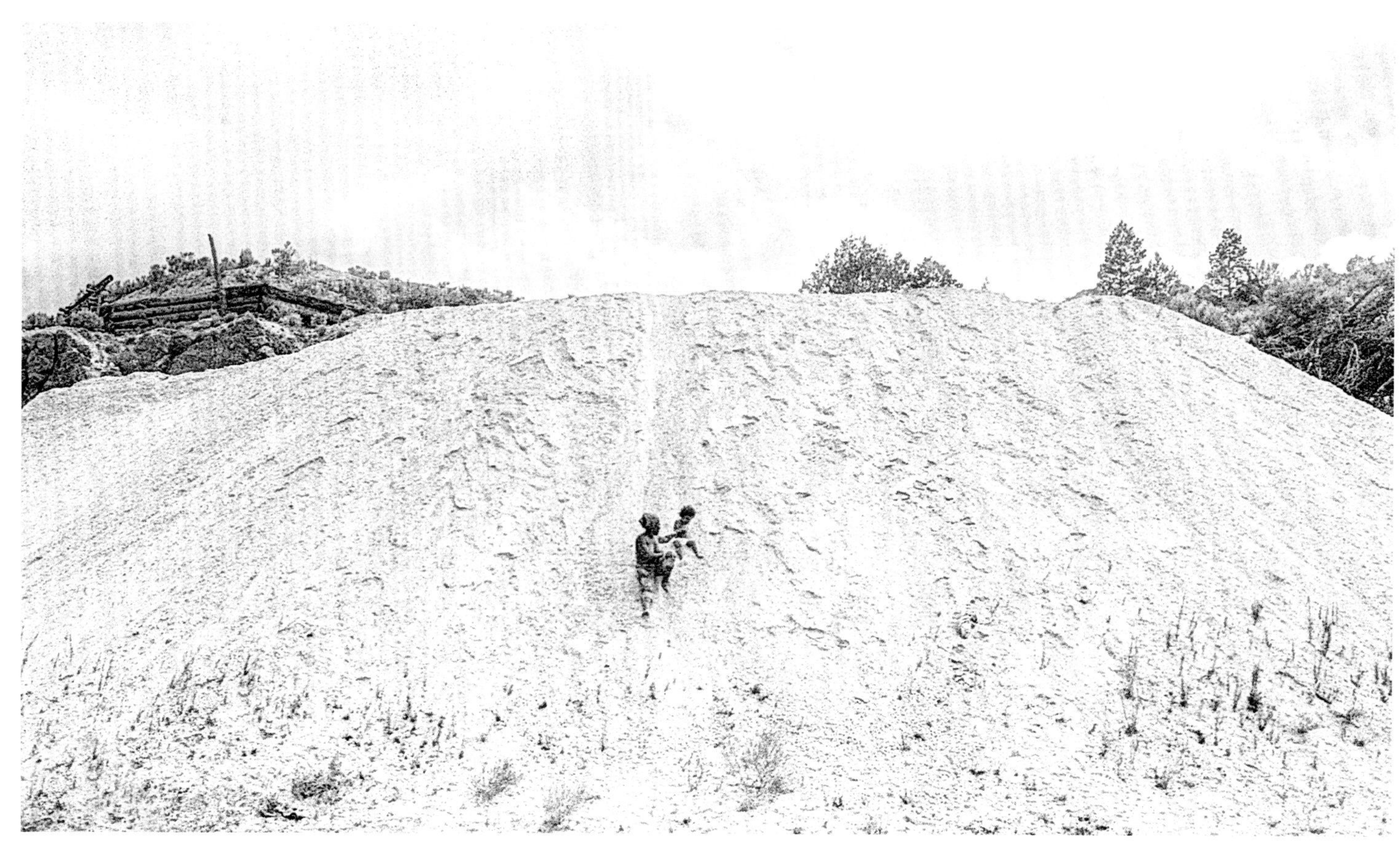

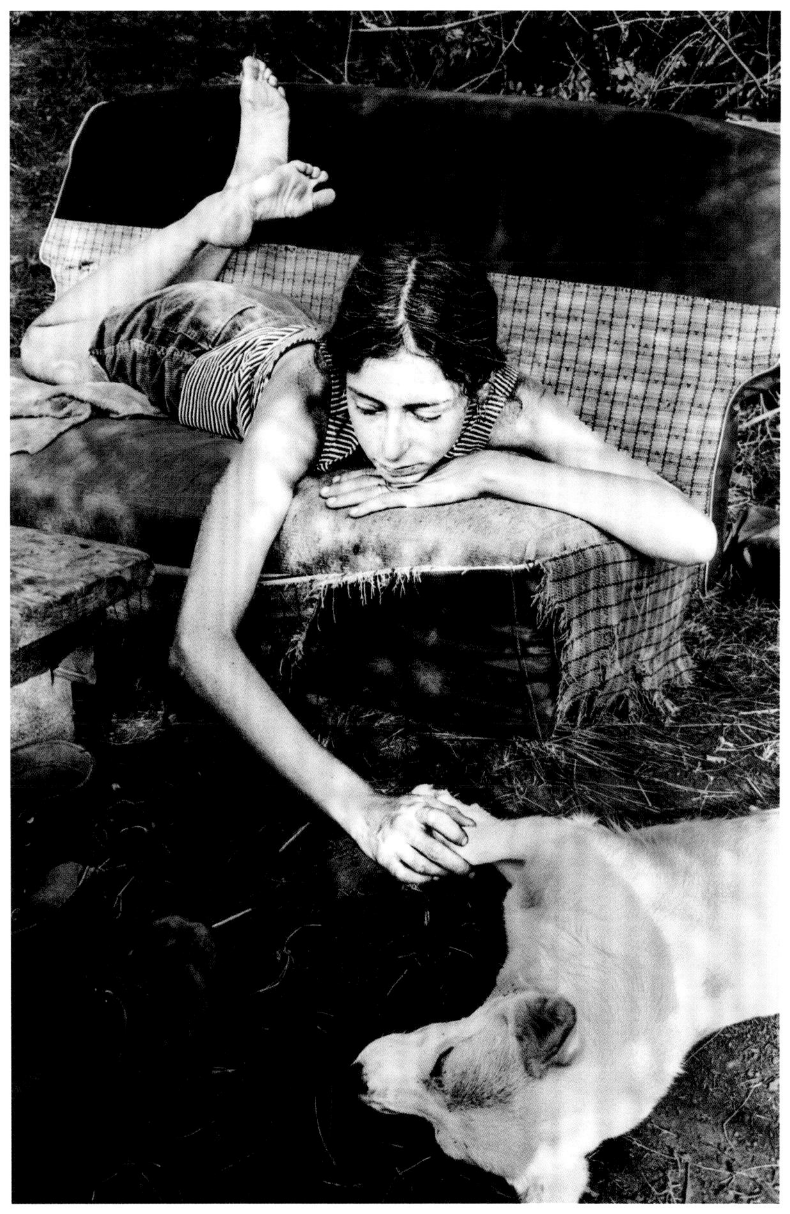

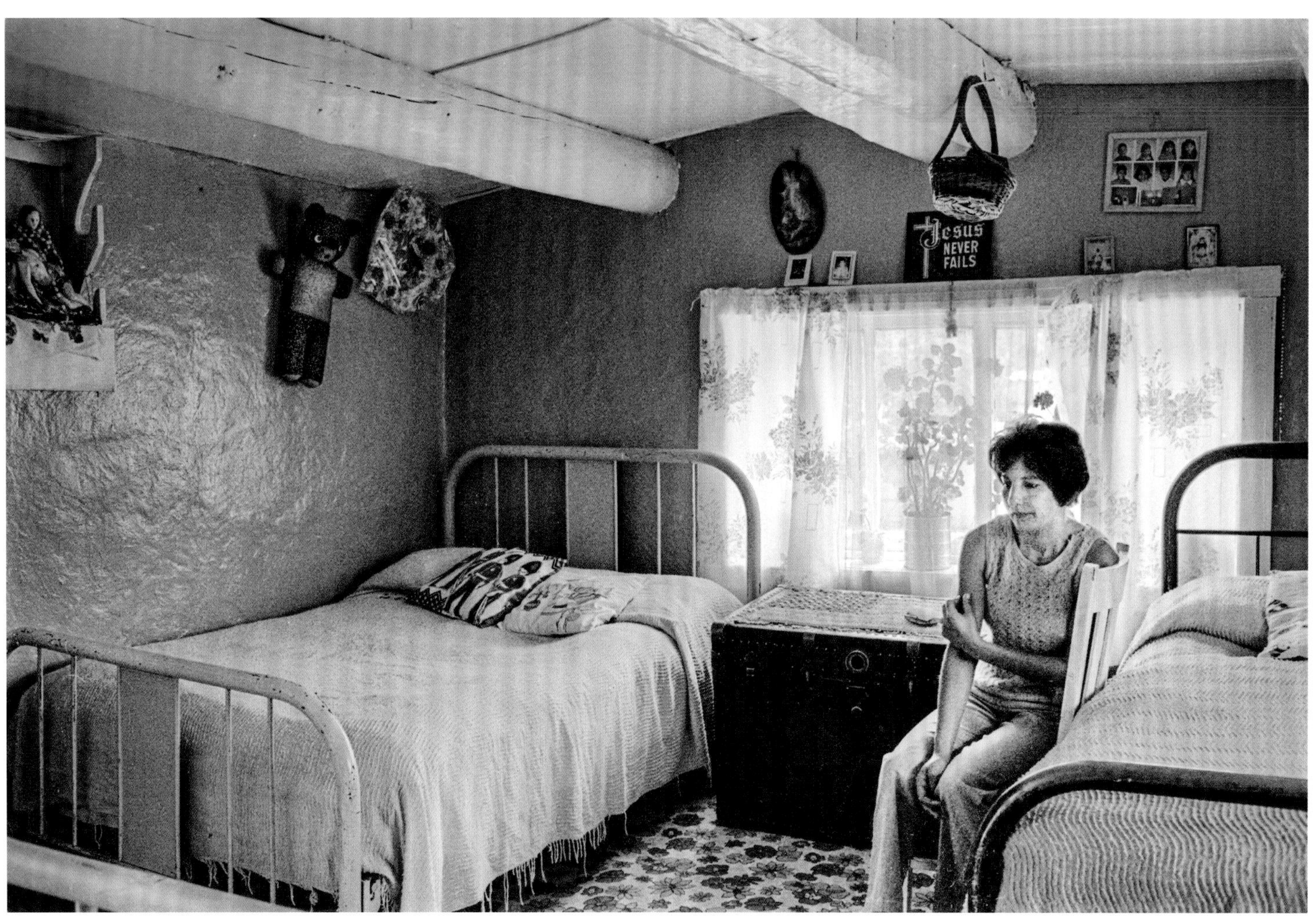
Jesus
NEVER
FAILS

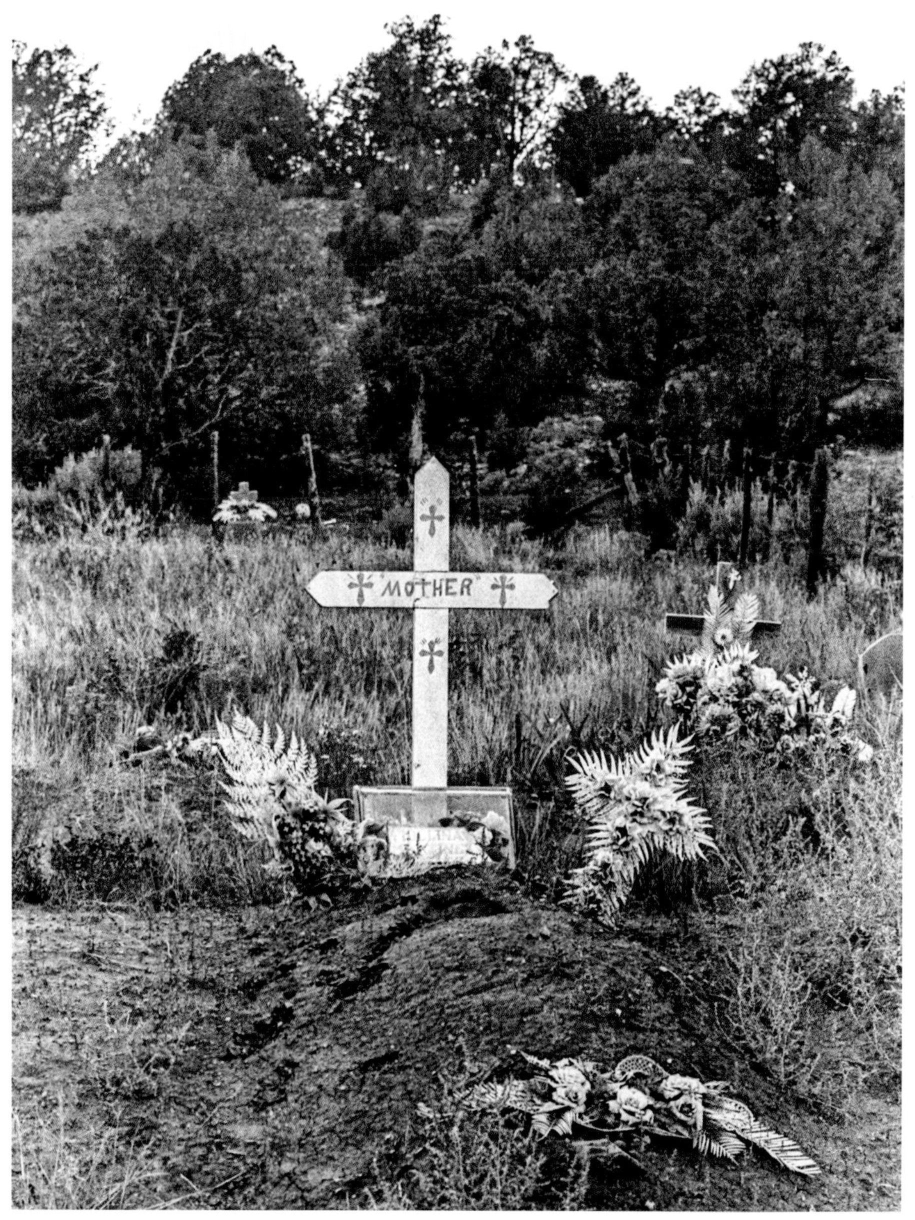
"MOTHER"

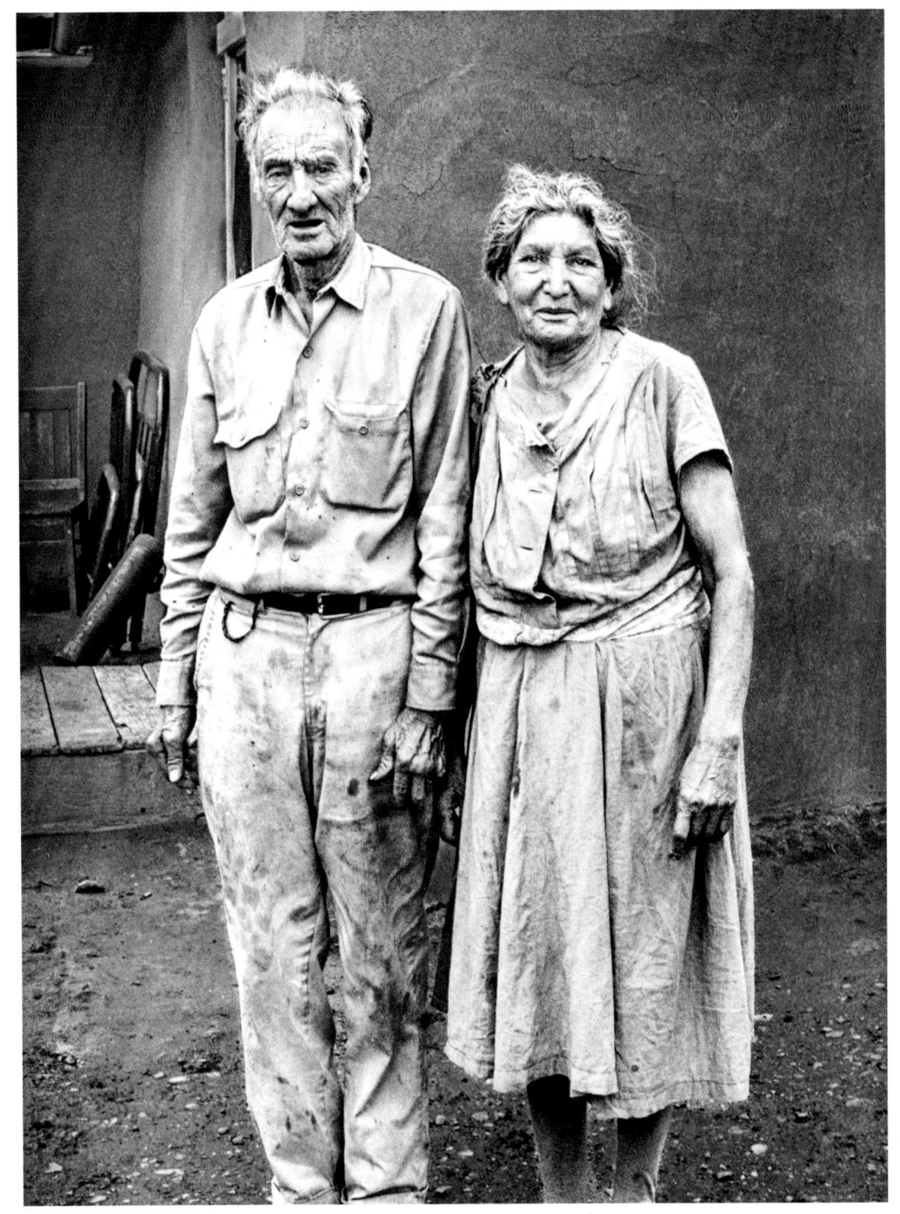

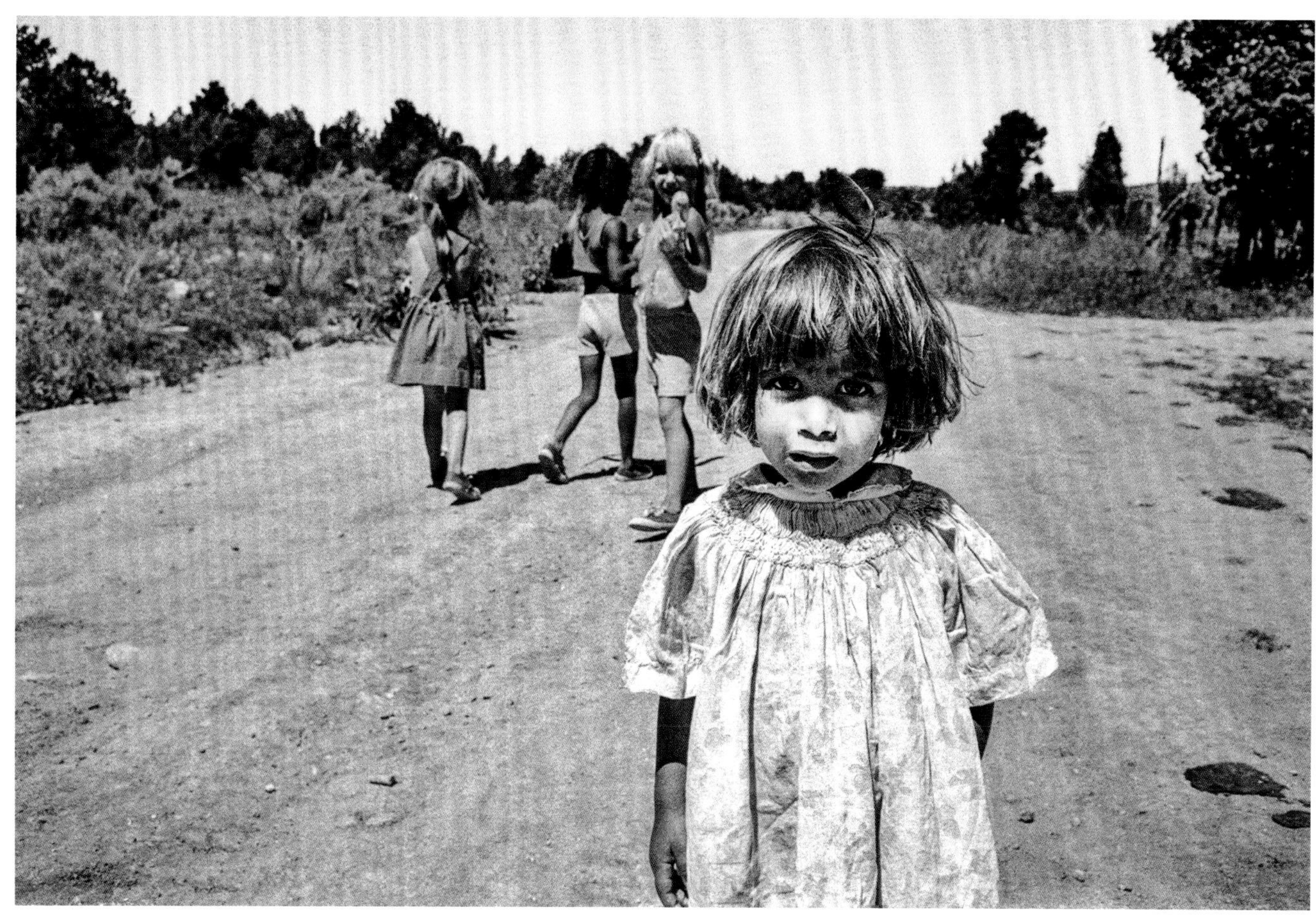

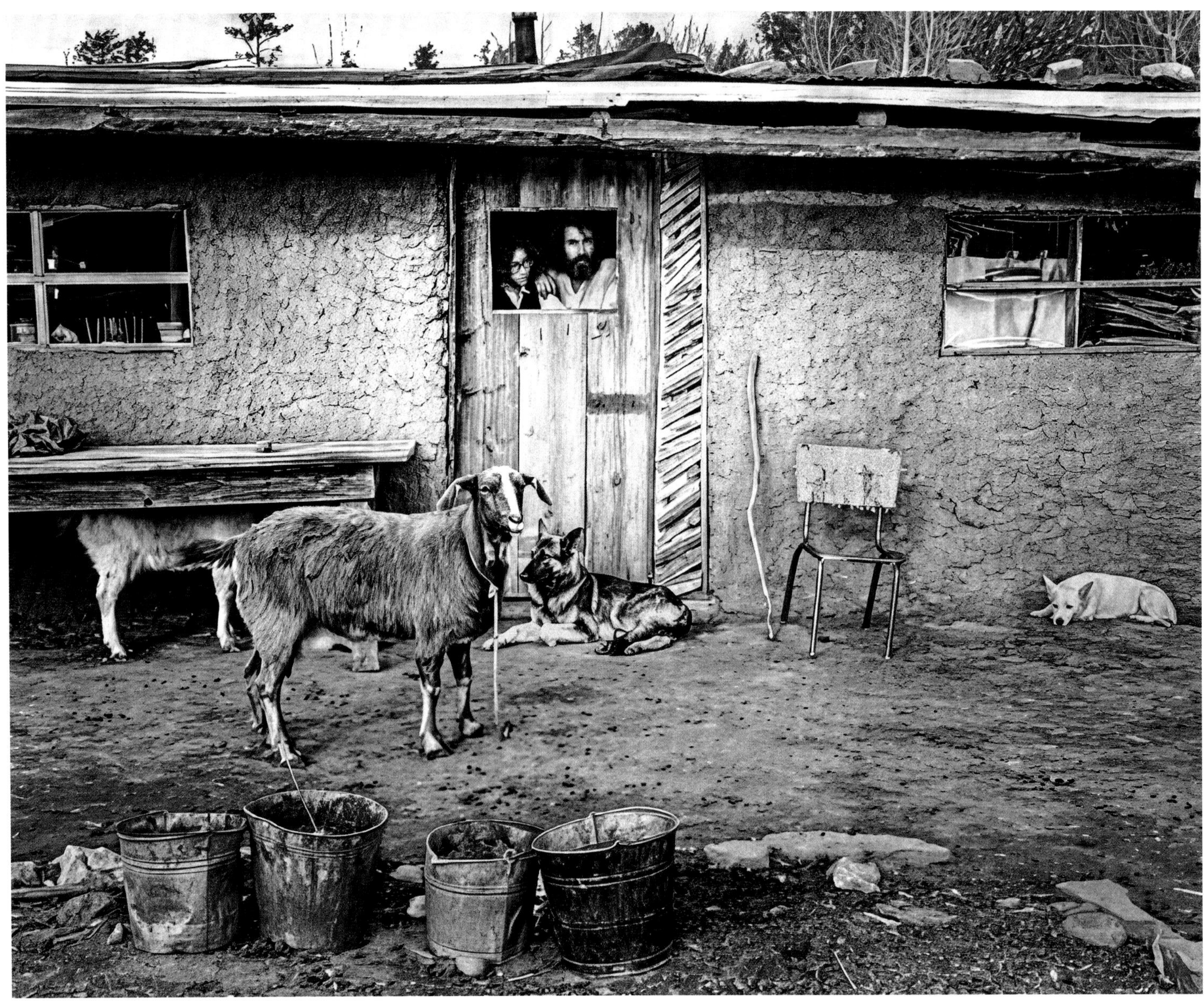

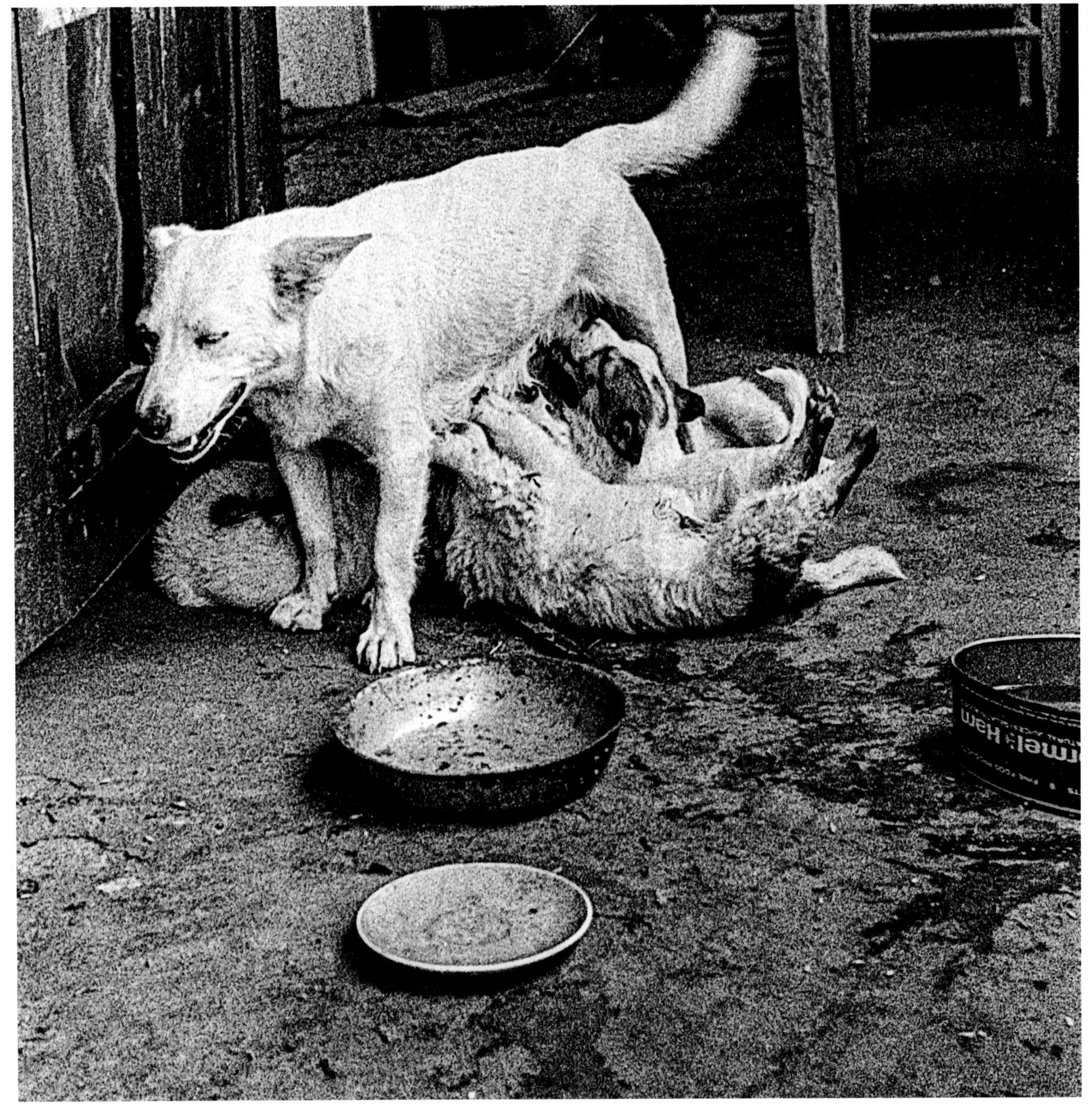

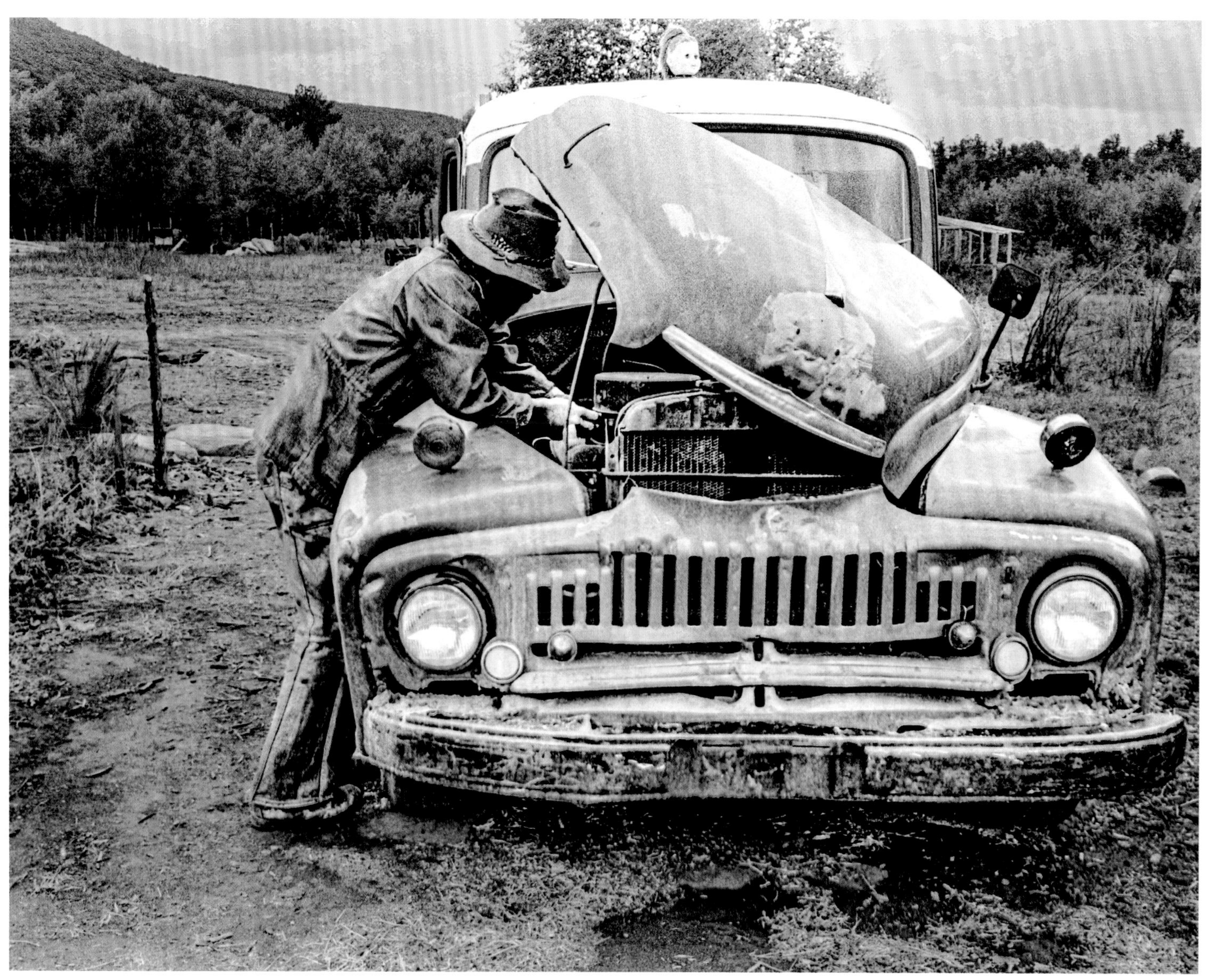

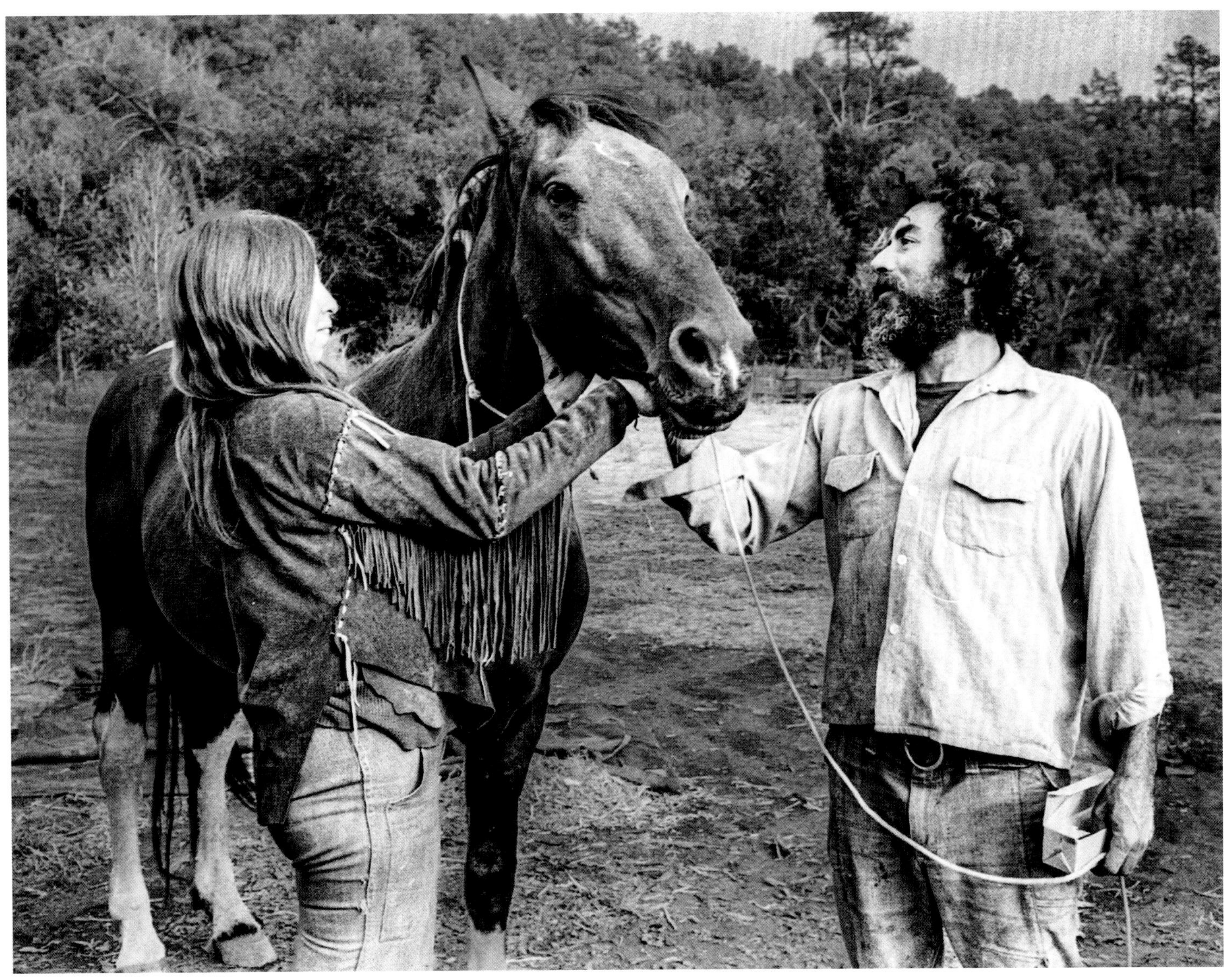

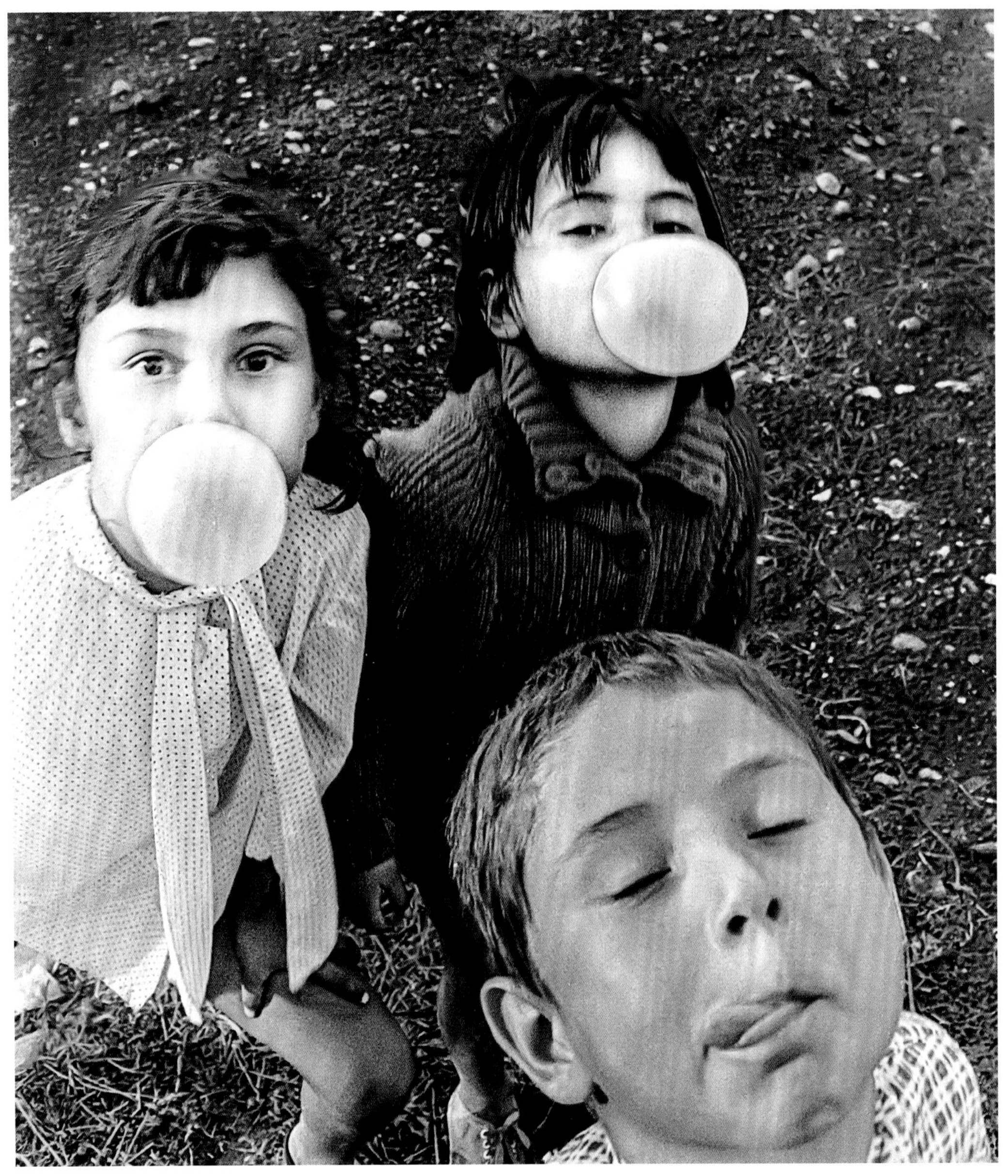

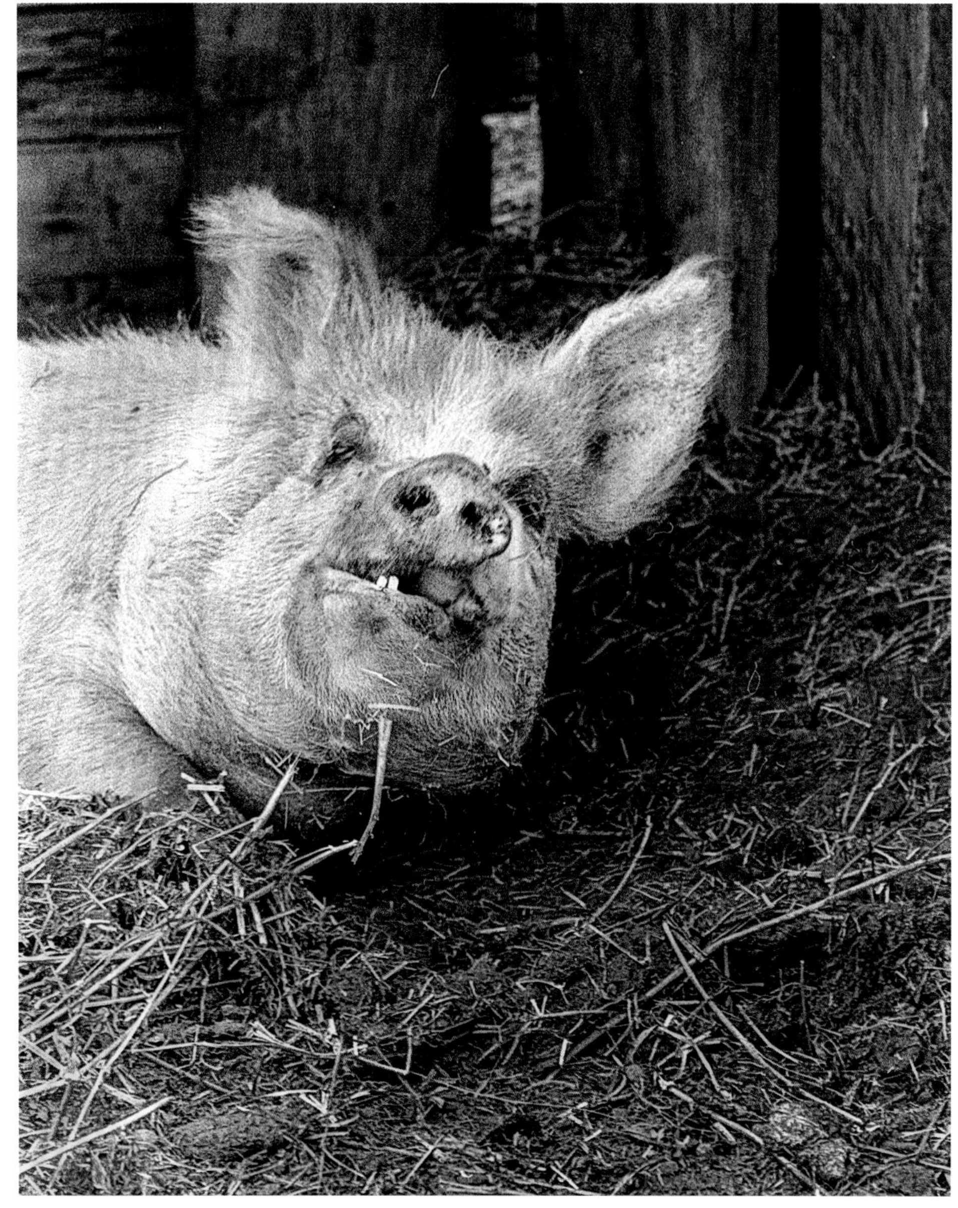

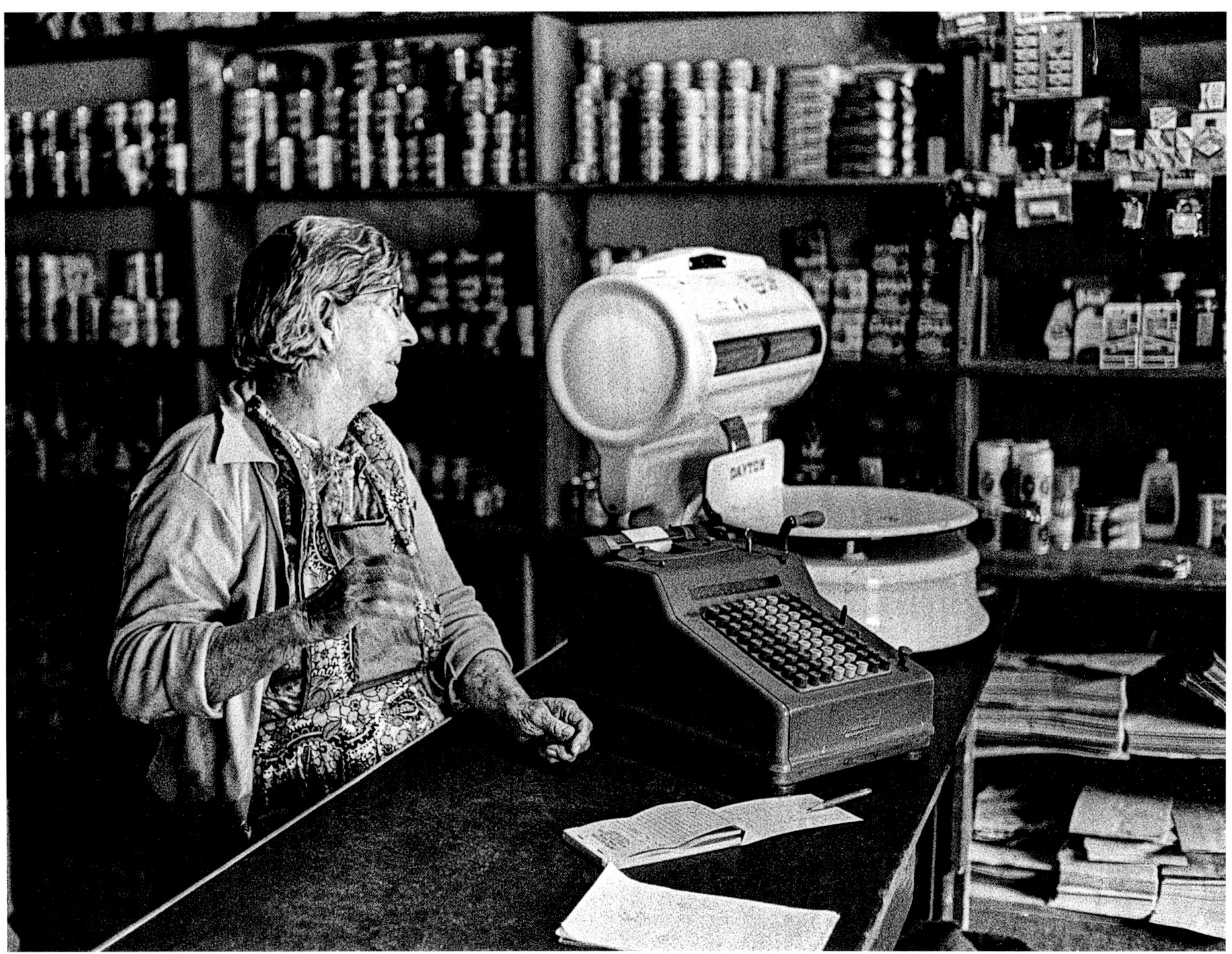

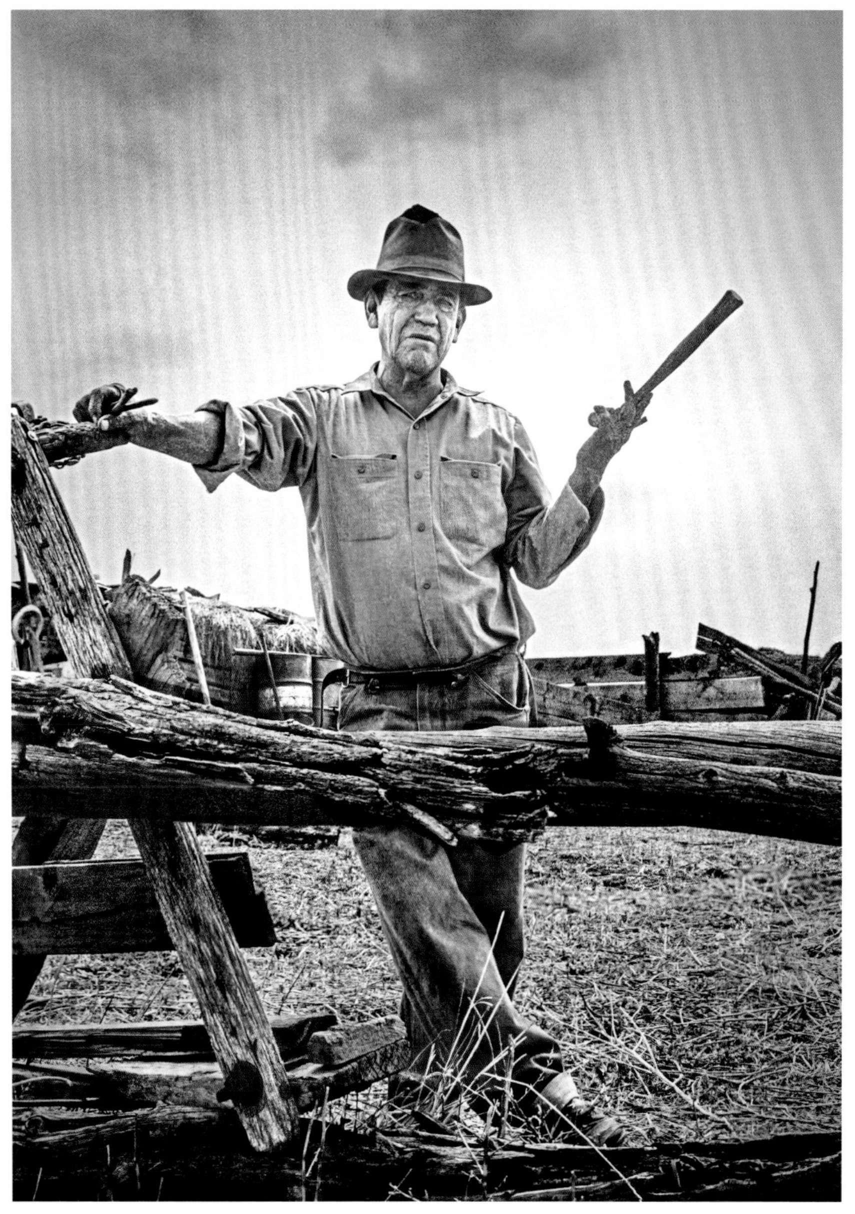

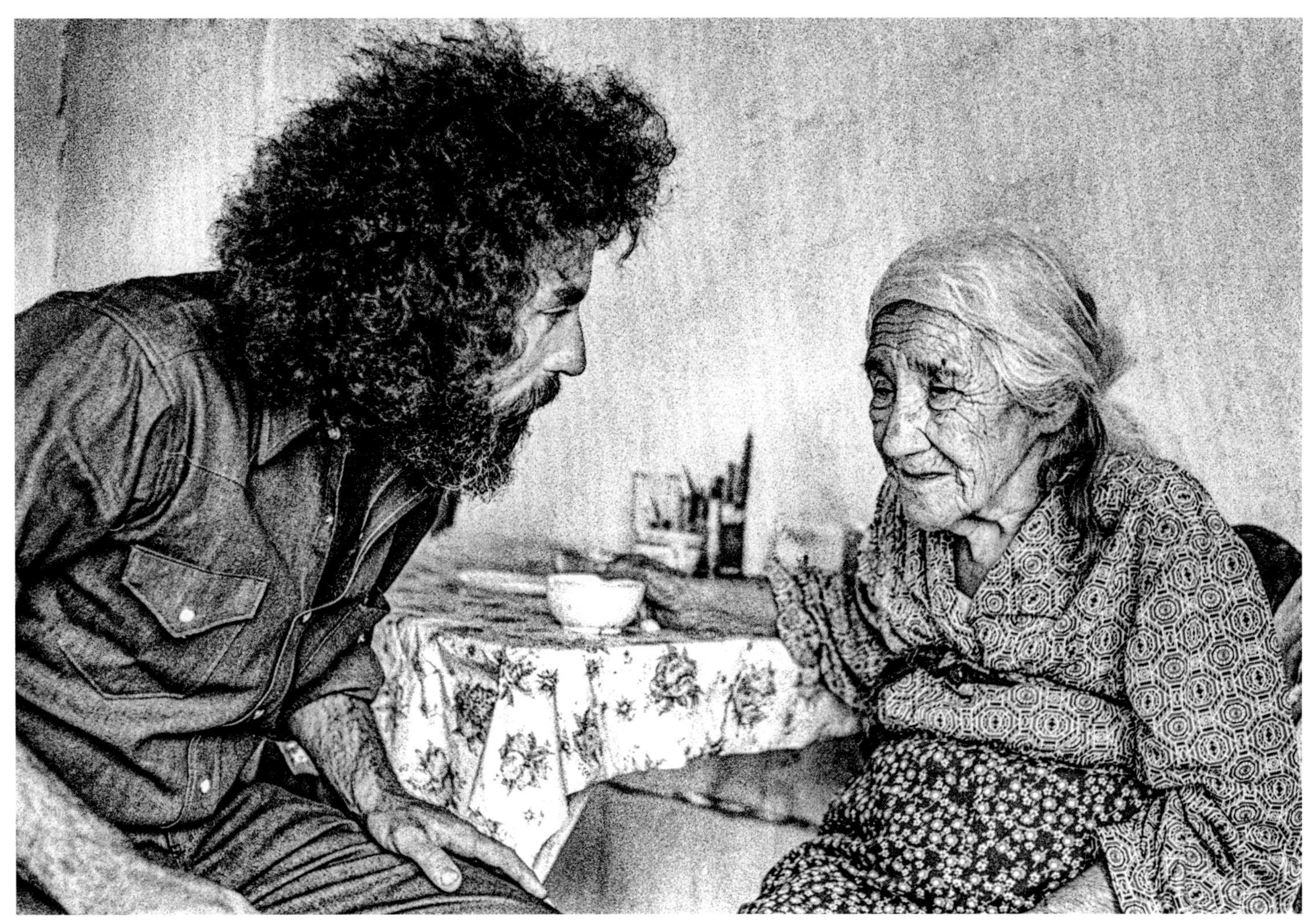

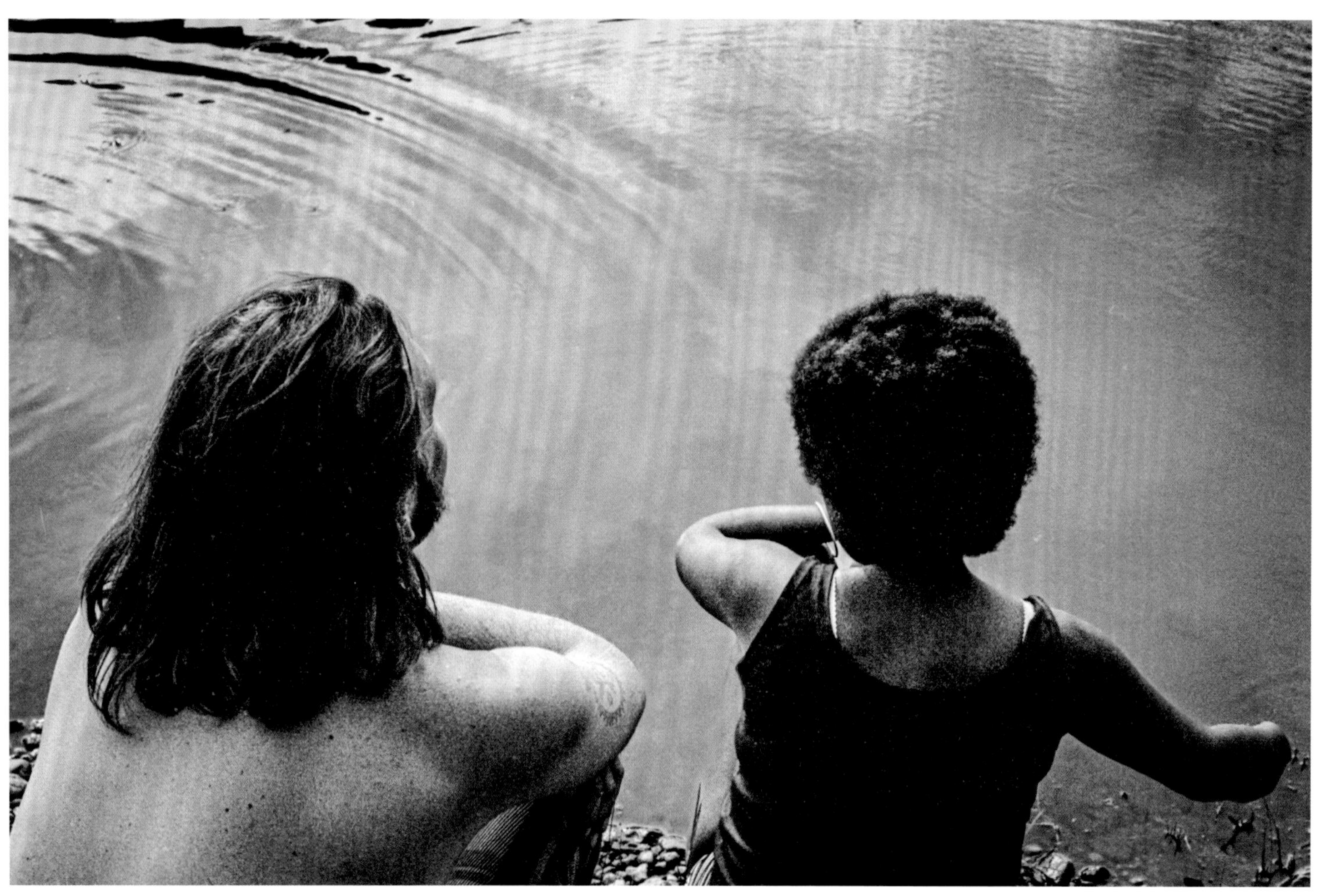

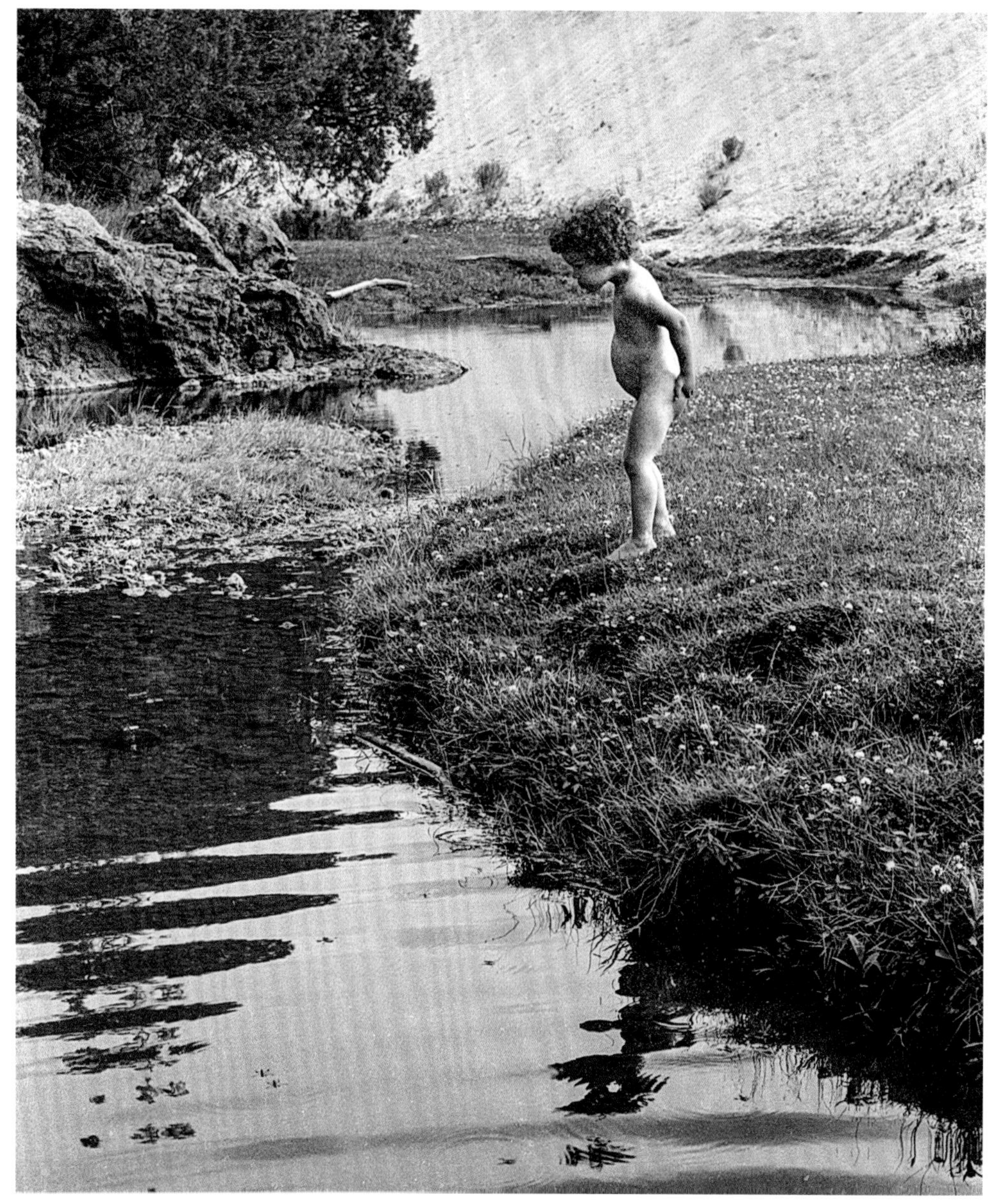

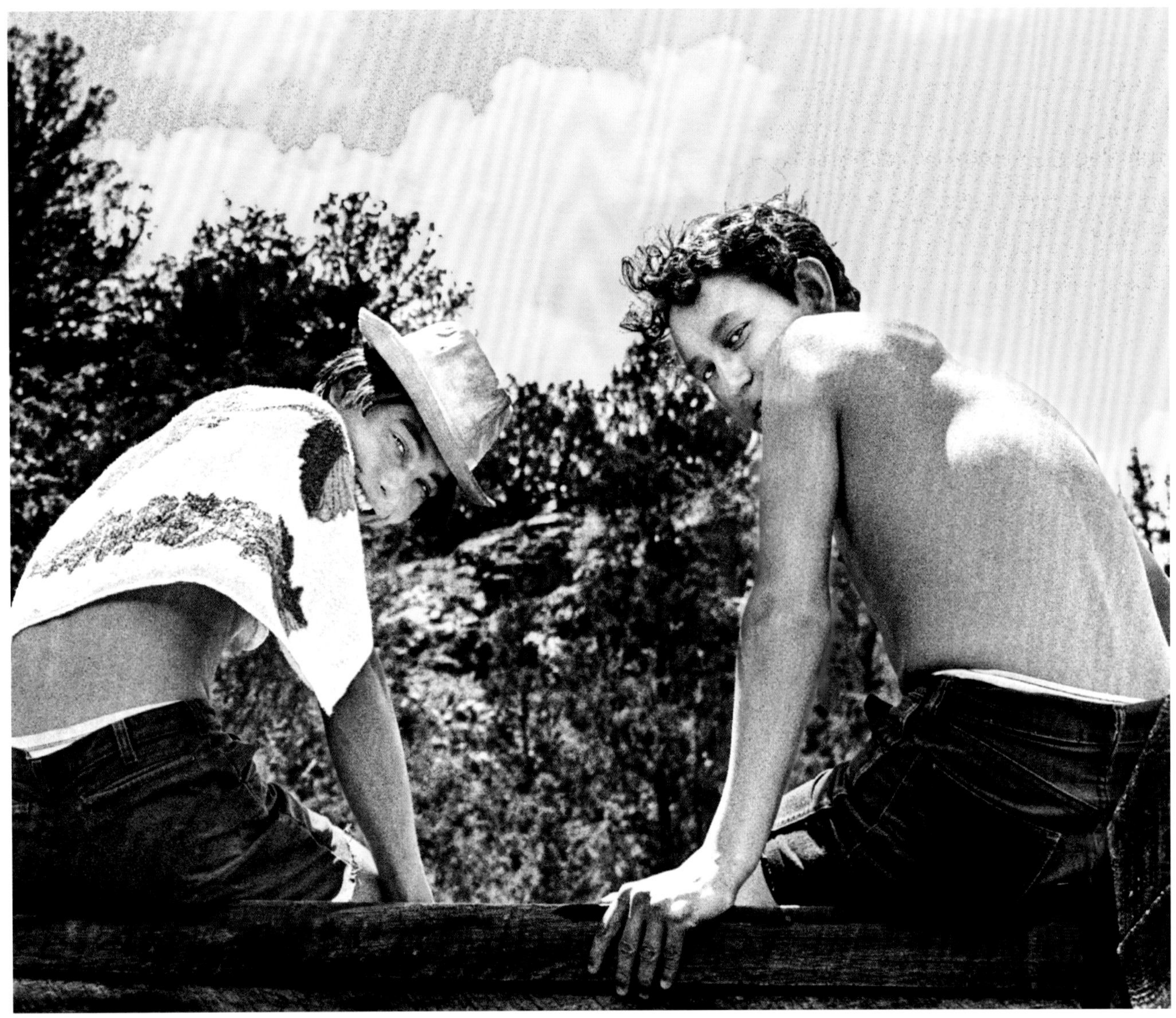

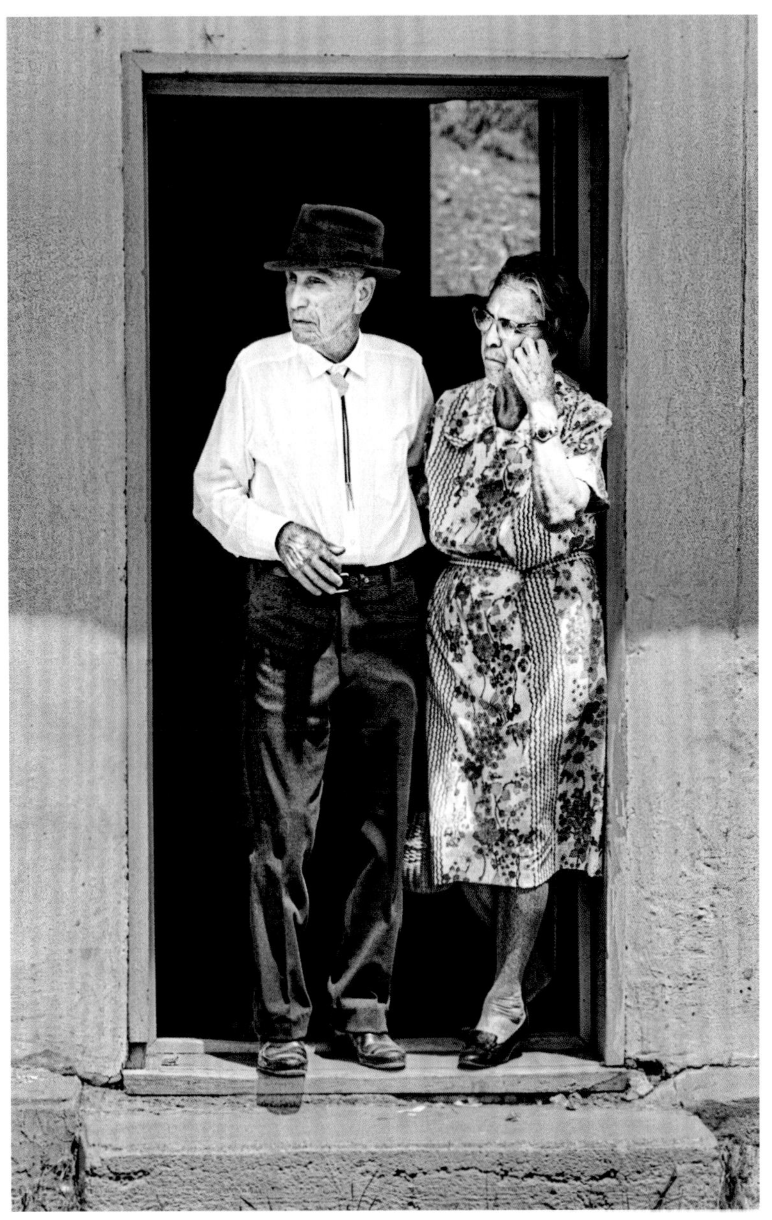

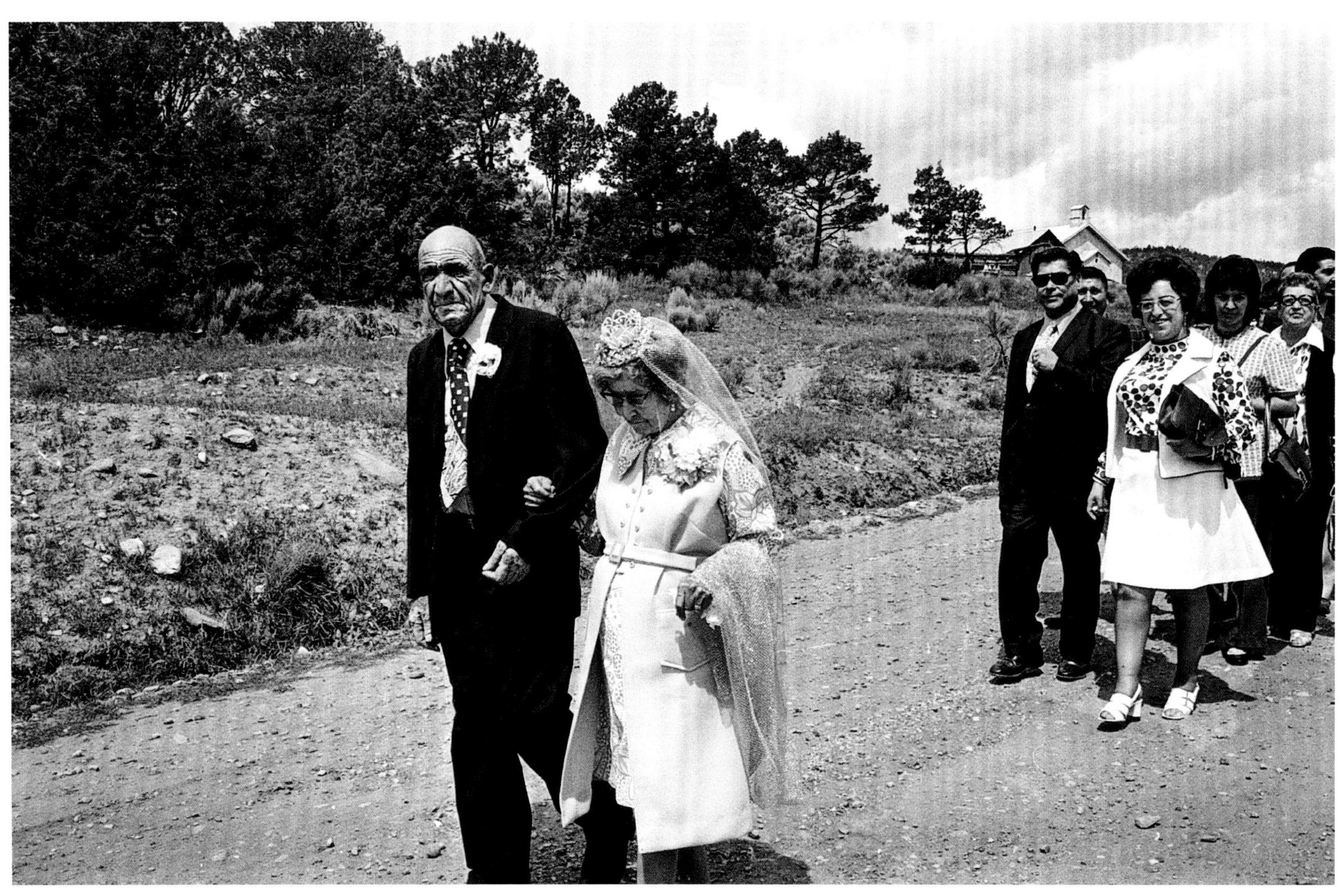

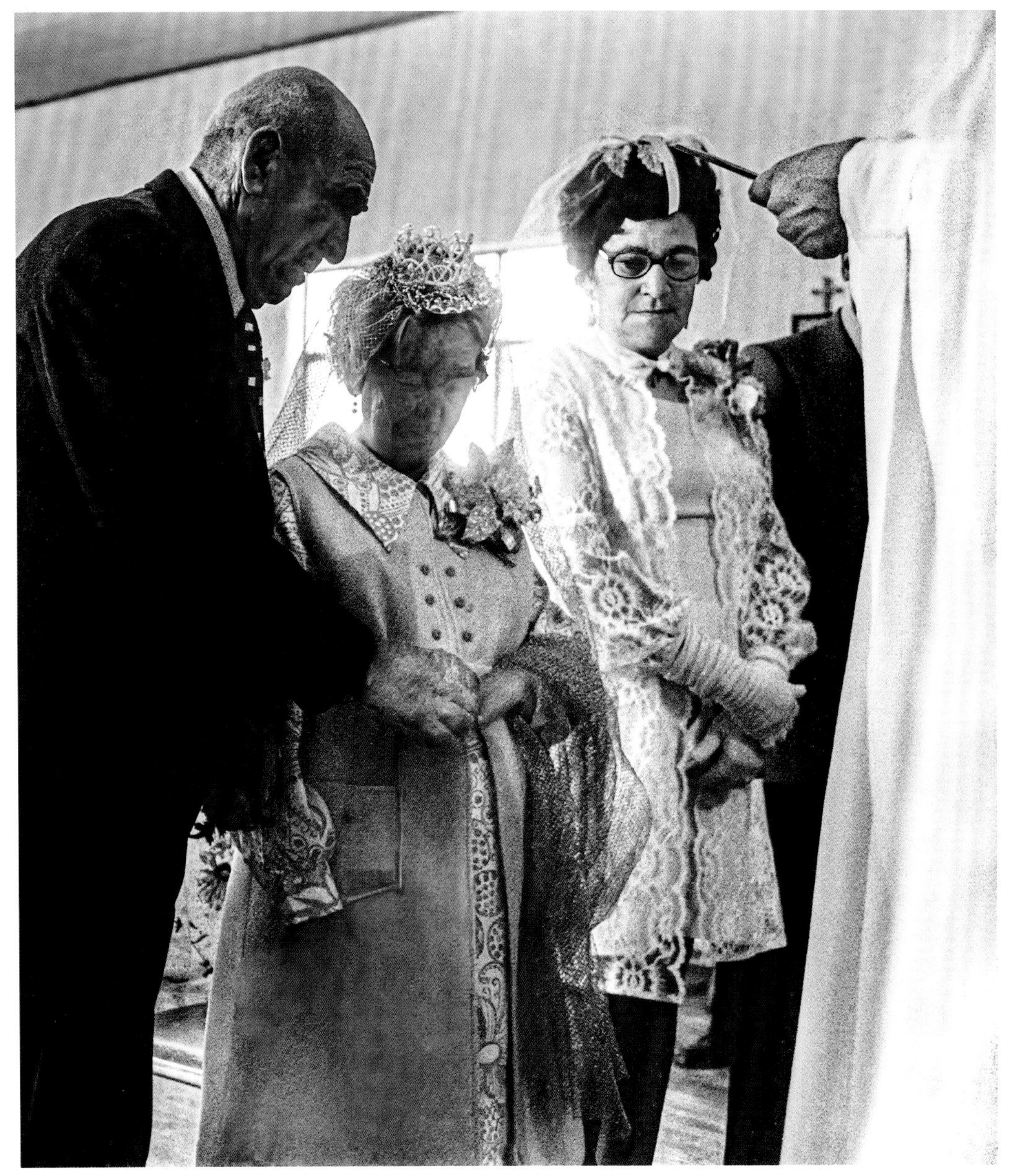

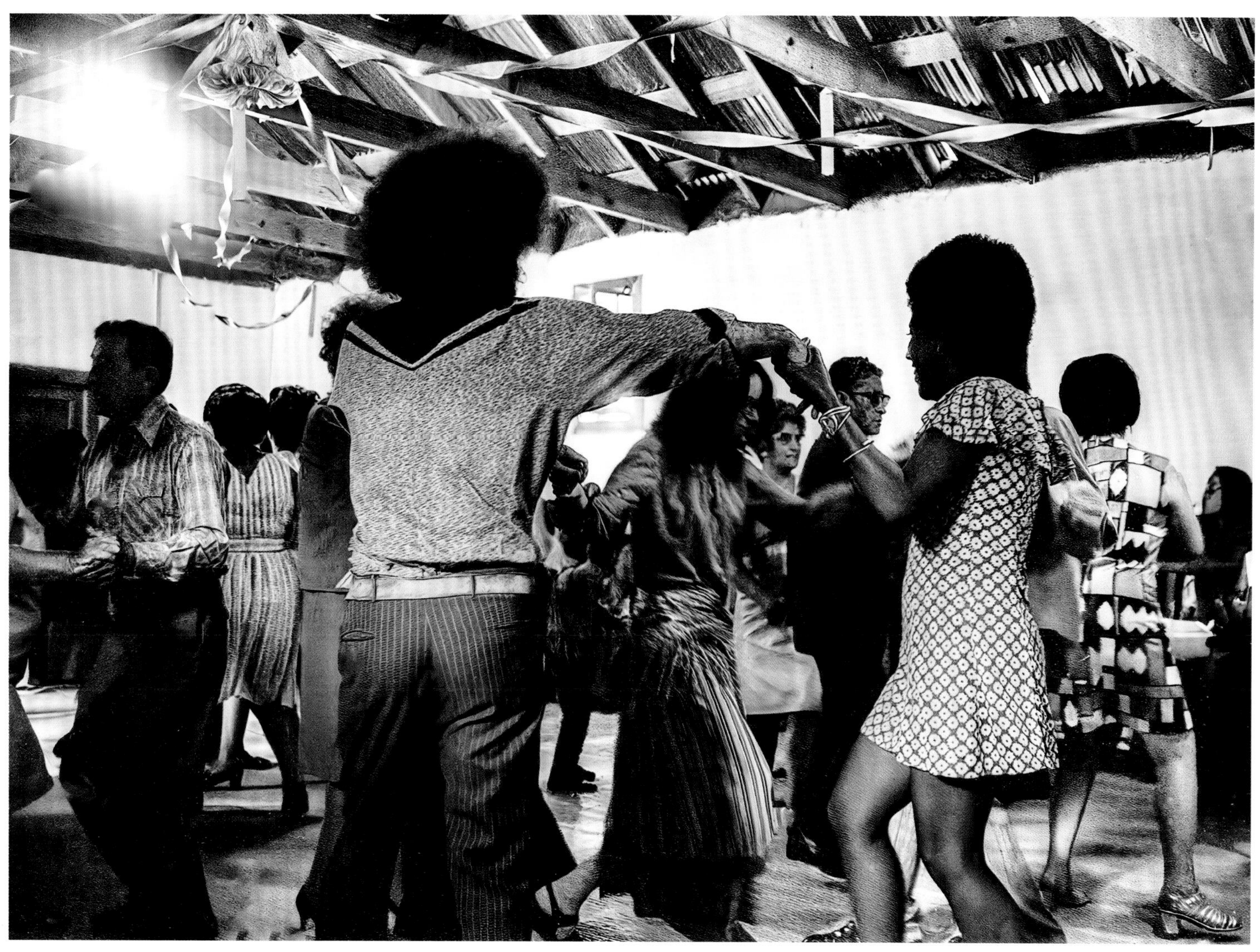

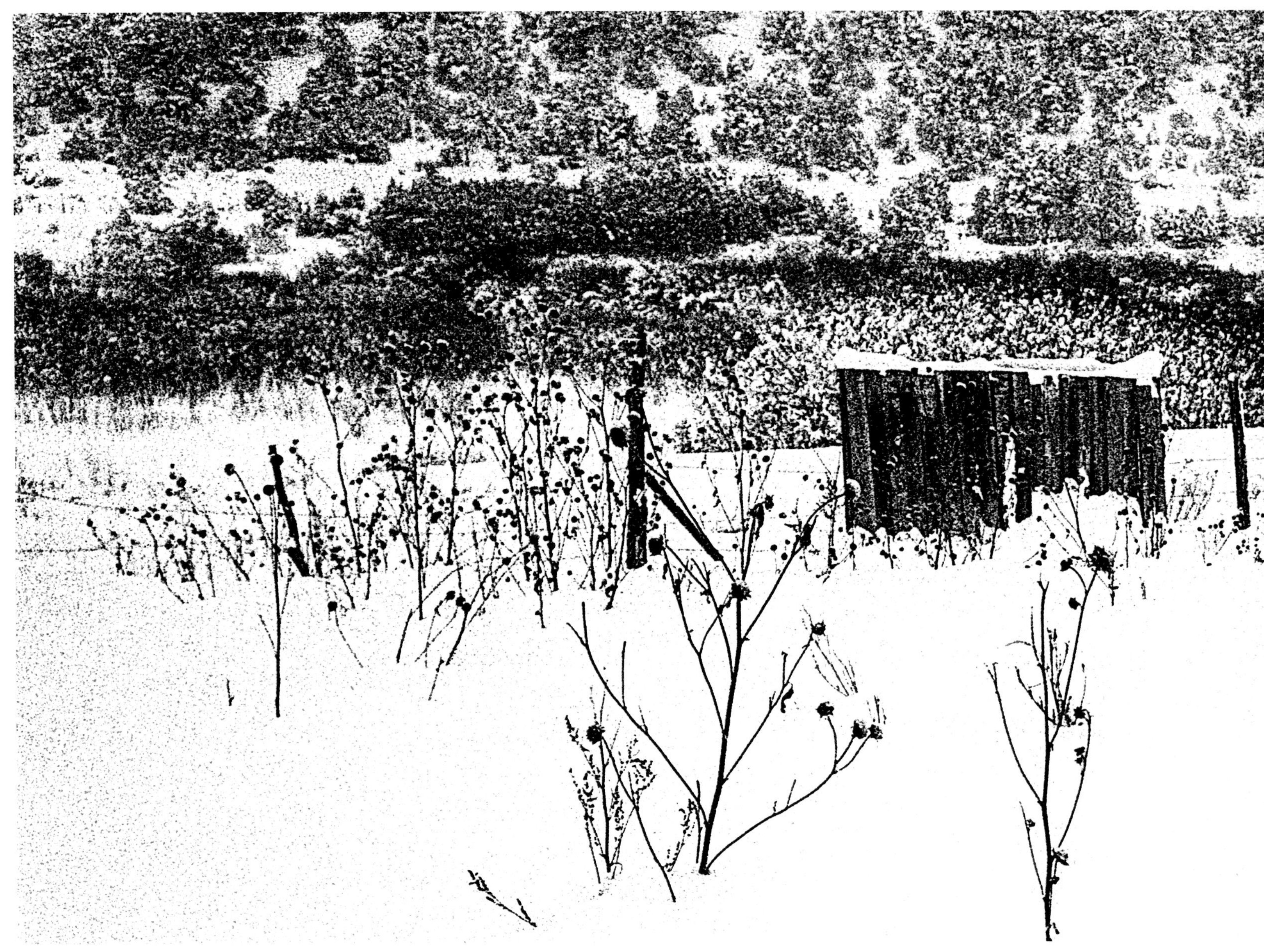

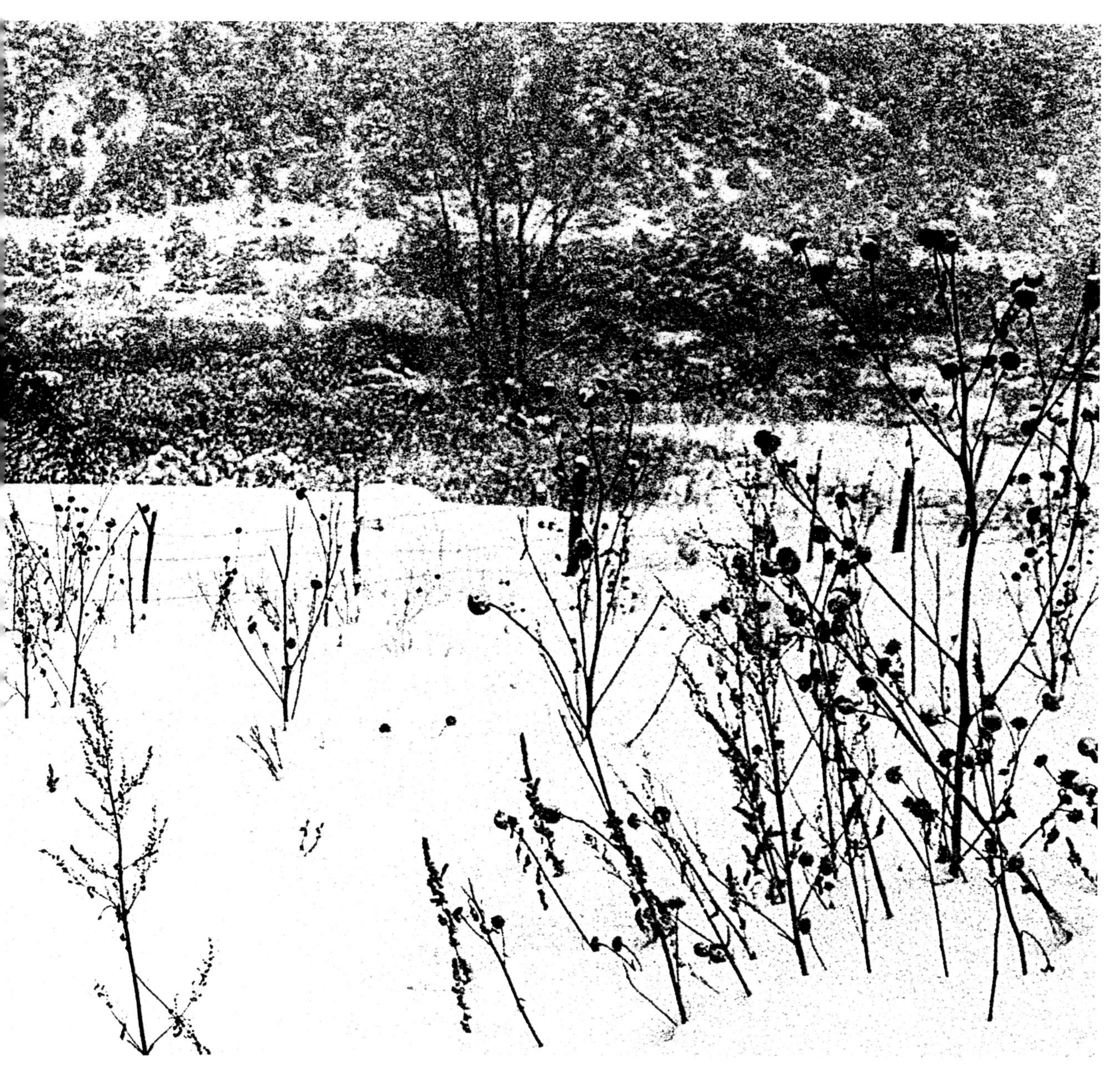

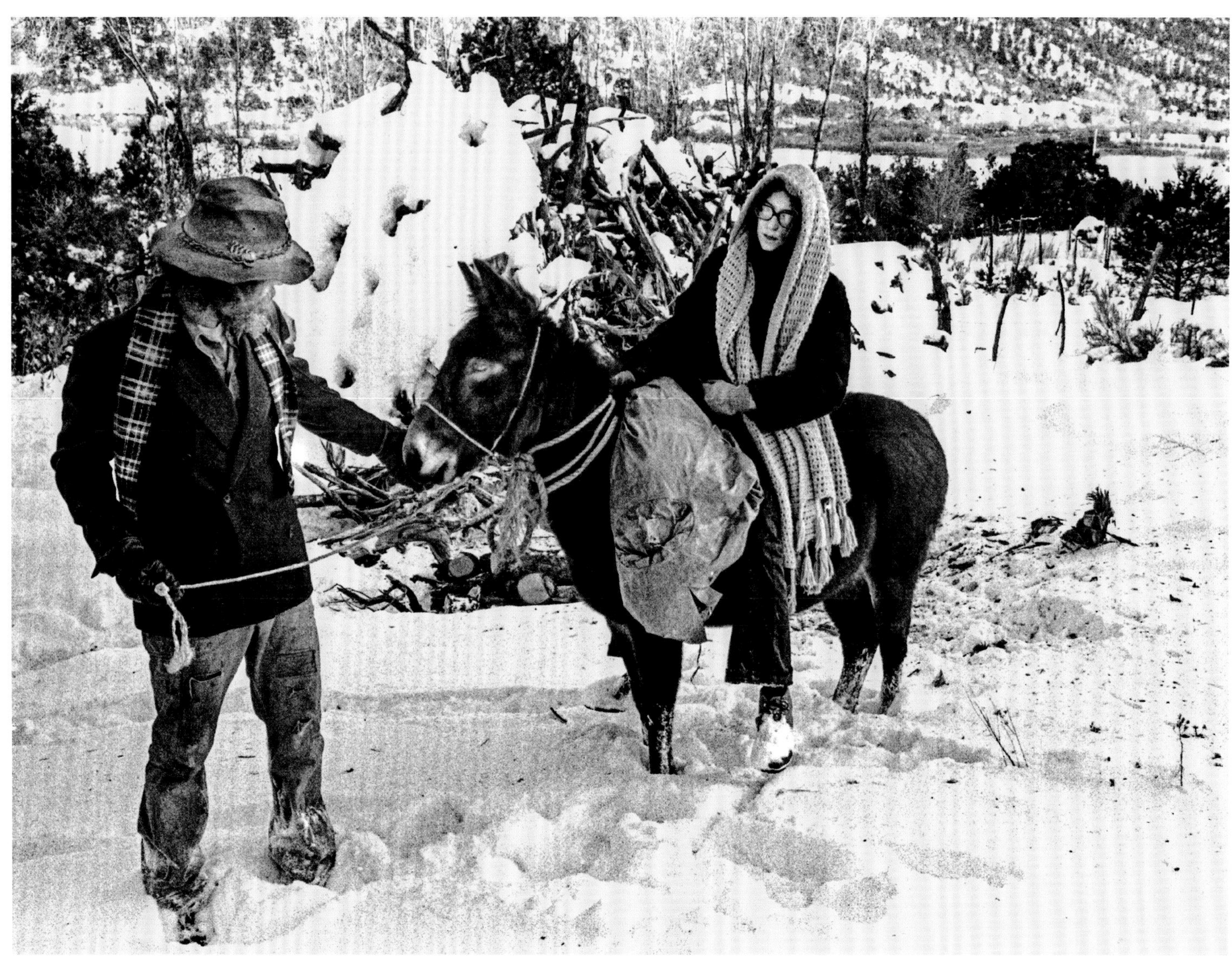

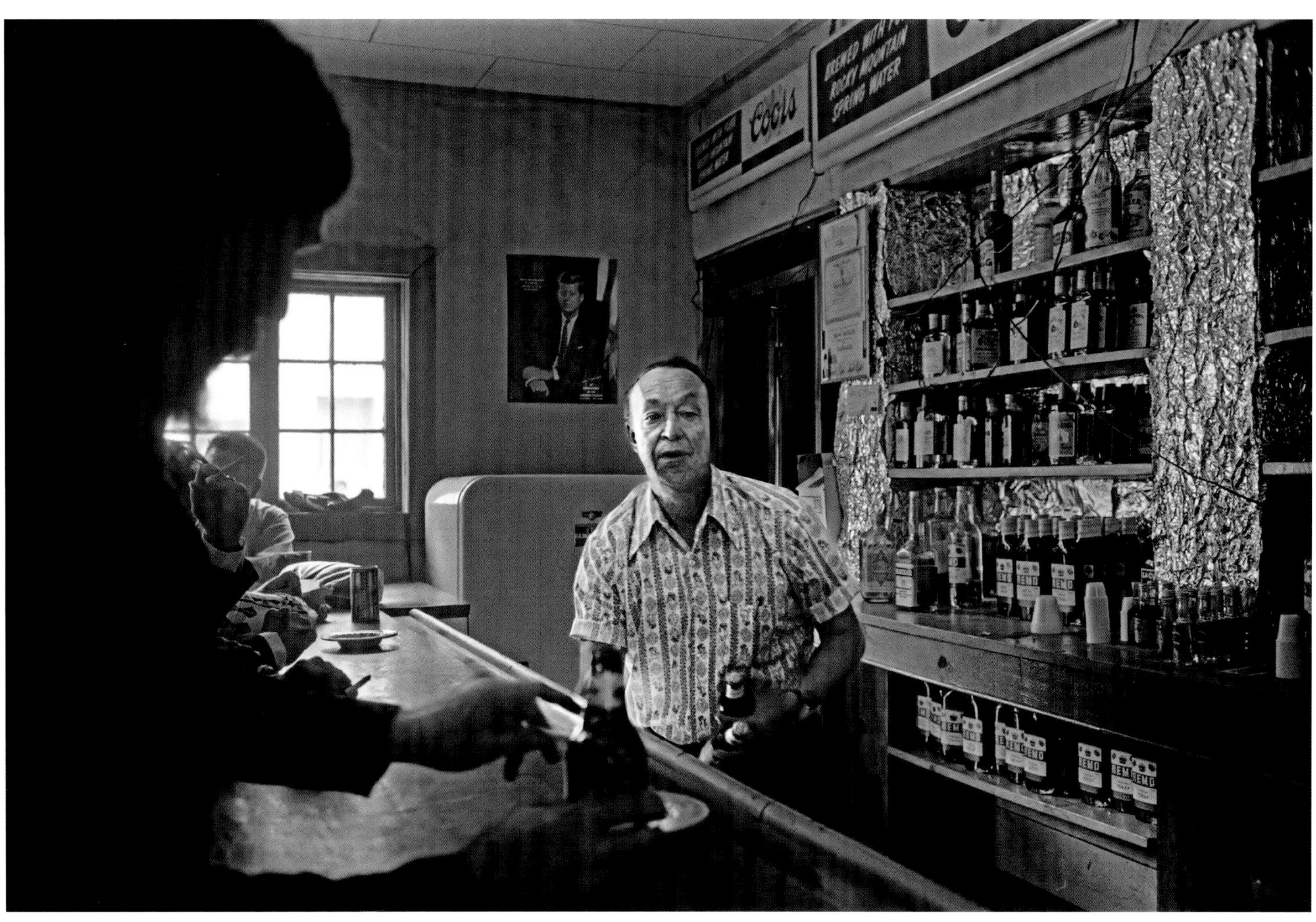
Coors
BREWED WITH
ROCKY MOUNTAIN
SPRING WATER

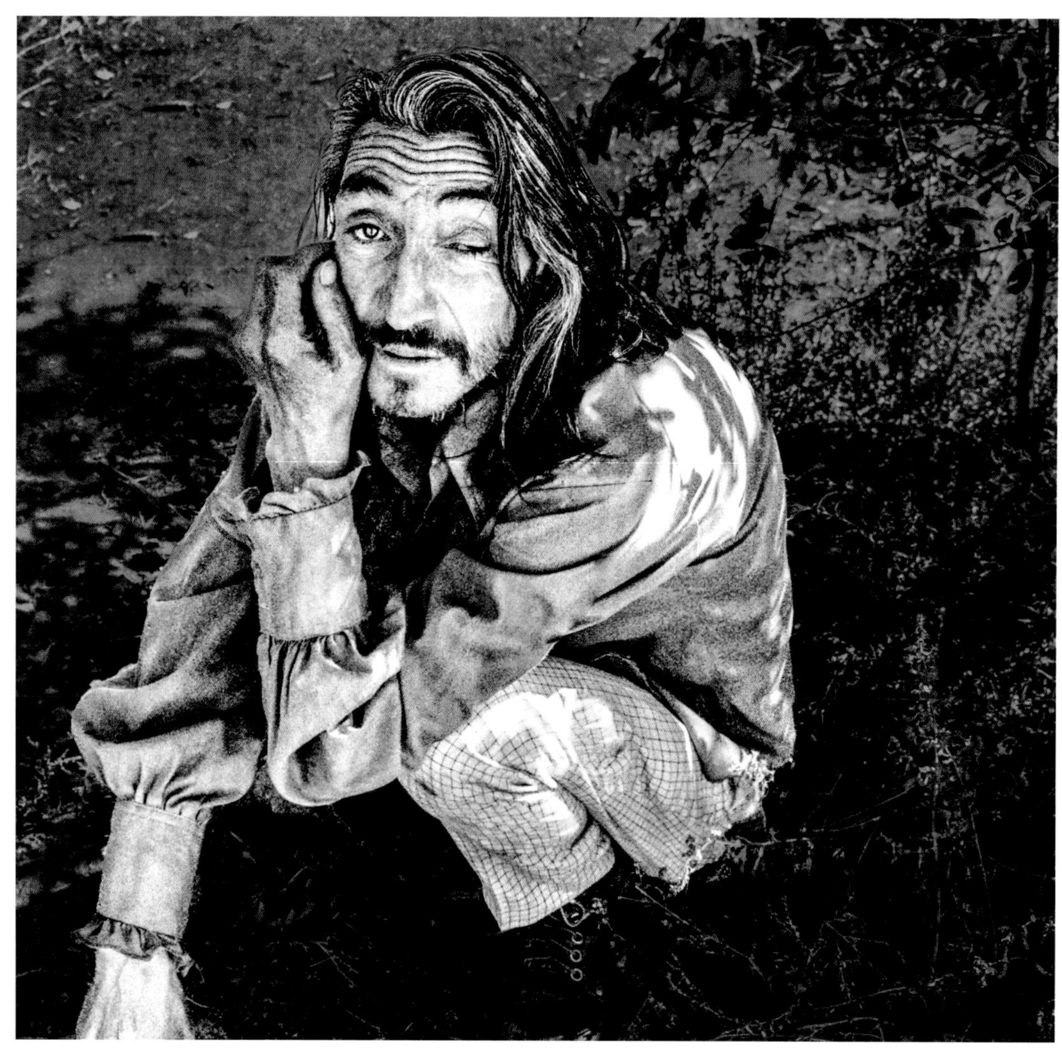

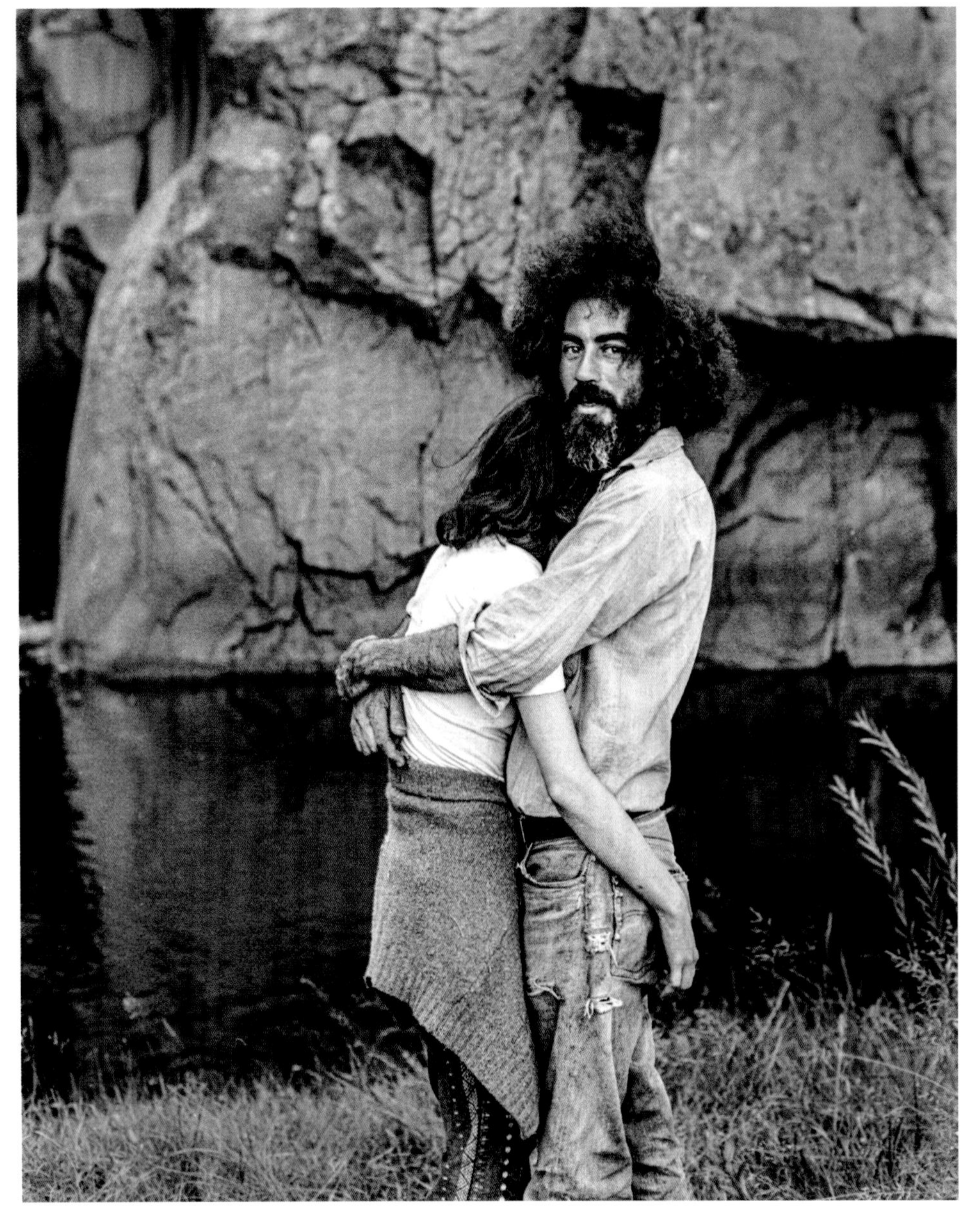

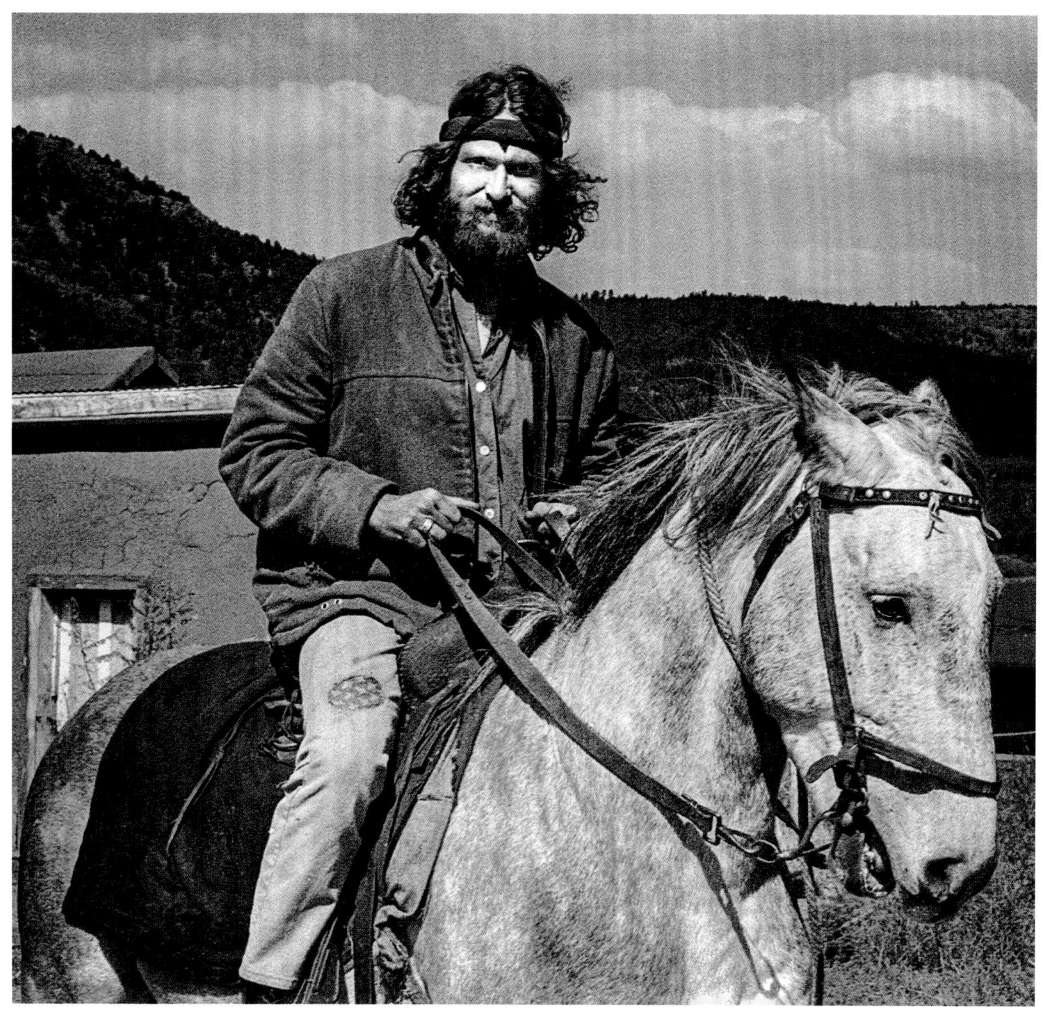

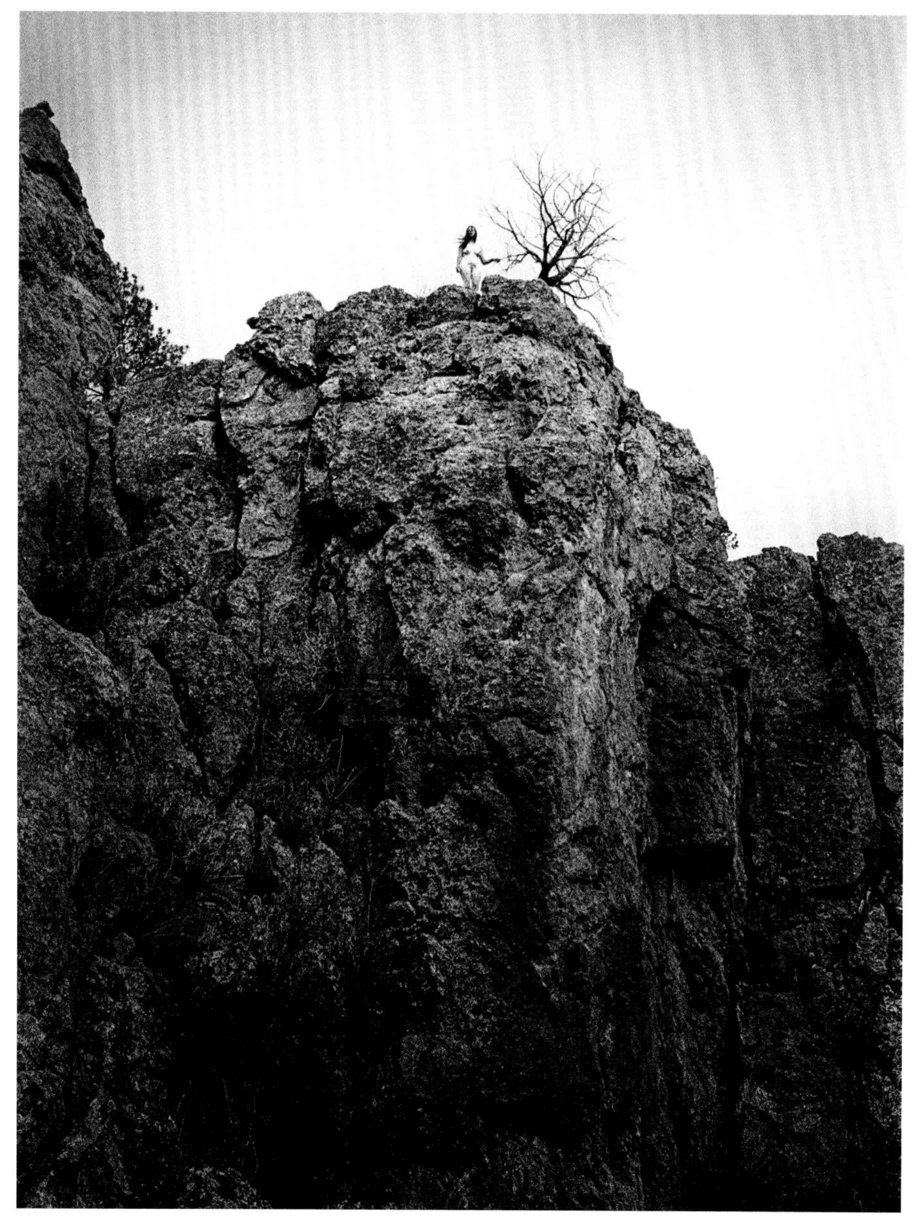

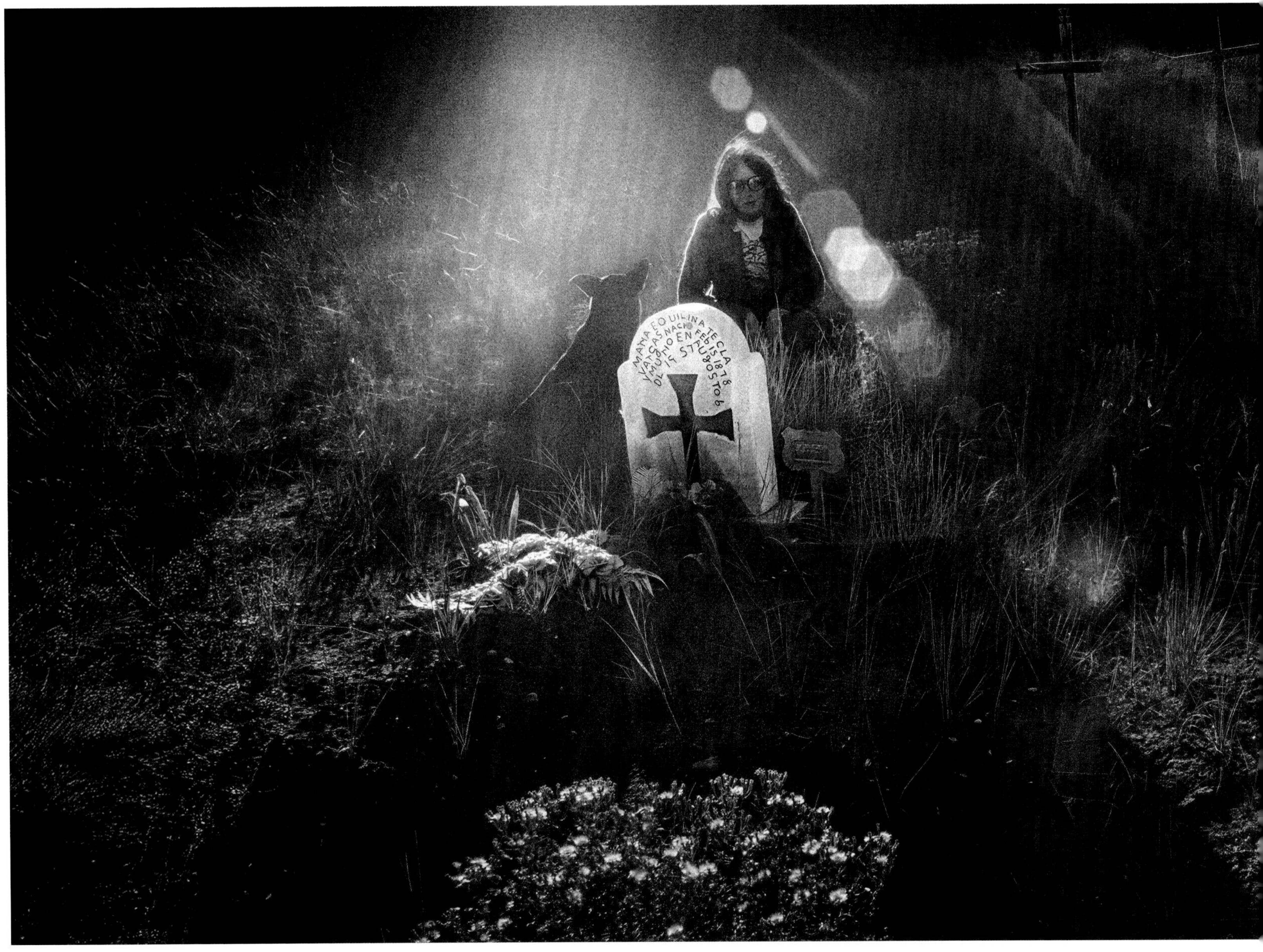
MAMA EQUILINA TECLA
FEB 15 1878

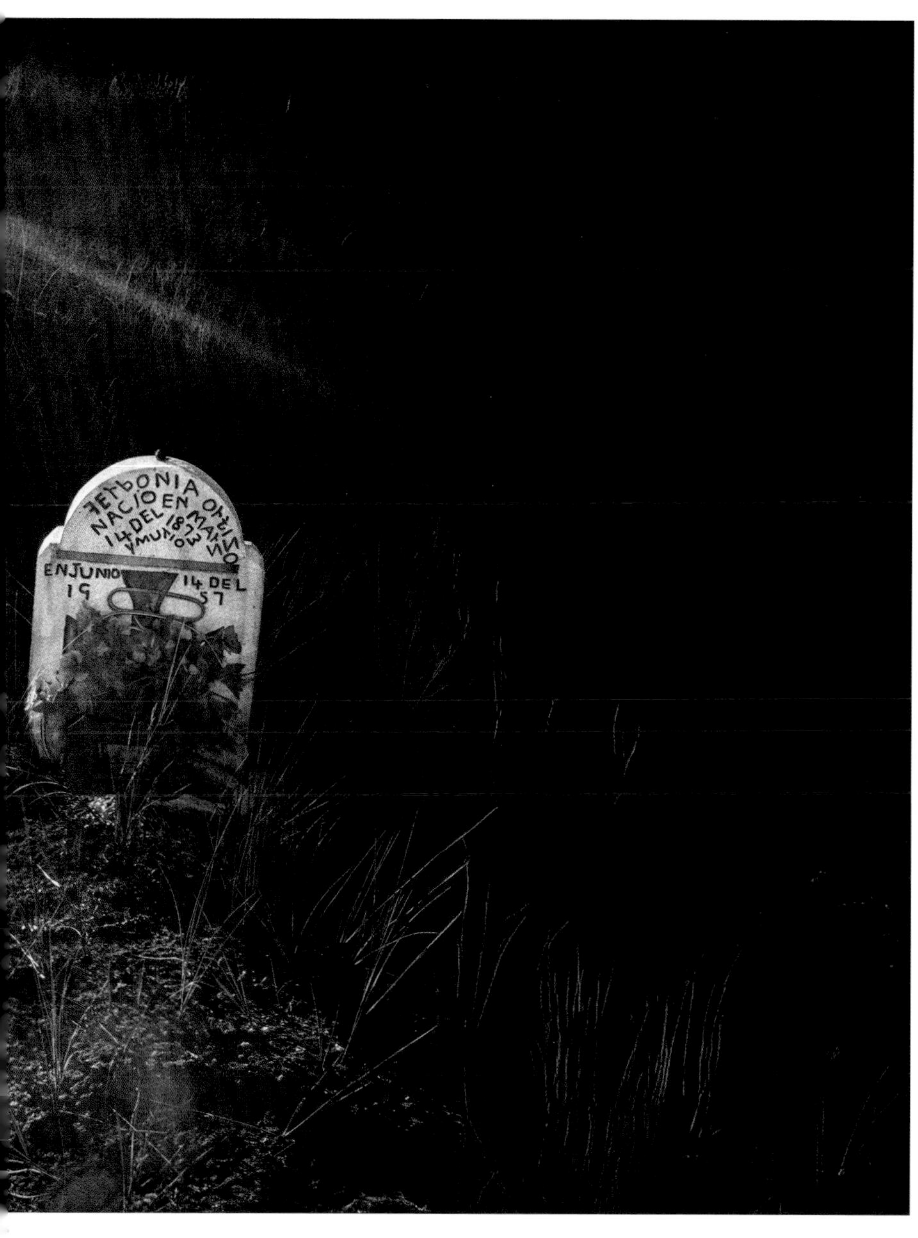
NACIO EN
14 DEL 1873
ENJUNIO
14 DEL
19
57

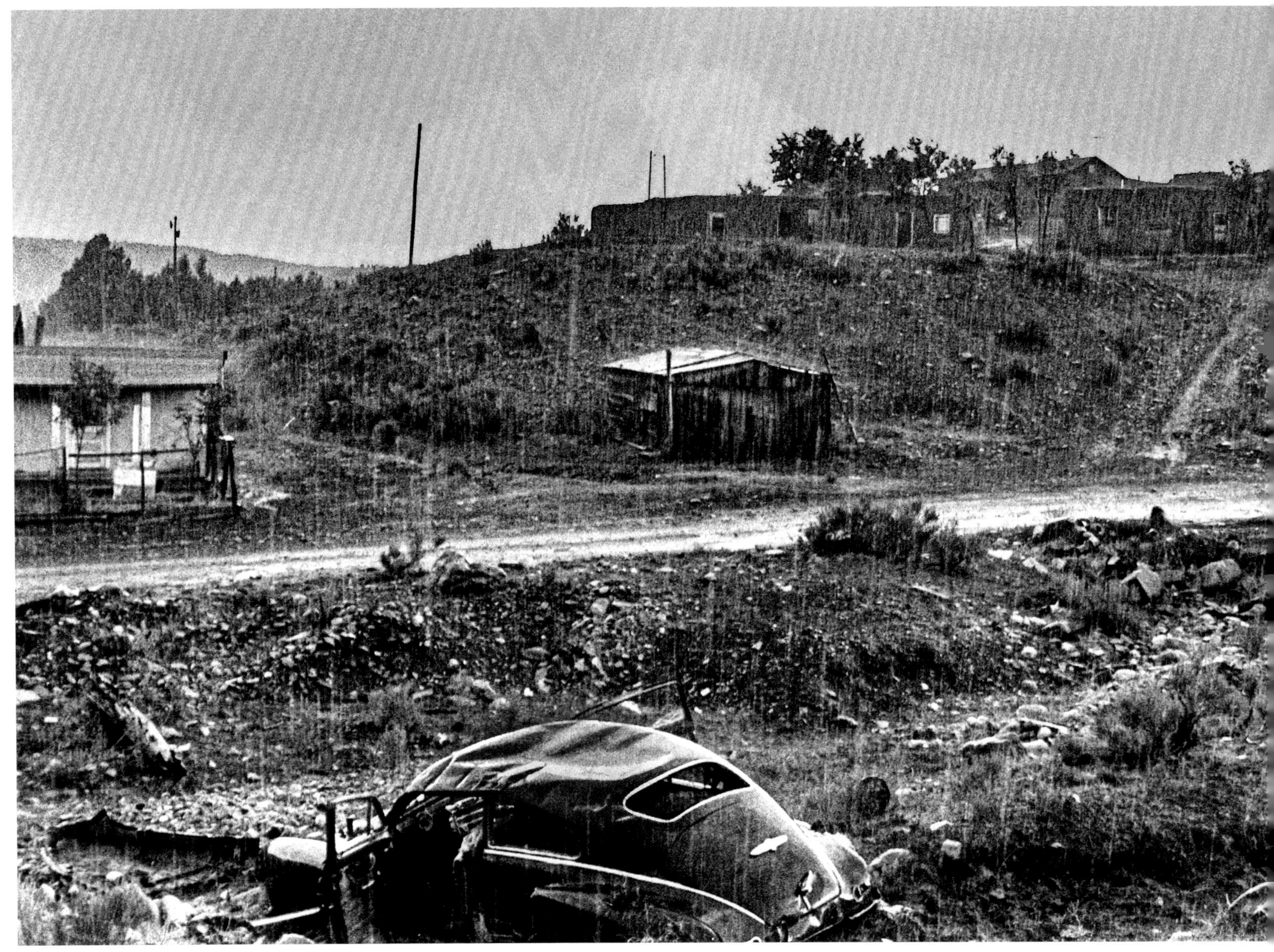

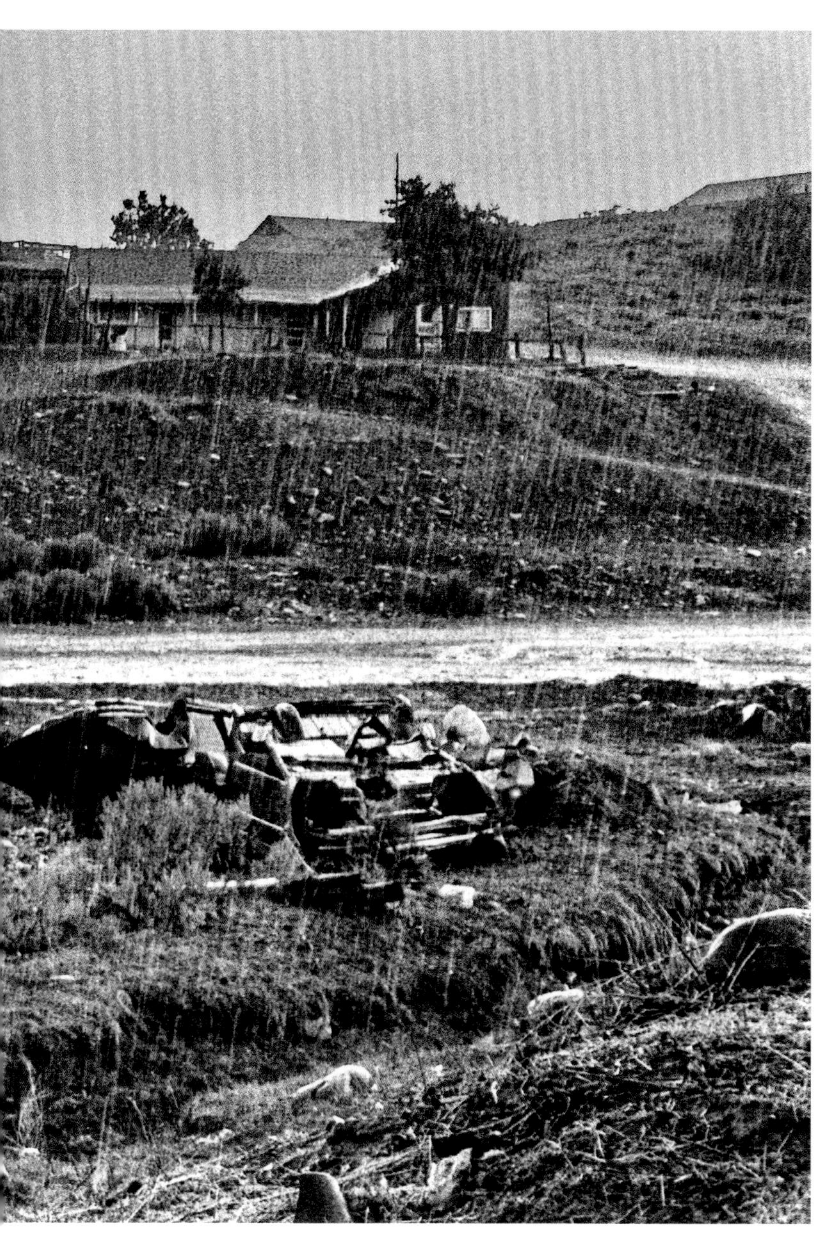

Once Upon a Time in Petaca

An Interview with Photographer Lynn Adler

Bill Shapiro

Late last fall, not long after the first snow had feathered New Mexico's Sangre de Cristo Mountains, I drove to Petaca. I'd been working with Lynn Adler on this book—and staring at her photographs of Petaca—for the better part of a year, and it was time to see the community for myself. As I bumped along a lonely forest service road, I found myself thinking of how, more than a half century earlier, in the summer of 1970, Adler, who was then just twenty-seven, had driven this same route, over these same ruts, past these same trees, in her red-and-white VW Bus. Over the course of a few days, she'd putt-putted 1,215 miles from her home in San Francisco, driving east on interstates and desolate two-lane highways before finally turning onto this dirt road and toward a flyspeck of a community that would, in many ways, change her life.

After I'd driven about twenty-five minutes, the dirt unexpectedly turned to rough pavement. A few homes appeared, pressed tight to the roadside. And then, where the road started to bend, a proper cluster came into view. There was no "Welcome to Petaca" sign. If there had been, it might have read, "Pop. 66., Elev. 7,274." Some of the structures seemed vaguely familiar from Adler's pictures—the church, a long building. Homes still dotted both sides of the road (although now many had boarded-up windows), but I saw no signs of life—no people, no barking dogs, no sounds from a television or radio—save for a few grazing cows and a wisp of smoke curling from a single home. Seeing the village today filled me with an intense appreciation for the pictures Adler made during her time in Petaca: of the people who lived here, of their homes and their animals, of their fences and fields, of her friends Marty and Gloria and Claudia and Sherie, of everything as it once was. After all, it's extremely unlikely that anyone has made more photographs of this remote village in Northern New Mexico than Adler has.

What follows is my conversation with Adler about what led her to Petaca and what it was like to make pictures there.

Bill Shapiro: What were your first impressions of Petaca?
Lynn Adler: I remember driving there but having no idea where, exactly, I was going, and not being sure I'd ever make it, because Petaca was barely on the map. Eventually I found the forest service road, which seemed to go on forever. But at some point I saw a group of kids—maybe ten, twelve years old—playing in the road. I slowed down and asked them, "Do you know where Petaca is?" I remember they just laughed and said, "You're *in* Petaca." And then one little boy, and I'll never forget this, said, "You must be looking for Marty and Gloria." He pointed to a little house. I remember the smoky smell in the air from wood-burning stoves and also the smell of sage, which was everywhere. Even today, when I smell sage, I have an immediate flashback to that moment.

Shapiro: What did those kids see? What were you like at the time?
Adler: My hair was long, maybe in pigtails, and I was probably wearing overalls and work boots. I was twenty-seven, living in the Haight-Ashbury neighborhood, seeing Janis Joplin and the Grateful Dead in Golden Gate Park. I was very political and had spent the last three years as part of the staff of Dr. Martin Luther King's organization, registering people to vote in rural Alabama and then working for fair housing in Chicago. At the time, I was drawn to the Cuban revolutionaries, the Weather Underground, the Vietnamese struggle for independence. I considered myself an organizer and an activist. We all did.

Shapiro: So what brought you to Petaca?
Adler: After Dr. King was assassinated, many of the people who worked with him organized the first Poor People's Campaign, a gathering he'd been planning for years. From across the country, thousands of representatives of poor communities traveled to Washington, DC, and created a tent city on the Mall.

Shapiro: That was the summer of '68?
Adler: Exactly, and that's where I met folks from the Alianza, the Federal Land Grant Alliance. It's also where I met Marty Greenhut, a community orga-

nizer from New York who was hanging out with the Alliance folks. They were recruiting people to come to Rio Arriba County [where Petaca is located], and I was ready to jump into whatever they needed. I came to Northern New Mexico with them and just fell in love with the visual beauty, the smell of sage, and the openness of the people.

Shapiro: What was so compelling to you about the land-grant situation?
Adler: Well, this was really about the unjust way the US government had taken land that had belonged to Hispano families for generations. When the Mexican-American War ended in 1848, Mexico ceded much of its territory to the United States—including what is now New Mexico. The US government claimed tons of land for the "public domain," and families who had farmed and ranched their land for generations lost it because their documents were incomplete, inconsistent, or missing. Some villagers lost their land because they were unable to pay land taxes under the new American system. And so Marty and I, and countless others, wanted to help right this wrong. And when I was in Petaca, I spoke with so many people who still felt deeply betrayed by what the government had done. The land represented a deep bond to their ancestors, and they wanted to reclaim what had been taken from them.

Shapiro: Before the Hispanos made their land-grant claim, who'd been living in and around the Petaca area?
Adler: For thousands of years, and long before the Spanish arrived in what is now New Mexico in 1598, this area had been occupied by Indigenous people. When I was in Petaca, I learned that the Capote Utes and Jicarilla Apaches had been the local Native groups, but I was young and more focused on the present than the past, so I didn't go much deeper than that.

Decades later, when I began revisiting my old photos from Petaca, I went deeper. I came upon a fascinating book called *Properties of Violence* by David Correia, a professor of American studies at the University of New Mexico, that described the complicated history of Rio Arriba County. In his book, and in other reading, I learned how the land grants, which began around 1860, involved vast tracts of land that encroached on traditional Native lands and resources. The Indigenous people were not consulted, of course, and from the beginning the Hispanos faced almost constant resistance from the Capote Utes and Jicarilla Apaches. The Hispanos tried to fortify their villages against attacks, but at the same time they also made alliances with other Indigenous groups including the Pueblo peoples. It was a violent, tense, complex time.
Shapiro: When you were in Petaca, did you see any evidence that Indigenous people had once lived in the area?

Adler: Actually, I did. Early on, I met Jesusita Martinez. She was the town healer and one of oldest people living in Petaca. In one of our first chats, she told me she was mixed Hispano and Jicarilla Apache, which really piqued my curiosity about how these two groups interacted. She told me that despite the hostilities, there had been periods of trade, negotiation, and, in some cases, intermarriage between the Hispanos and Native peoples. Jesusita was a master potter who made traditional Jicarilla Apache–style cookware using the same clay that her Indigenous ancestors had, clay that was embedded with a singular glint of mica.

Shapiro: Marty was the spark that inspired you and your friends to come to Petaca. What was he like?
Adler: Incredibly charismatic, incredibly idealistic, grandiose, dogmatic, and, looking back, maybe not so realistic. I mean, if I met him now, I'd probably think he was full of shit on many levels. But at the time I was sort of fascinated by his energy and his vision. He had endless plans: create a school for the kids, start a print shop with a printing press for a monthly newsletter, build a farmhouse and a toolshed and a garden full of vegetables that he and Gloria could live off of. And on and on.
Shapiro: Did he accomplish his goals?
Adler: Well, he built a small home and started a garden, although there wasn't really enough to live on. The rest of it, no, that didn't come to pass. It was harder than he expected. But he *did* accomplish one thing: He became part of the Petaca community. In terms of intercultural relations, I think that was very significant.

Shapiro: Who else was there?
Adler: Marty and Gloria were the first ones to move to Petaca. And later, Claudia and her daughter, Maya, and Sherie and her son, Sarmod. I was very close to Claudia and Sherie, having worked with them for a couple of years on Dr. King's staff in both the South and in Chicago. Claudia, who is the Black woman in the photos, was very intense and could be hostile unless you got to know her, but once I did we connected completely. Both Claudia and Sherie were adventurous, fearless. There were a few other stragglers over the years, but that was the core group.

Shapiro: Let's talk about your photographs. In 1971, there weren't a lot of women who were documentary photographers. What prompted you to bring a camera?
Adler: Well, at the time, I'm not even sure I knew what a documentary photographer was. And it's funny because, you know, in 1965, just as I was about to get on a train for Alabama to be part of the summer

voter-registration drive, a photographer friend handed me a camera, insisting that I document the events. I ended up putting the camera under my bed and never took a single frame. I clearly had no understanding of the power of images.

Shapiro: Obviously *something* changed . . .
Adler: Well, yeah. A few years later my mother had a stroke, and I flew home to Philadelphia. Right after she died, I had this weird and I guess life-changing dream. My mother had recently built a darkroom, which I'd never seen, and in the dream I walk into the darkroom, see a bureau, open a drawer, and there's this camera, so I pick it up. Then I woke up. The next day, I raced back to her house and went straight to the darkroom. It looked just like it did in my dream, and just as in the dream, there was the bureau. I opened the drawer, and there was the same camera from the dream—an Olympus. Look, I'm not a woo-woo-hippie-bullshit kind of person, but I just was, like, *How could this be?* I decided to start taking pictures and soon became obsessed. Back in San Francisco, I got together with a few photographers, and we formed a collective and called it Optic Nerve.

"I found that approaching the locals with my camera made it easier for me to engage with them, brought me closer to them."

Shapiro: When you landed in Petaca, you had very little experience behind the lens. So I'm curious: What were you looking for when you lifted your camera?
Adler: Honestly, I wasn't really looking for anything in particular. I wasn't thinking about making a book. Nothing like that. I was just taking pictures of my friends in this strange new environment. But I found that approaching the locals with my camera made it easier for me to engage with them and brought me closer to them. And that's really what I was interested in at that point, much more than taking a good picture.

Shapiro: How did it help you connect with the locals?
Adler: In two ways, I guess. I wouldn't say they were flattered, but they were definitely amused that I would even want to take their picture, so that sort of opened them up to a conversation. But there was something else. Petaca was very poor, and no one had a camera, not even a Brownie or an Instamatic, and no one had photographs of themselves. You'd walk into their homes, and there's a cross on the wall and an icon but no family photos. So I'd go back to San Francisco, drop into the public darkroom there, make a bunch of 8 × 10 prints, and send them to Marty and Gloria, who would then give them to whomever was in the pictures. And the people really appreciated that, appreciated seeing pictures of themselves. It was a way that I could share my feelings toward them.

Shapiro: So what did you find yourself drawn to shooting?
Adler: The older people. The children, I guess. But I really, really didn't have an agenda. It wasn't like now, when I go into a situation and have an idea of what I want to capture. I was just there. If someone had asked me, "Why do you want to shoot my beans?" I wouldn't have had a very good answer other than, "I like you. I like what you're doing. I want to remember this. I want to be able to share it with you." Of course, no one ever asked. It was all so fascinating to me. I'd traveled a lot for my age, but I'd never really been in a community like this. There were things I'd never encountered.

Shapiro: Like what?
Adler: Few people had electricity, and no one I knew had indoor plumbing. They got their water from the well or from the acequia that ran through the town. I'd never heard of acequias before, but they're an amazing system of communal irrigation canals. It was also the first time I'd met a *curandera*, a healer.

Shapiro: When I first saw your pictures, one thing that struck me was that you never shot what today might be called "poverty porn." You know, unwashed children, a tumble-down outhouse, cracked windows. Instead, your photos carry a lot of warmth.

“If someone had asked me, ‘Why do you want to shoot my beans?’ I wouldn’t have had a very good answer other than, ‘I like you. I want to remember this. I want to be able to share it with you.’”

Adler: I wasn’t blind to the poverty, and I’d been to places where the poverty had been horrific. I just wanted to document what was meaningful to me, and what was meaningful to me, what I was very moved by, was the generosity I found in the community. No one had much of anything, materially, but when someone needed a fence rebuilt, they had no trouble getting people to join.

Shapiro: What did you learn about yourself?
Adler: Well, I learned that I didn’t know shit about surviving in a rural situation and that my way of life was not typical of how most people were living in the world. I mean, to be in a place where nobody had anything but I had so much gave me an understanding of what a life built around sharing can look like. I learned how important that is. I learned that these people could teach us things that we didn’t even know we needed to learn. There was also plenty that we *knew* we needed to learn. The locals helped Marty and Gloria build their house, construct their fence, know what to grow and how to grow it, how to stay warm, and on and on. I mean, Marty and Gloria didn’t even know how to cook.

Shapiro: Looking back at your pictures, I wonder if there are a few that stand out to you that you feel really tell the story of Petaca?

Adler: Interesting. [*Pause.*] Okay, yes, three come to mind, and, in a way, they're actually connected. The first photo shows beans drying on a farmer's small, simple bed just after he'd harvested them (page 27). To me, it's an intimate picture that speaks to the close relationship the farmers had to their land and their crops.

I've always felt drawn to the picture of Jesusita standing in her doorway, listening to the village (page 14). Jesusita, as I mentioned a moment ago, was very old, but she was also nearly blind. She was part Apache and was the last living person in the region who knew the secret of making the traditional hand-formed clay pots used to cook beans. The pots were unique because they were made from a special clay found only in Northern New Mexico. The clay contained a high percentage of mica, a mineral that strengthened and insulated the clay so that the pots could be placed directly on an open fire without cracking from the heat. Some say they also gave the beans a perfect creamy texture. The last image shows the ruins of the abandoned mica-processing facility where, before the plant was shut down, many of Petaca's men worked to separate mica from the tailings (page 66). When the facility closed and the men lost their jobs, it brought further hardship to Petaca. These photos speak to me of tradition and exploitation.

Shapiro: In later years you would become a documentary filmmaker and producer. Do you think your experience in Petaca had an impact on that?
Adler: Filming a documentary puts you in a place where you would never expect to go. We used to call it "culture leaping." It's the same with documentary photography: It somehow gives you permission to join a different culture and become part of it for a period of time. Petaca was really the first time I experienced that, and, yes, I think it gave me the bug.

Shapiro: You visited Petaca over the years and stayed for extended periods of time. But you never moved there. Why not?
Adler: At the time, I remember feeling pretty torn. There were moments when I wanted to move, but I had formed this photography collective in San Francisco, and we'd rented space to build a darkroom and studio in an old, abandoned candy factory. That building was an important part of the counterculture of the '70s and housed dozens of artisans, sculptors, and filmmakers. That was really my focus at the time.

Shapiro: And yet you kept coming back. Why?
Adler: Because I was interested to see how my fish-out-of-water friends were going to figure things out. I mean, none of them knew what they were doing. None of them had any money—I think they ended

up on food stamps—and I wanted to see how things between my friends and the community would unfold.

Shapiro: How did they unfold? How did the Petaca adventure end?
Adler: The people in Petaca had come to accept my friends. They still might have thought they were in over their heads and maybe a little nuts, but they were definitely accepted. And yet there were other factors we didn't fully understand at the time. Like, the Forest Service was slowly encroaching on nearby land, which set people in the community a little on edge. And, of course, a lot of hippies had moved to communes in Northern New Mexico, and some of them could be provocative. They began coming to Petaca on horseback and just camping out, getting high, and selling drugs. My friends, of course, were not into that. But this was a very traditional town, and there seemed to be a growing sense of distrust among the locals. They'd heard about how other areas had been taken over by Anglos. And after my last time there, in the winter of 1974, things got worse. There was one sort of notorious hippie commune called the Hog Farm, and some of its members would rove around and set up teepees, and they had drugs and, we heard, guns. They tended to attract the cops. So there was a lot of tension. Marty—and I think everyone—felt like this disrespect for the community was going to lead to some kind of disaster. And it did.

Shapiro: What happened?
Adler: One night when Sherie was away, her house in Petaca was set on fire and burned down. It was actually the first house Marty and Gloria had rented when they arrived in town four years earlier. It was terrifying. I found out about it weeks later in a letter from Claudia. The old people wanted my friends to continue living in town, but it was like a switch had been flipped in Petaca, and my friends no longer felt comfortable. And then two more houses burned. My friends packed up and just fled. It was depressing because their spirit had been so strong. I mean, we felt like we were building a new world and that nothing was going to stop us. But after the fires, my friends kind of went their separate ways. It all ended so quickly.

Shapiro: You made these photos half a century ago. Where have they been all this time?
Adler: I rediscovered them during the pandemic. They were tucked away in the darkroom I'd built in my garage. I hadn't seen them for at least twenty years, but there they were, in a three-ring binder labeled "Petaca, New Mexico." My photographic career never took off because I got sucked into documentary filmmaking, and I really sort of regret that.

> *"It would have been so easy for these pictures never to have been made. I was a kid and could have just left the camera at home. And the negatives could have been lost or damaged. So I feel incredibly grateful that these people who might otherwise have been lost to time have been preserved."*

Shapiro: When you opened the binder and started looking at your contact sheets—at pictures that were made a lifetime ago—what did you feel?
Adler: I immediately started wondering, *Where are these people? Could they still be alive?* When I met some of the older residents, they were probably in their sixties or older. I realized that Jesusita, Santiago, and Maria couldn't possibly still be with us, but maybe some of the kids were still around. So I started researching, and I learned that a lot of those children ended up dying in car accidents or by gun violence. The more I looked at the pictures, the more moved I felt. It was a very important chapter in my life.

Shapiro: In all, you spent a handful of months in Petaca. And you're eighty-one now. So that's a tiny portion of your life—
Adler: But you know how some days feel more special than all the other days . . . ?

Shapiro: What do you see as the legacy of the Petaca photos?
Adler: It would have been so easy for these pictures never to have been made. I was a kid and had no idea what I was doing, and I could have just left the camera at home. And of course, in the fifty years that followed, the negatives could have been lost or damaged. So I feel incredibly grateful that, somehow,

these people who might otherwise have been lost to time have been preserved. Over the last few years, as I've gotten in touch with the relatives of the people I knew who lived in Petaca, I've been able to give them pictures of their ancestors. Some had never seen their great-grandmother or their great-grandfather before. These pictures? They've become a way to connect people, which, I guess, was the reason we all came to Petaca in the first place.

BILL SHAPIRO is a former editor in chief of *LIFE* magazine.

Petaca's People

The Photographer Looks Back at the Small Town's Most Memorable Characters

Lynn Adler

My time in Petaca was marked by my relationships with both my Anglo friends and some of the local townspeople. The following pages highlight a few of the people who played a major role in my life at that time.

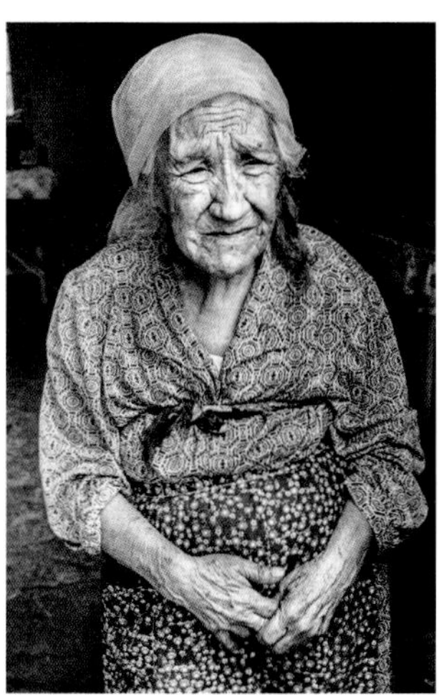

JESUSITA MARTINEZ

Born in 1886, Jesusita was Petaca's *curandera*, or healer. She was an incredibly skilled potter and, when I was in Petaca, she was also the last person in the area who knew how to make traditional Jicarilla Apache–style cookware, using mica-embedded clay. (She passed on her knowledge to a few who carry on the tradition today.) When I met Jesusita, she was nearly blind, but her door was always open to the young newcomers looking for advice, and I remember sitting in her home listening to her many stories. Sometime after I left, I learned that she'd been murdered. Someone thought she had money hidden in her tiny, tidy home.

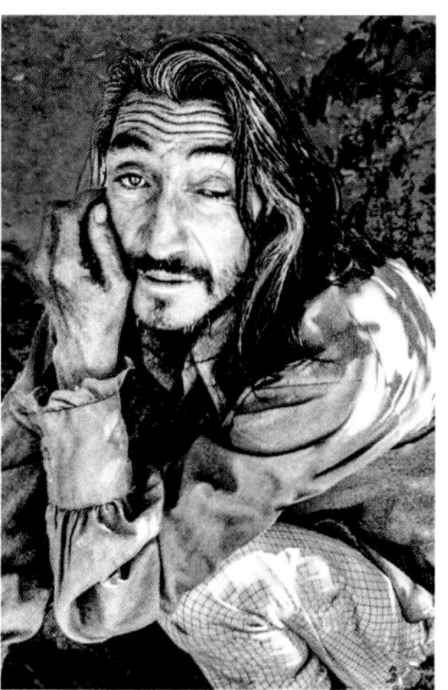

ELMO LIDO

Elmo was easy to spot. He had long hair—not common for Hispanos in this traditional town—and often dressed like he'd just come from Haight Street, with paisley or ruffled shirts and cool, patterned pants. Even though he was much older than we were—I'm guessing he was in his late fifties—he came by to visit with us often, to hang out and to drink beer. He was incredibly friendly, incredibly kind, but there was a certain sadness about him. It had been a while since he'd worked; like many other men in town, he'd lost his job when the sawmill in nearby Vallecitos shut down. Maybe he saw us as less judgmental than his peers.

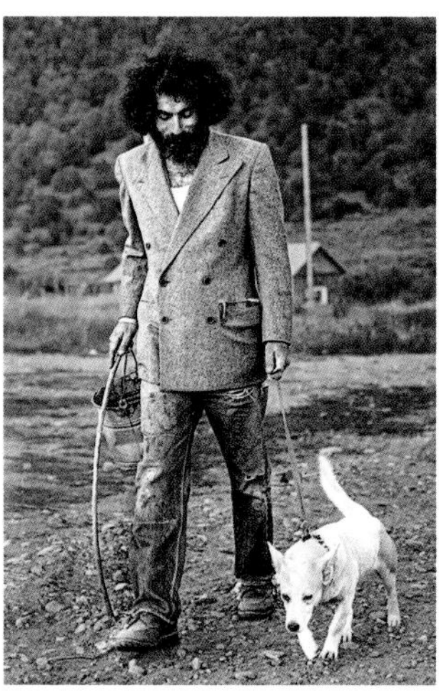

MARTY GREENHUT

I met Marty in 1968 during the Poor People's Campaign at Resurrection City in Washington, DC. It was a month-long encampment on the Mall, inspired by Martin Luther King Jr. to secure economic justice for those struggling financially. We were both in our mid-twenties and caught up in the spirit of the times. There, Marty and I learned about La Alianza Federal de Mercedes, a group from Tierra Amarilla, New Mexico, that fought for the land rights of traditional Hispano New Mexicans. Marty wanted to support their efforts.

In San Francisco, Marty and his wife Gloria met people involved in the "back to the land" movement. Inspired, they left the city for rural Northern New Mexico. In moving to Petaca, they wanted to connect with the locals and learn how to survive away from the turmoil of urban life. They wore their hair long but rejected the term "hippie"; instead, they called themselves "urban activists."

And they had big dreams. A letter Marty wrote me in November of 1971 read, in part, "We plan to build chicken and goat sheds, an outdoor kitchen, a bathhouse with sauna, a workshop with living quarters, water irrigation systems, root cellar . . ." They had no idea how difficult all of this would be.

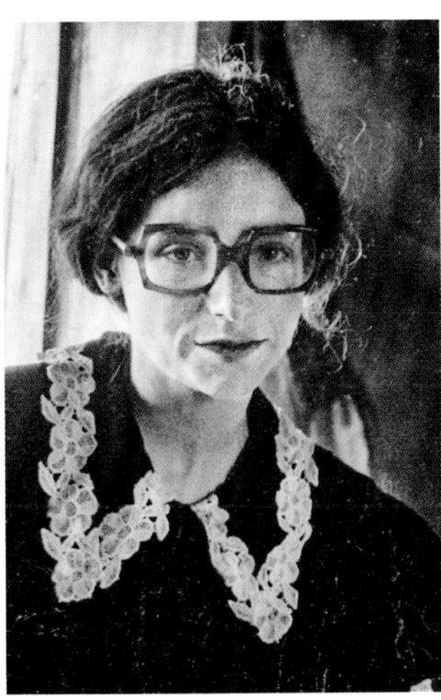

GLORIA GREENHUT

Gloria was in her early twenties when and she and Marty piled into their car and drove to Petaca. Homesteading in an off-the-grid community where not everyone spoke English took both persistence and resilience. As Marty began building a simple home, Gloria focused on the garden they hoped would supply much of their food. The trouble was, Gloria had been raised in New York City and knew exactly nothing about raising crops. She made up for her lack of experience with energy and enthusiasm, asking the locals about the best crops to plant (potatoes and purslane, or verdolagas, which grew like a weed) and organizing work parties to clear a small area of land in front of their not-yet-finished house.

The old tractor they bought fell apart, their ancient plow horse couldn't really plow, the fence that was meant to keep out the predatory animals was always in disrepair, but Gloria never got discouraged. And in the end, she successfully learned how to can beets for winter and bake bread in an outdoor *horno*.

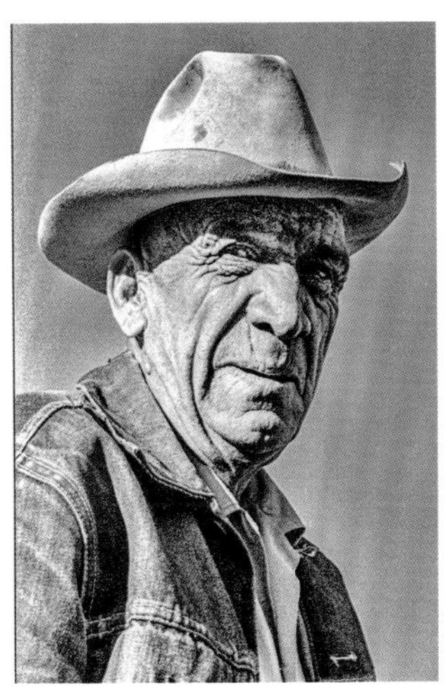

SANTIAGO ROYBAL

The Roybal family helped settle Petaca in the 1860s. Santiago, a rancher with a small herd of cattle, was very respected in the community and was often called to settle land disputes. He and I liked to talk politics—unlike others in town, he was fluent in English—and we tended to return to the tricky history of land grants and what that meant in the '70s. He and the others welcomed my friends, but he also wanted me to know that there was an underlying fear of losing more of their land to the Anglos. I was honored to be invited to Santiago and his wife Maria's fiftieth wedding anniversary, which included a parade through the town and a reception at the old dance hall. Santiago knew the local politicians and was instrumental in getting a new road for Petaca. Years later I learned that his great-grandson, Marcos, attended graduate school at the University of New Mexico and published a study about the history of land grants, which I know would have made Santiago proud. The other notable thing about Santiago: His pet goose, Lugar, had a habit of nipping Sherie's legs when she passed by carrying water from the well.

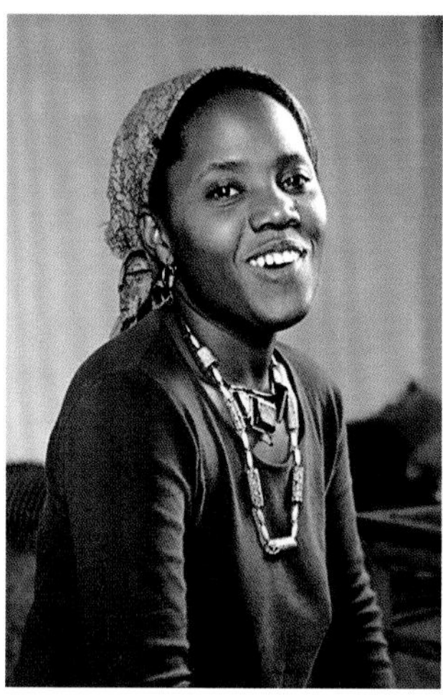

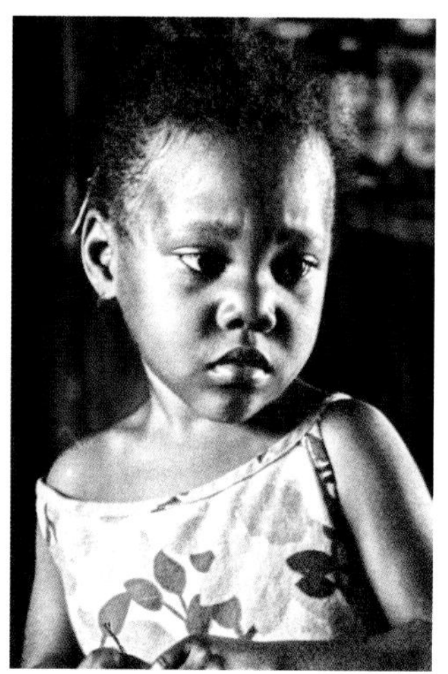

CLAUDIA KING

Fearless, outspoken, and independent, Claudia grew up in Chicago and, between 1965 and 1967, worked on Martin Luther King Jr.'s staff. That's where I met her. She was not happy living in San Francisco, finding it neither affordable nor welcoming for single mothers, so when I happened to tell Claudia and our friend Sherie, also a single mom, about Petaca, they were up for the adventure. As a single Black mother in a remote Hispano village, Claudia truly stood out, but she became good friends with the other young mothers in town. After being forced to leave Petaca, she and her young daughter Maya moved seventy miles away to the town of Chamisal, where she eventually married a local Anglo, added "Yunker" to her last name, built an adobe house, and had two sons. Claudia once told me that she never wanted to leave New Mexico, and she didn't: She lived out her life on the land, in Chamisal, until she died in 2023.

MAYA

Maya moved to Petaca as a toddler with her mother, Claudia. She was doted on by the town elders and made friends with the local kids, whom she loved to join when they swam in the Rio Tusas or climbed up the white piles of tailings that surrounded the old mica mill. I remember one of the older local kids, Patricia Lopez, who was probably twelve or thirteen at the time, used to play with Maya in a big sister role. Years later, as a young adult, Maya moved to San Francisco, fell in love with a British humanitarian aid worker, and now lives in Oxford, England. She has two teenage sons and is politically active.

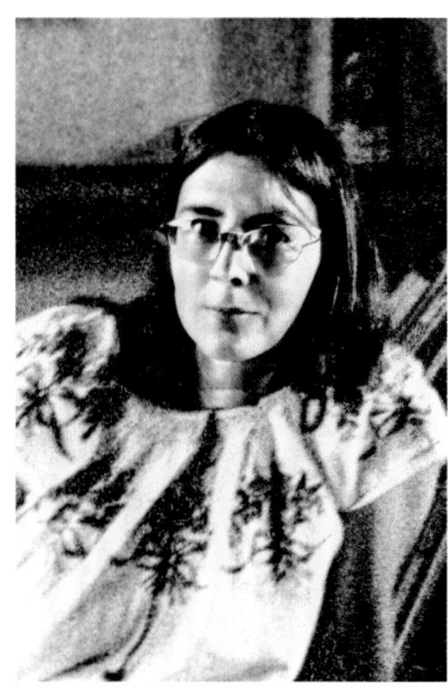

SHERIE LAND

Sherie grew up in Orange County, California. She met Claudia through a mutual friend, and in 1965 the two of them traveled to Selma, Alabama, to take part in the historic march from Selma to Montgomery. I met her in Chicago, where we all worked on the staff of Dr. King's organization. While there, she fell in love with Jimmy Collier, a well-known Black folk singer in the movement. Dr. King married them in the funky apartment that she and I shared. Together they had a son, Sarmod. Not long after Sherie and Jimmy broke up, Sherie moved to Petaca.

In a phone conversation a few years ago, Sherie shared with me her vivid memories of the night, close to the end of her time in Petaca, when a group of aggressive young Anglos came to town and, carrying guns, demanded that she drive them an hour south, to Española. She refused.

After Sherie's home and the homes of other Anglos in Petaca were burned down, Sherie, Claudia, and their children moved to Chamisal. Several years later, Sherie moved to Santa Fe and became a landscaper; recently, she left for Fresno to live with her son Sarmod and his family.

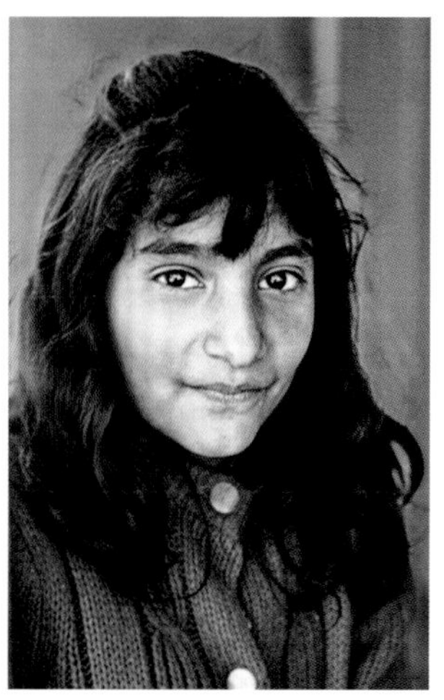

LOUELLA TORREZ

Louella, whom you see on the book's cover, was sort of the leader of Petaca's pack of kids. She had serious charisma. Her face always struck me as being extremely expressive, and I liked watching her—with and without my camera. She wasn't shy about hanging out with my friends and playing with their young kids, and I remember that she loved dogs. When Marty and Gloria's dog had puppies, Louella was thrilled to be given one, and she treated it with incredible tenderness. I later learned that she married Flaviano Gutierrez, a Petaca native, became Louella Torrez Gutierrez, had two kids, and moved to a nearby town, Ojo Caliente. She worked at the Los Alamos National Labs for fifteen years and passed away in 2021.

What They Saw

For the Locals, the Young Transplants from the Haight-Ashbury and New York City Raised Questions—and Eyebrows

Lynn Adler

The Anglos in Petaca were something of a spectacle. Here's how the residents of a remote, traditional town saw—and tried to make sense of—the long-haired activist newcomers.

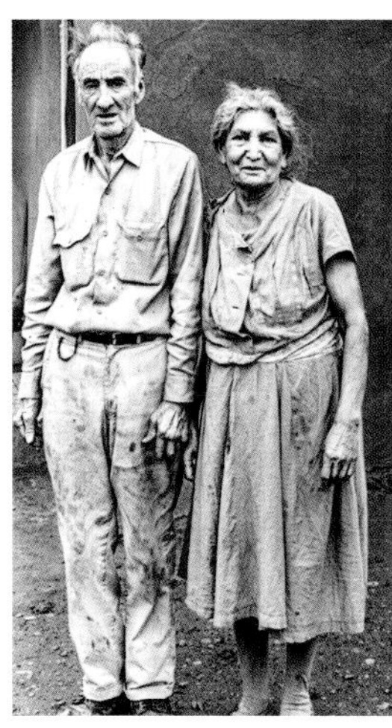

EUPHEMIA AND MAX TORRES

Euphemia and Max lived near the center of town. She was warm, engaging, and always kind to the newcomers. Whenever she visited Sherie or Claudia, she expressed concern for their children. "*Por favor*, remind your *hijas* to watch out for rattlesnakes" was her refrain. She liked to tell us about the old days in Petaca: "*Sabes*, we used to have a *clinica* here, but *no mas*. We had places to work, like the old lumber mill in La Madera, *pero no existe ahora*." In fact, none of the local mills or factories existed anymore.

From time to time, her husband, Max, would drop by and offer to lend a skilled hand. He was in his early seventies but insisted on climbing atop Sherie's roof to fix her leaks. "I may look old," he said, "but I have been doing this kind of work *todo mi vida*." Like nearly everyone else in town, the couple was befuddled by the fact that these city Anglos would actually move, on their own accord, to Petaca. "Our little town no longer has a school, and most of us have no indoor plumbing or electricity," Euphemia once said. "Why would you choose to move here?"

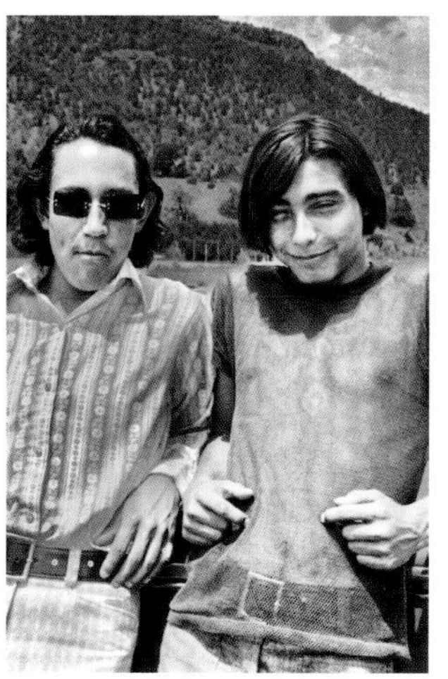

GERALD ESQUIBEL AND BILLY CISNEROS

When they weren't driving their beloved late-model cars up and down the dirt roads, Gerald and Billy were usually parked and hanging out inside them. Sometimes the two teens would take the Anglos to their secret spots, like to the waterfall that seemed to appear as if by magic after hiking through fields of sage or to the top of the nearby mesa with its sweeping views.

Unlike their more guarded parents, Gerald and Billy didn't hesitate to ask the Anglos personal questions. They were curious about Claudia's daughter, Maya, and Sherie's son, Sarmod. "What happened to their dads? Why would you leave them and bring little kids to a place like this where there's nothing to do?"

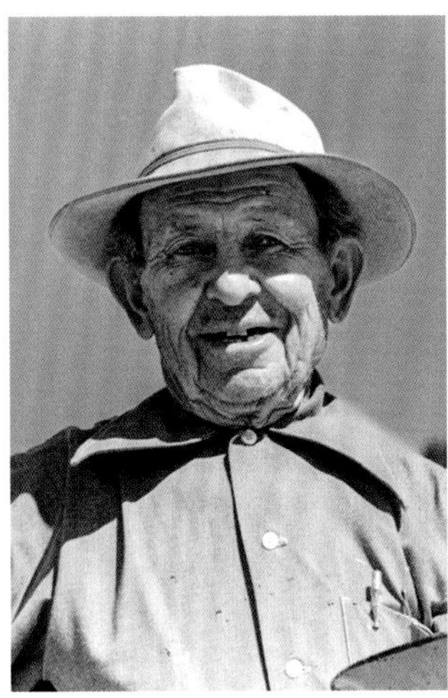

THEODORO MARTINEZ

When I first met Theodoro, I was walking by his weathered home with my friends Marty and Gloria as he was harvesting beans in the backyard. "Do you want to help?" he asked. "I am sure you have never seen this way of harvesting, but you need to know how we do things here." We said yes, of course, and, following Theodoro's lead, began to sort and spread the beans on the ground, which he then carried into his home and laid out to dry on his bed.

In a good-natured way, Theodoro and his friends poked gentle fun at the Anglos, often in their native Spanish. They couldn't fathom that Marty and Gloria, who were long on energy but short on practical know-how, were going to try to build a house. I remember Theodoro telling his friends, "*Vamos a tener que mostrarles como hacer adobes, y esperar que no se caigan de la escalera*" (We're going to have to show them how to make adobes, and hope they don't fall off the ladder).

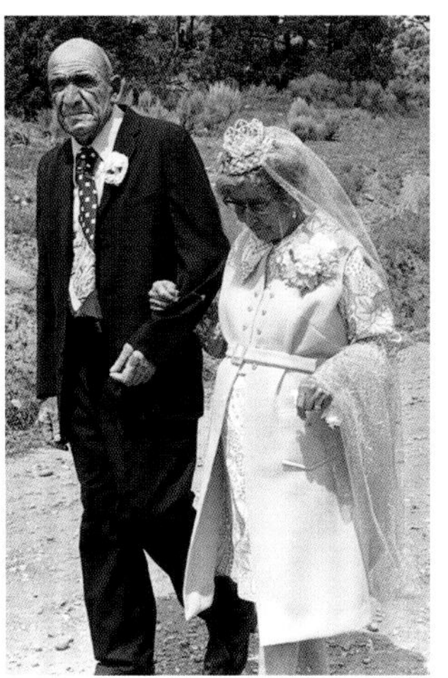

SANTIAGO AND MARIA ROYBAL

Santiago and Maria lived in a small adobe home in the center of town. From their porch, they could see everyone in town coming and going. As it happened, my friend Sherie moved in next door, and they kept an eye on her as well. With a mixture of pity and amusement, Santiago and Maria looked on as Sherie and the other Anglos struggled to raise crops, mend fences, and handle the other daily chores of rural life.

Like most of the women in this traditional town, Maria was a skilled cook, and she worried that the young Anglos weren't getting enough to eat. "These kids are too *flaco*," she once said to me, using the Spanish word for *skinny* as she prepared enchiladas that she'd soon walk over to Sherie. Another time, I remember her showing Sherie her tricks for making breakfast burritos. Santiago used to come by and sit on Sherie's porch, sharing his observations, concerns, and questions. "Why would you leave your homes with dependable electricity and running water to come to my little village?" he once asked me, genuinely perplexed. And also, "I know you don't know much about wood-burning stoves, but we can teach you how to keep it going all night. It gets very cold in the winter, and that will be your only heat."

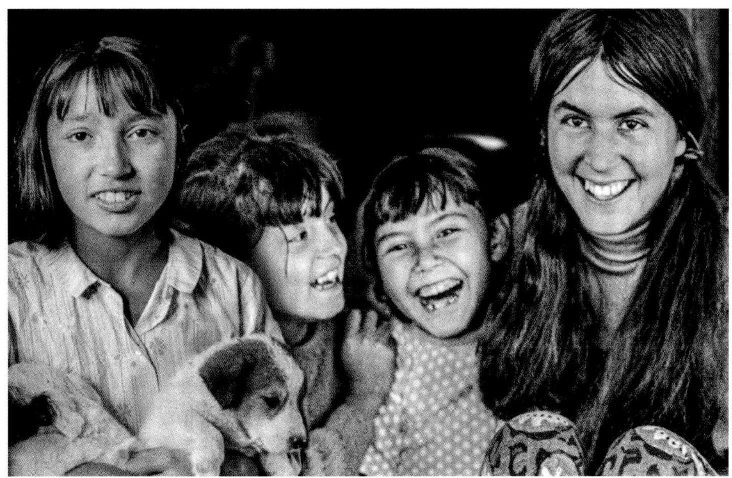

PETACA'S YOUNGSTERS

Perhaps no one was more fascinated with the strange, wild-haired Anglos than Petaca's many children. I was often there in the summer, when school was out and the kids ran around making their own fun. The Anglos became their focus and their entertainment. They'd arrive at Sherie's house early in the morning, hoping to play with Sarmod and Maya, and then beg us to go with them to the nearby Tusas Creek. They were endlessly curious about where we came from and had concocted fantastical ideas about our lives before Petaca. They were sure we'd lived in mansions with swimming pools.

Patricia Lopez was about twelve when I took her picture holding a puppy (above). I spoke with her a few years ago, and she remembered playing hopscotch and Hula-Hoop, swimming in the river, and catching fish. "My sister, Paulina, was the same age as Maya and Sarmod, so they played together a lot," she said. "[The Anglos'] long hair and strange clothes didn't bother me. They were nice people, and my parents liked to help them, teaching them how to do the laundry, how to warm up the water for baths, how to use a wood-burning stove. I never wondered about why they came; it was just good to have more people in our town."

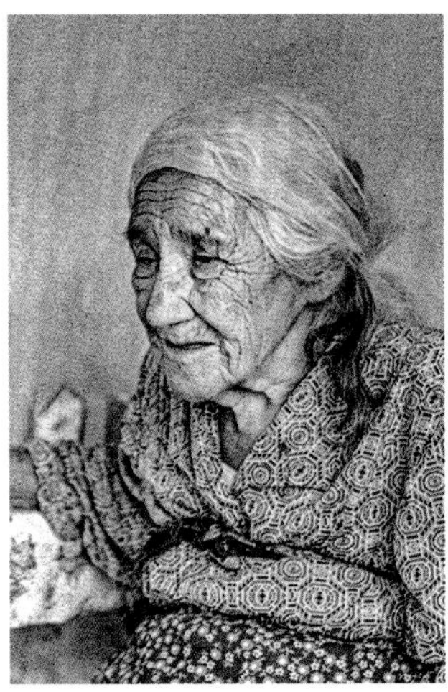

JESUSITA MARTINEZ

Jesusita was a small, frail-looking woman who appeared to be in her eighties. She lived by herself near the town's only public well. I would often see her standing in her doorway, and one day I asked if she would mind if I took her picture. Cameras were not seen in Petaca, and she was genuinely shocked by my request. "Why would anyone want a picture of an old woman?" she asked. "You have a wonderful face," I told her, which was true. She found this deeply amusing.

Jesusita was known as the town healer—an important role in a community without healthcare services—but, as she often said, she couldn't fix a broken bone. "You come from big cities where there are doctors," Jesusita once told me. "Here, when kids get sick or have a bad accident, they have to go many miles to find a hospital." Her English was limited, but she and Marty were able to communicate using a mix of simple English and Spanish words, and she enjoyed telling him about Petaca's past. I listened one day as she said, "Did you know that we had a dance hall next to the little store?"

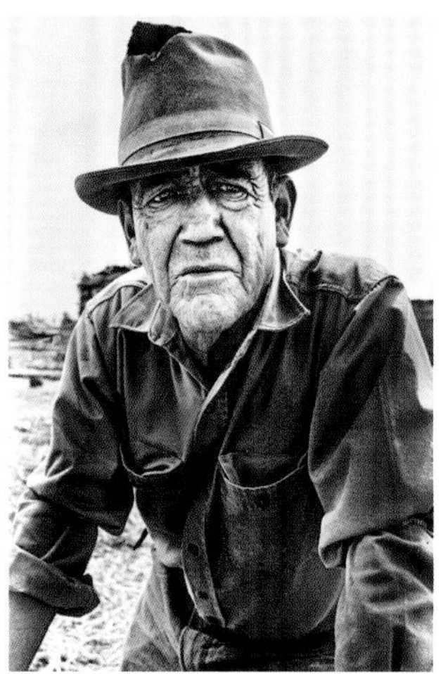

FRED ESQUIBEL

Fred was the very first person I met in Petaca. When I drove into town for the first time, he was standing in front of his house, driving nails into an old fence. There were no street signs, but, after some local kids pointed me in the general direction, he graciously guided me to Marty and Gloria's house.

In a hot, dry place like Petaca, everyone was focused on water, and Fred felt he had to teach the Anglos the rules and rituals surrounding its use. He took us to the acequia, an irrigation canal at the edge of town, which is how the community managed water distribution. "I bet you never thought about these issues in your entire lives," he said. "But if you're going to live here, you need to understand how we do things."

Acknowledgments

A heartfelt thanks to the people of Petaca, who graciously shared their expertise in off-grid living as well as their own histories, which played a crucial role in deepening my friends' understanding of the age-old struggles over land-grant issues in Northern New Mexico. And thanks to my activist friends—Claudia King, Sherie Land, Marty Greenhut, and Gloria Greenhut—who relied on their previous community-organizing skills to build meaningful relationships with their Hispano neighbors. Their tenacity and openness to learning new ways, along with their respect for the traditional culture, still inspire me.

Thanks to my son, Cody Sai Adler-McAllister, who nudged me to start posting on Instagram, which eventually led to the birth of this book. Thanks to Bill Shapiro, who discovered my work on Instagram and has been instrumental in shaping the book into its final form. His knowledge of the photography world and enthusiasm for my images has been invaluable. He is much more than an editor, and I sincerely appreciate his support and guidance.

To Jim Locker, who recognized the value in my work and motivated me to create this book. As my creative and technical consultant, his generosity and enthusiasm have been absolutely indispensable.

To my dear friend, the author Summer Brenner, who has been a longtime supporter of my work and has always offered enthusiastic encouragement and wise feedback. And, of course, to Stephen Hull, James Ayers, Felicia Cedillos, and the rest of the brilliant, hardworking editorial team at the University of New Mexico Press, without whom this book wouldn't exist.

I would also like to express my deep gratitude to the relatives of the Petaca residents featured in this book. Their willingness to share background information and offer insights into the lives of their ancestors helped create a more comprehensive, meaningful narrative: Kimberly Herrera, Sheryl Lambert, Deirdre Landers, Patricia Lopez, Felicia Lujan, Larry Roybal, and Rose Volpe.

Index of Plates

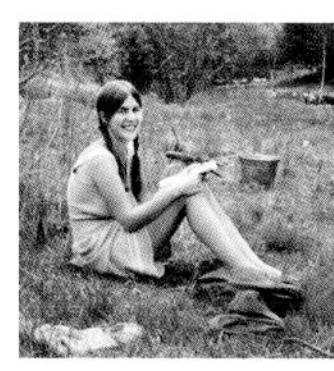
Photographer Lynn Adler in Petaca, circa 1971. 2

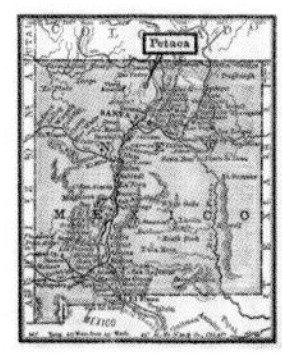
New Mexico map, from *Pocket Atlas of the World*, 1887; courtesy of Art Source International. 4

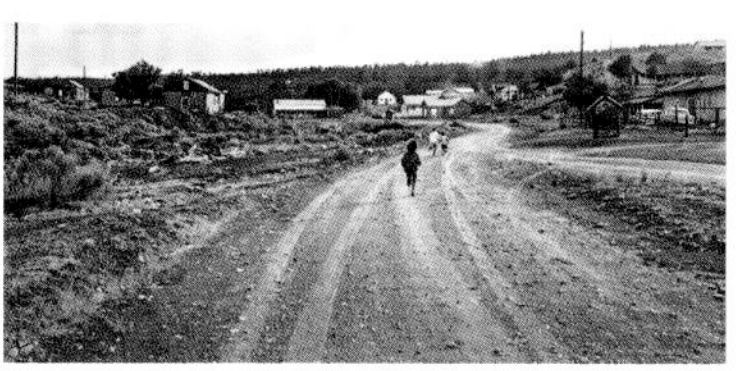
Entering Petaca. 7

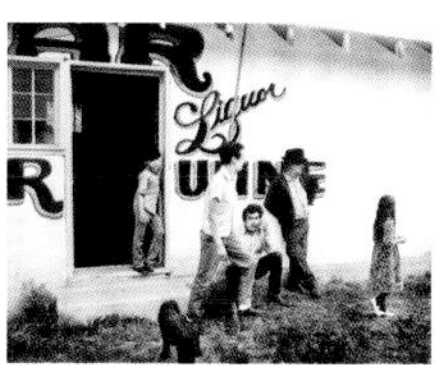
At the saloon. 8

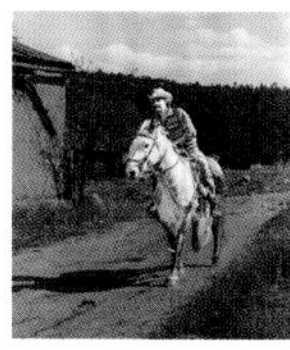
Morning ride. 9

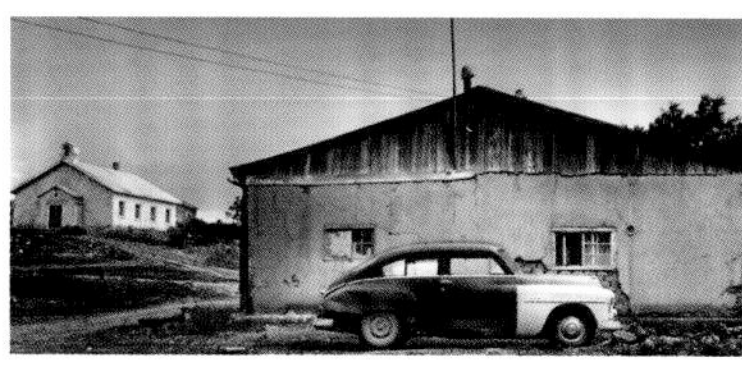
Church parking. 11

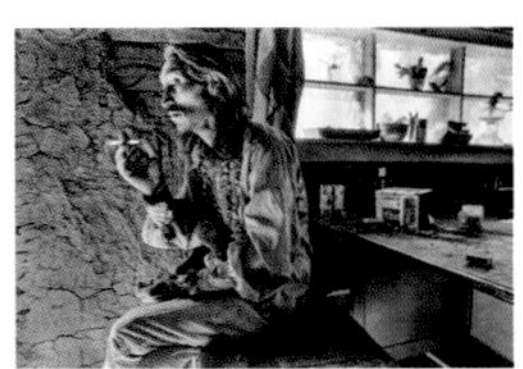
Elmo Lido visits Marty and Gloria Greenhut's home. 12

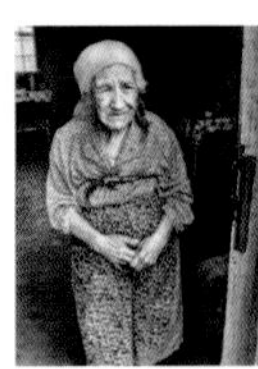
Jesusita Martinez listens to her village. 14

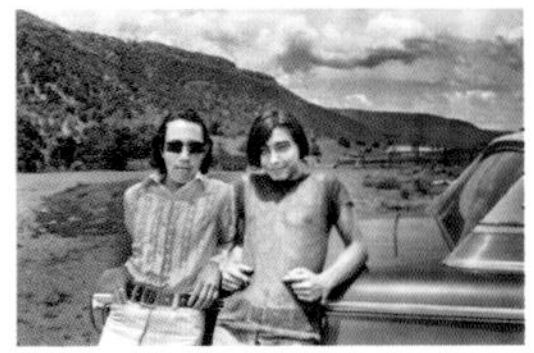
Gerald Esquivel and Billy Cisneros dreamed of lowriding in Santa Fe. 15

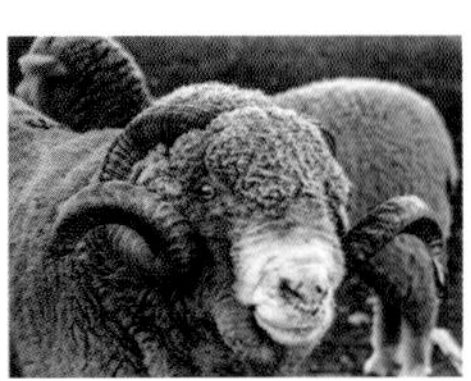
The churro, a breed of sheep brought to New Mexico by Conquistadors, is a reminder of the Spanish conquest. 16

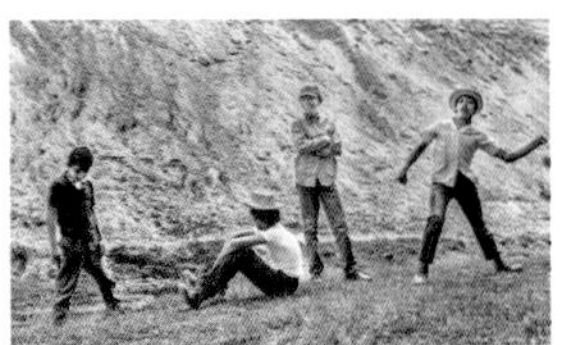
Playing in front of mountains of Mica. 17

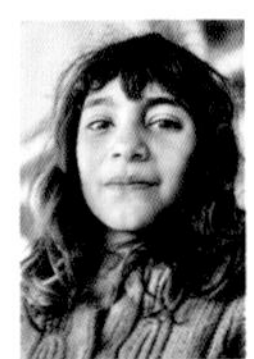
The charismatic Louella Torrez. 18

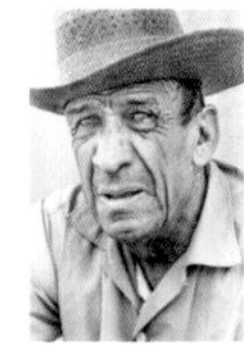
Santiago Roybal, unofficial alcalde, or mayor. 19

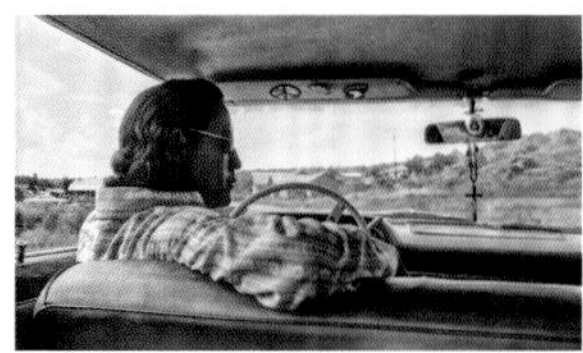
Gerald Esquivel in the driver's seat. 20

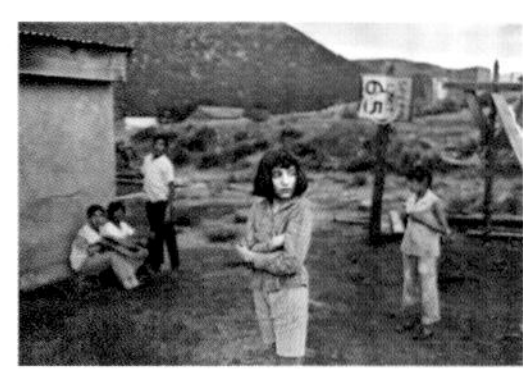
Louella Torrez at sundown. 23

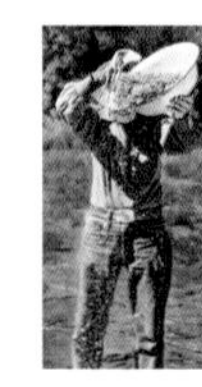
Theodoro Martinez in his bean field. 24

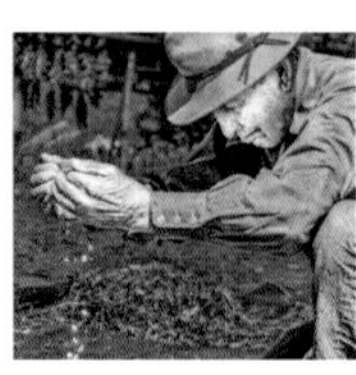
Theodoro Martinez examining his beans. 25

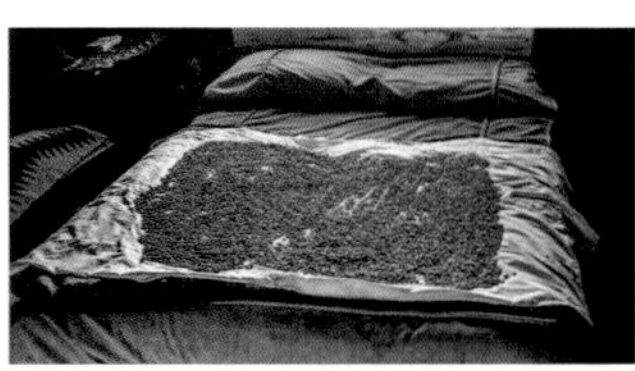
Beans drying on Theodoro Martinez's bed. 27

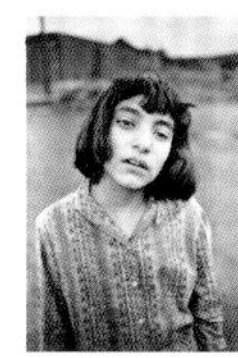
Louella Torrez. 28

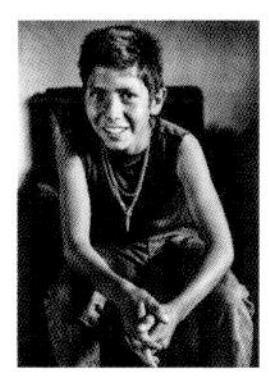
Julian Lovato, always on the go. 29

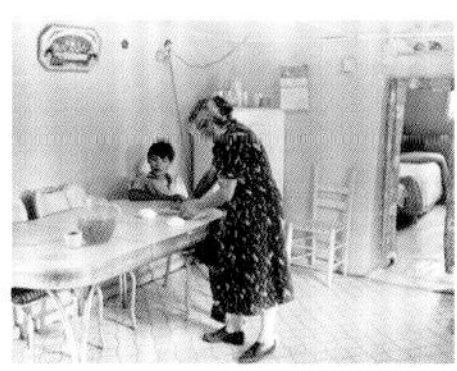
Euphemia Torrez making tortillas. 30

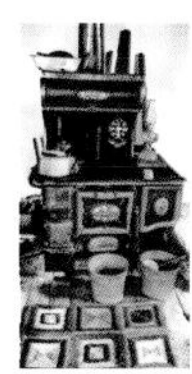
Most homes had an old cast-iron stove for cooking and heating. 31

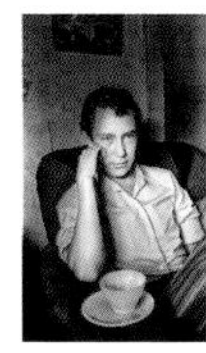
Gerald Esquivel taking his morning coffee at Sherie's house. 32

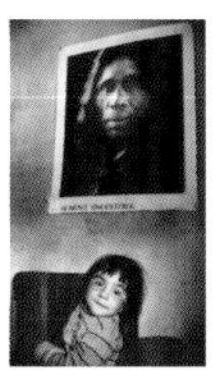
Paulina sits under an Edward Curtis poster of an Indigenous Californian. 33

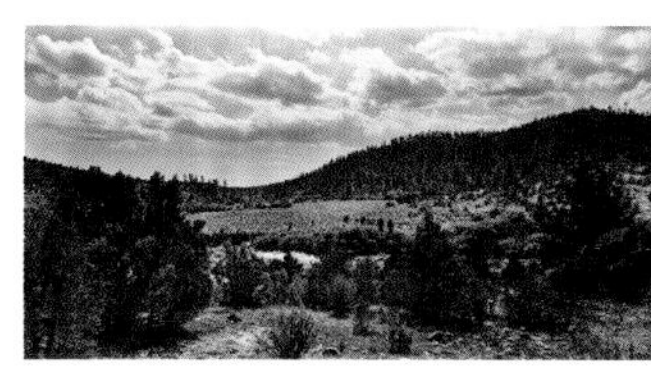
Petaca's sweeping spring views. 35

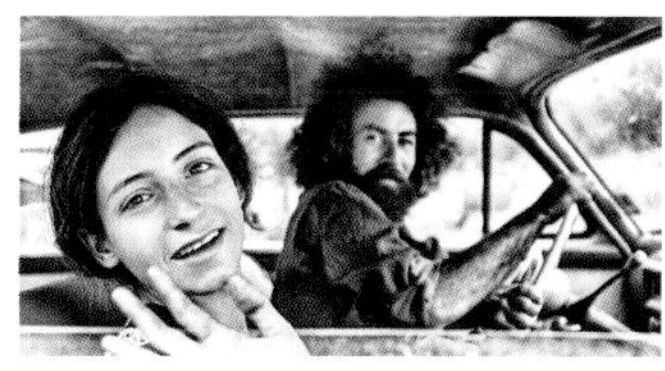
Marty and Gloria in their 1951 Plymouth Concord. 36

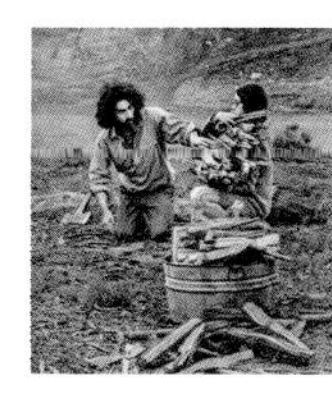
Marty and Gloria prepare for the long winter. 38

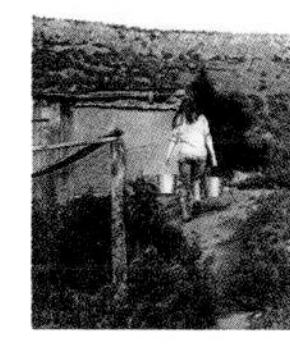
Sherie Land carrying water, hoping to avoid Santiago's snapping goose, Lugar. 39

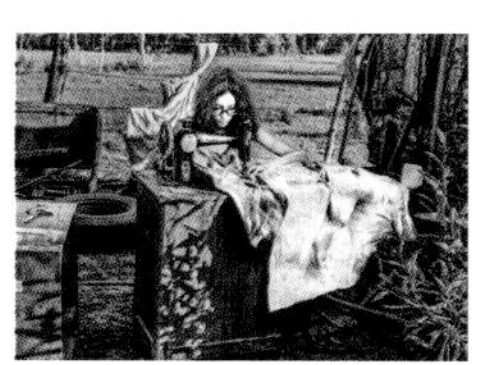
Gloria sews a wedding dress. 40

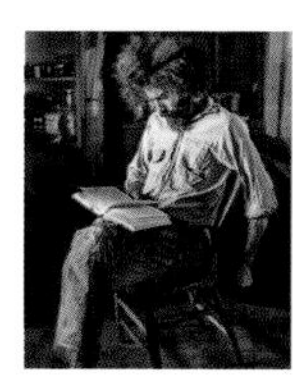
Marty reading a book about horse-drawn ploughing. 41

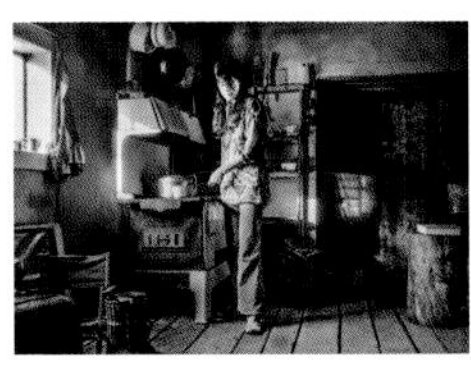

Photographer Lynn Adler brews morning coffee. 42

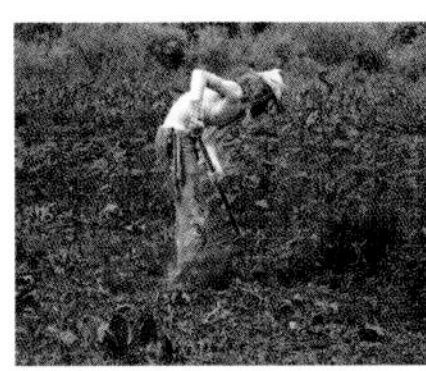

The hoeing and weeding never end. 43

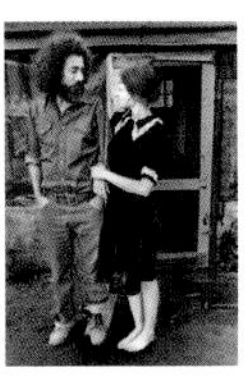

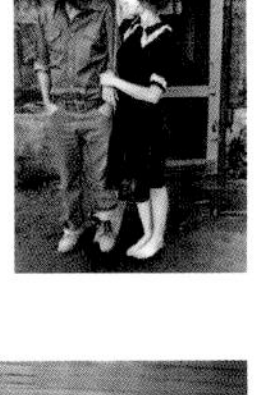

Marty and Gloria in front of their home. 44

Bathing in the Rio Tusas. 47

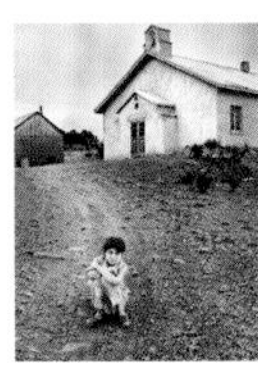

Ida Herrera in front of Petaca's church. 49

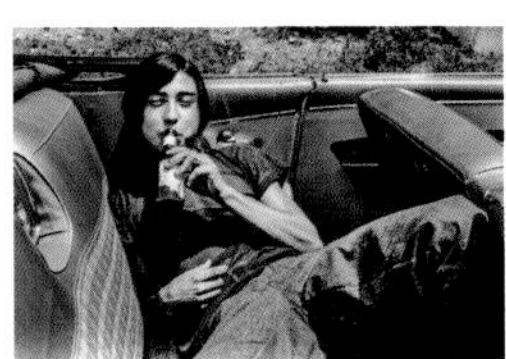

Billy Cisneros killing time in his favorite ride. 50

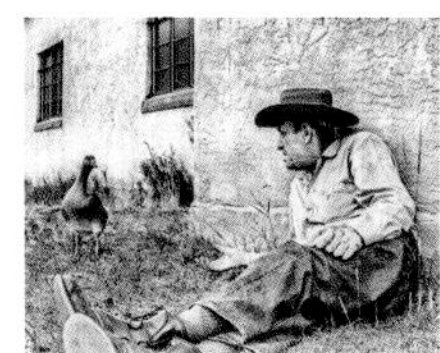

Santiago Roybal's guardian goose, Lugar. 51

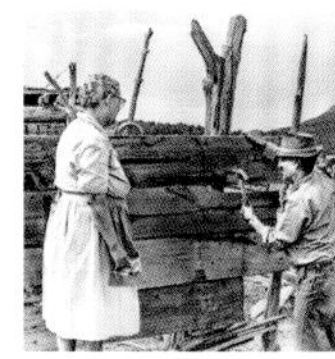

Mending fences brought members of the community together. 52

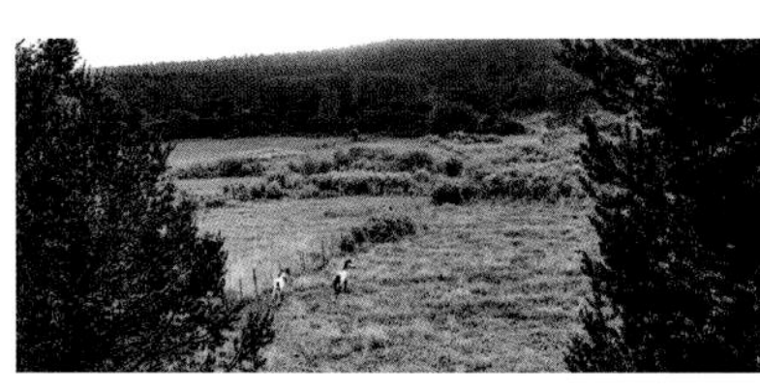

The horses were very hard to catch. 54

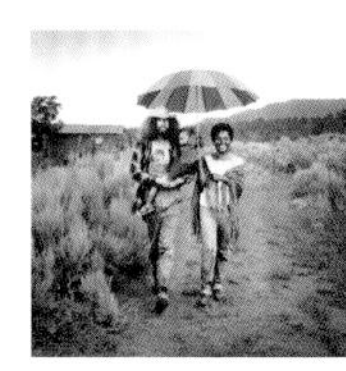

Claudia King, Maya, and friend Gary Sullivan with protection from summer's blazing sun. 56

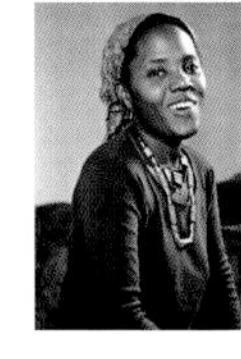

Claudia: fierce on the outside, gentle on the inside. 57

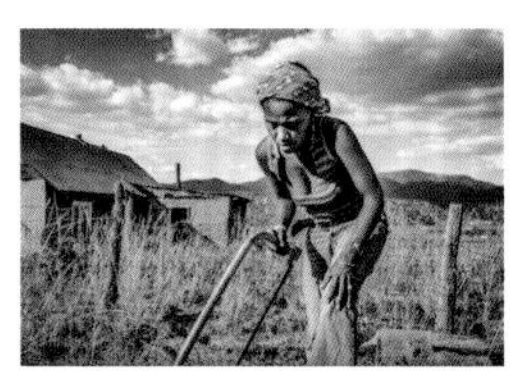

Claudia sawing fence posts, a necessary skill. 59

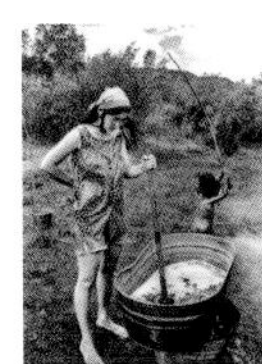
Clothes were often washed with water from the river. 60

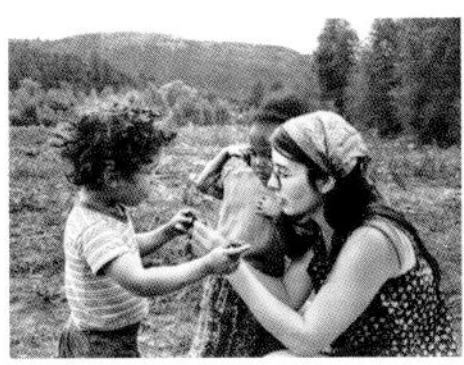
Sherie Land, Sarmod Collier, and Maya. 61

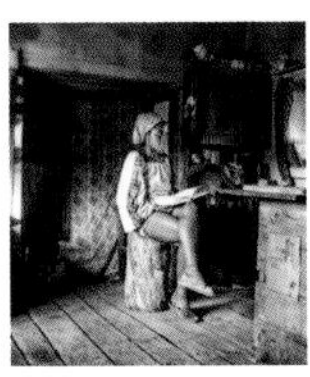
Claudia searching for a tamale recipe. 62

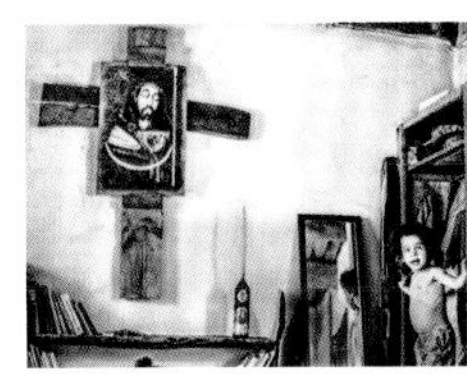
Where a Jimi Hendrix poster once hung, a painted icon looms over Sarmod. 63

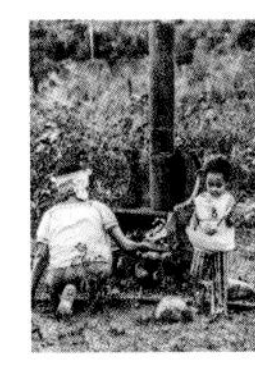
Claudia and Maya using an outdoor stove in the summer. 64

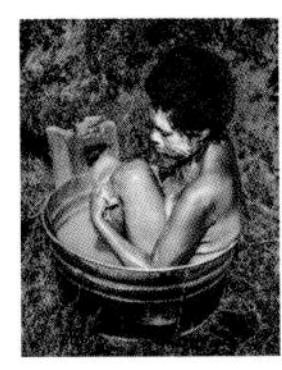
The smaller the tub, the less water needed. 65

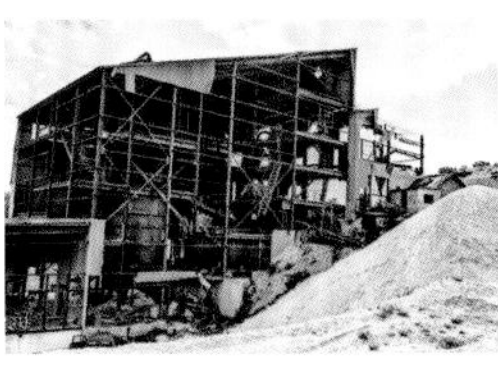
The old mica mine once employed many of Petaca's men. 66

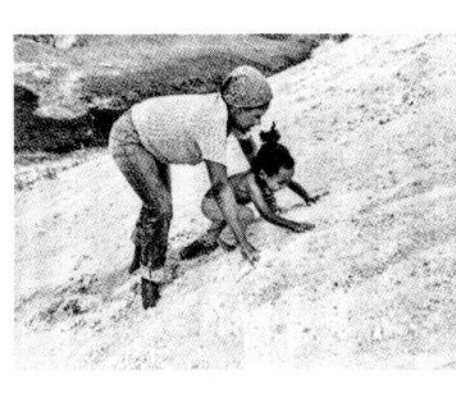
Claudia and Maya, up and down the mica hills. 68

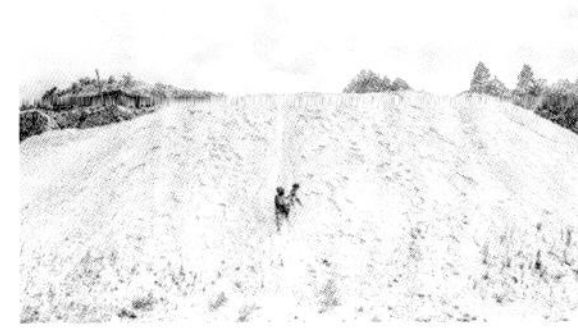
Claudia and Maya, endless fun. 69

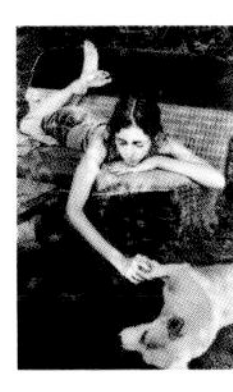
Gloria taking a rest with her favorite old dog. 71

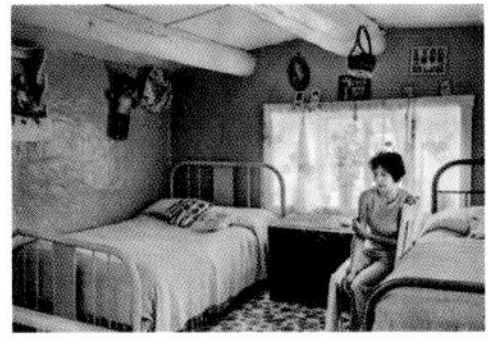
Inside Senovia Mendoza's traditional adobe home. 72

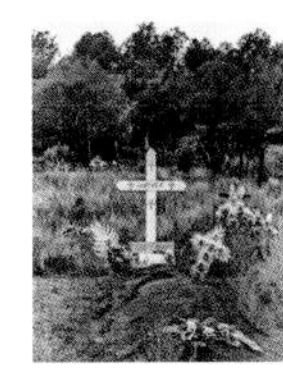
Petaca's main graveyard. 73

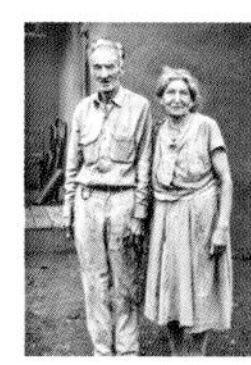
Max and Euphemia. 74

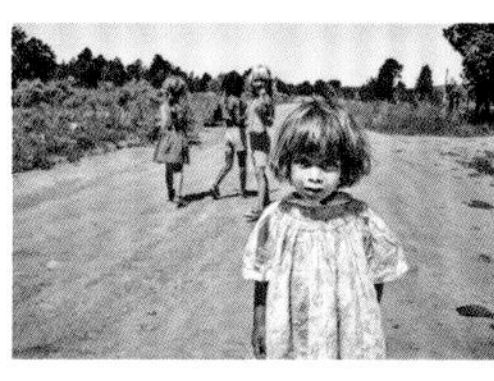
Children wandered freely, often out of sight of their parents. 75

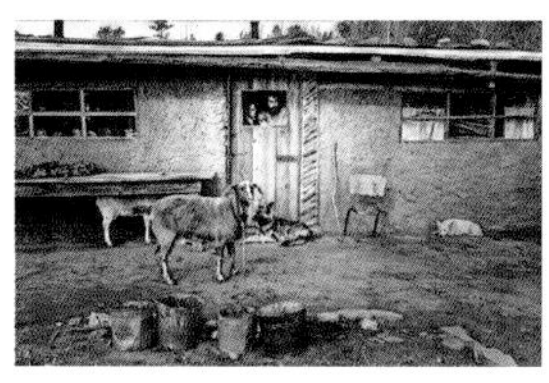
Marty, Gloria, and the adobe home they built by hand with clay, sand, straw, and water. 76

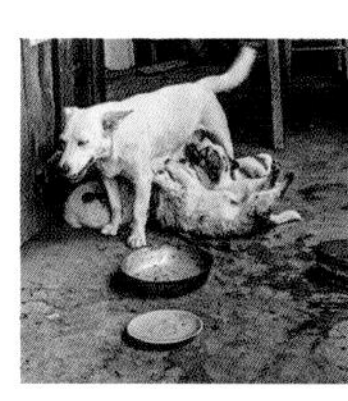
Petaca's much-loved pets. 78

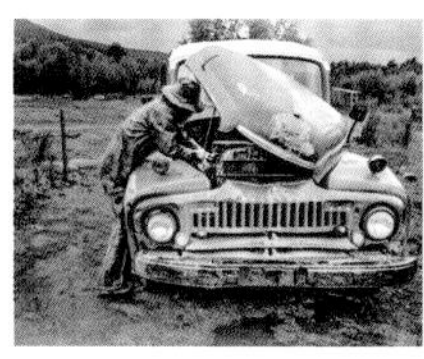
Marty's old International Harvester required constant work. 79

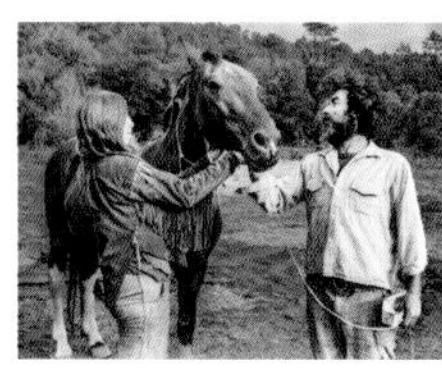
Marty shops for a horse. 80

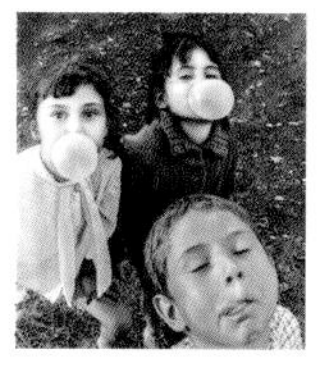
Blowing bubbles. 82

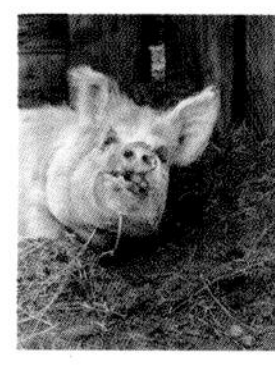
When a pig was slaughtered, neighbors received a share and drank some blood. 83

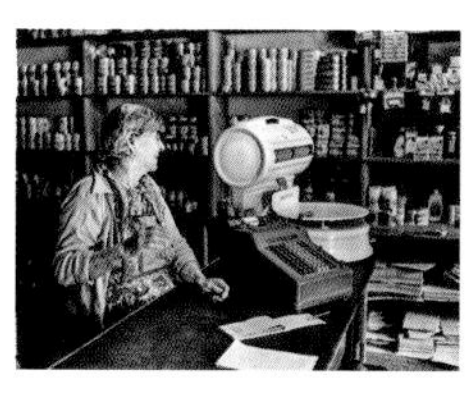
Inside the town's only general store. 84

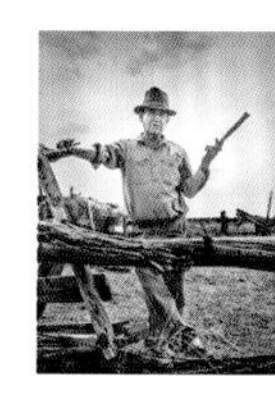
Fred Esquivel at work. 85

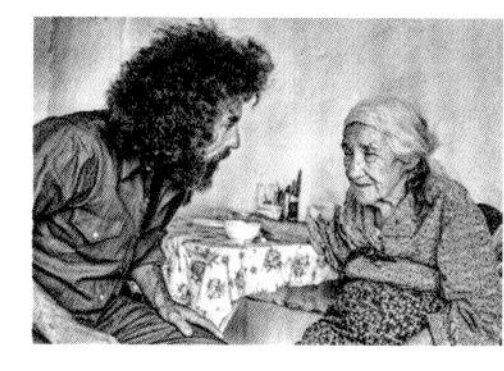
Jesusita Martinez advises Marty. 87

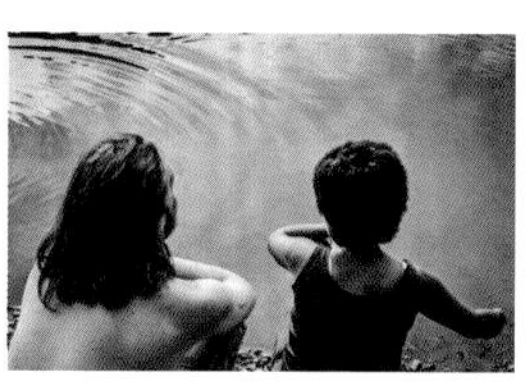
Passing time by the river. 88

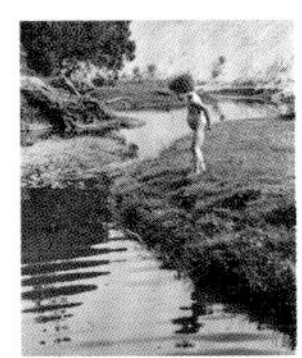
Sarmod along the Rio Tusas. 89

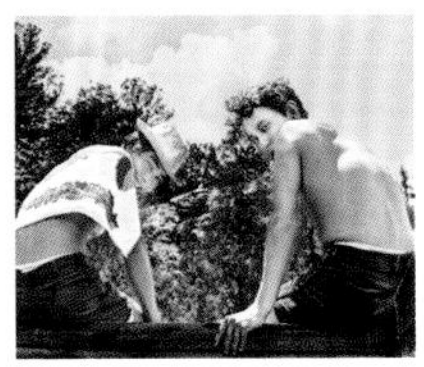
Ready for a swim in the Rio Tusas. 90

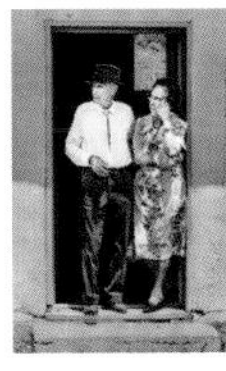
Well-wishers before the anniversary procession. 91

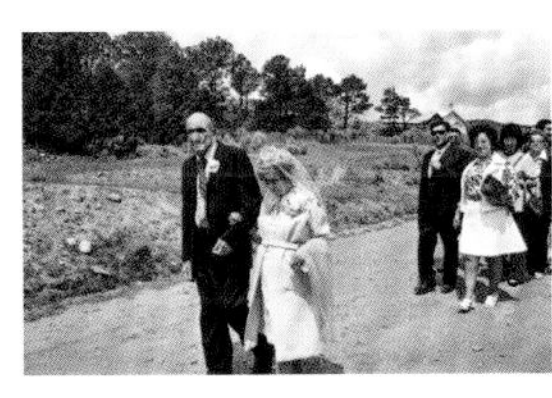
Maria and Santiago's anniversary procession snakes through the village. 92

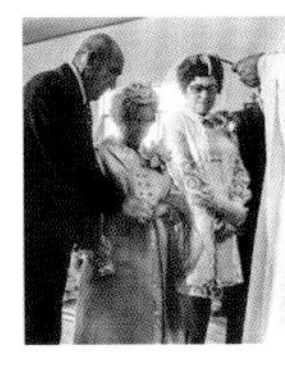
On their fiftieth anniversary, Maria and Santiago renew their vows. 94

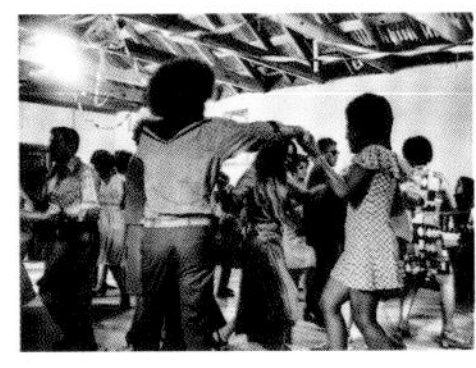
Celebrating in the dance hall. 95

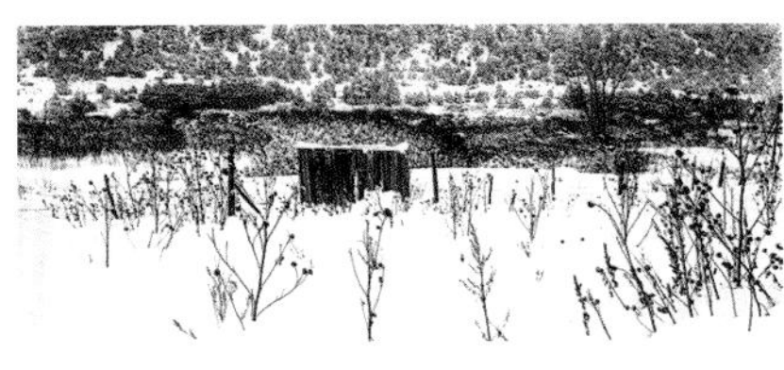
January snow fills the corral. 96

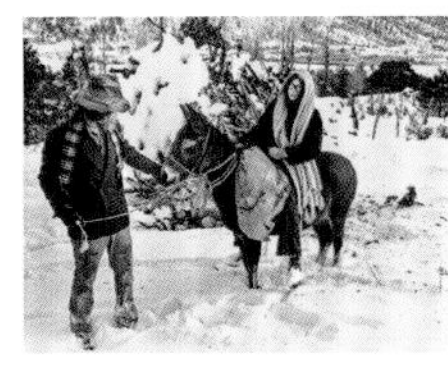
The stove is out, the house is cold, and a trip to the woodpile is required. 99

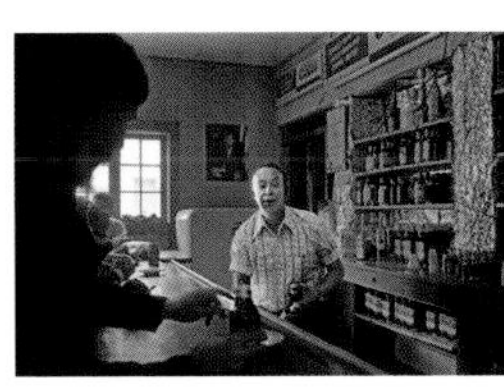
A cold beer at the bar. 100

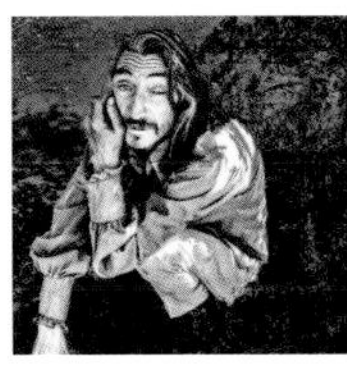
Elmo Lido, a frequent visitor at Marty and Gloria's. 101

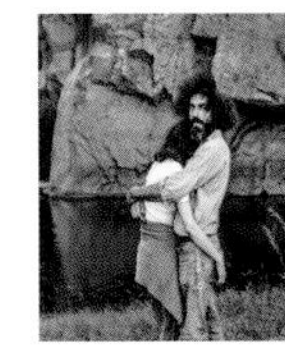
Moments after a narrow escape from a flash flood. 102

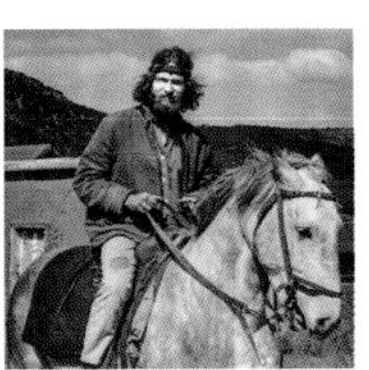
A stranger rides into town. 104

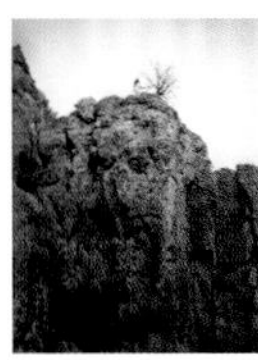
Sherie on the edge. 105

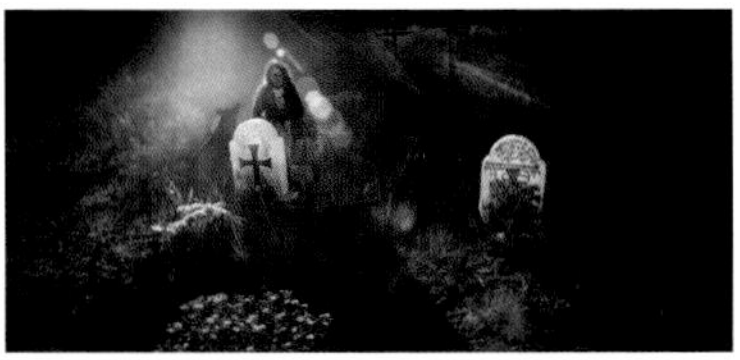
Gloria among the tombstones 106

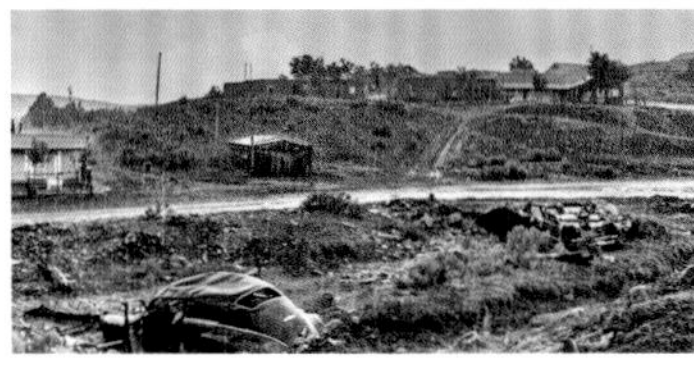
Junked cars in a cold rain. 108

Further Reading

The history of Northern New Mexico—and especially that of the Rio Arriba County—is fascinating, layered, and complex. For those wishing to know more, these books and articles are a good place to start:

Mario Barrera, *Race and Class in the Southwest: A Theory of Racial Inequality* (University of Notre Dame Press, 1979).

David Correia, *Properties of Violence: Law and Land Grant Struggle in Northern New Mexico* (University of Georgia Press, 2013).

William deBuys, *Enchantment and Exploitation: The Life and Hard Times of a New Mexico Mountain Range* (University of New Mexico Press, 1985).

Roxanne Dunbar Ortiz, *Roots of Resistance: A History of Land Tenure in New Mexico* (University of Oklahoma Press, 2007).

Erlinda Gonzales-Berry and David R. Maciel, eds., *The Contested Homeland: A Chicano History of New Mexico* (University of New Mexico Press, 2000).

Charles Montgomery, *The Spanish Redemption: Heritage, Power, and Loss on New Mexico's Upper Rio Grande* (University of California Press, 2002).

Peter Nabokov, *Tijerina and the Courthouse Raid* (University Of New Mexico Press, 1969).

Sherry Robinson, *Apache Voices: Their Stories of Survival as Told to Eve Ball* (University of New Mexico Press, 2000).

Marcos Roybal, *The Court of Private Land Claims and the Petaca Grant: Case Study Summary* (University of New Mexico Digital Repository, 2012).

Mike Scarborough, *Trespassers on Our Own Land: Structured as an Oral History of the Juan P. Valdez Family and of the Land Grants of Northern New Mexico* (Dog Ear Publishing, 2011).

Printed in China

ISBN 978-0-8263-6963-5 (paper)

Library of Congress Control Number: 2025054176

Founded in 1889, the University of New Mexico sits on the traditional homelands of the Pueblo of Sandia. The original peoples of New Mexico—Pueblo, Navajo, and Apache—since time immemorial have deep connections to the land and have made significant contributions to the broader community statewide. We honor the land itself and those who remain stewards of this land throughout the generations and also acknowledge our committed relationship to Indigenous peoples. We gratefully recognize our history.

Cover photographs by Lynn Adler
Designed by Felicia Cedillos
Composed in Adobe Garamond Pro